ROME—OPPONENT OR PARTNER?

TO THE CHURCH OF SCOTLAND

ROME

OPPONENT OR PARTNER?

RUDOLF J. EHRLICH

THE WESTMINSTER PRESS

PHILADELPHIA

CONTENTS

5

PART III

Barriers to Christian Unity

PREFACE

THE question of the unity of the Church and even of the eventual reunion of the churches is very much to the forefront today. Therefore an account, as faithful and accurate as possible, of the debate between Rome and the Churches of the Reformation, may, in the light of recent developments, be not without interest and value. While I offer in this work my own critical comments, what is of prime importance is the debate itself. Accordingly the Roman and Reformation arguments and pronouncements have not been relegated to footnotes; the views expressed on both sides from the time of the Reformation in the sixteenth century up to the present day have been given their due place in the body of the study so that they may speak by and for themselves.

It is hoped that the book will be of some service to the reader who desires to be informed about the present state of a dialogue which has been carried on in varying moods and with different degrees of intensity for 400 years; where he disagrees with my findings he will yet profit, I trust, from the *verbatim* reports of what has been and is being said.

Practically all the citations in this study are in English— either from authorized translations of Latin, German and French originals, or, failing these, in renderings of my own. In some cases it has been considered advisable to cite both original and translation.

I thank my friends, the Rev. Professor Thomas F. Torrance M.B.E., D.D., D.Theol., Chair of Christian Dogmatics, New College, Edinburgh, and the Rev. John P. Smith, M.A., B.D., St. David's, Viewforth, Edinburgh, who put their time and knowledge ungrudgingly at my disposal. Without their interest, encouragement and advice this book would never have been written. I also acknowledge my indebtedness to the following: the Rev. James C. Strachan, M.A., B.D., Colmonell, for his careful reading of my manuscript; the Rev.

7

Professor Gottfried W. Locher, D.Theol., Chair of Systematic Theology, University of Bern, for several valuable suggestions, and the Editors of the *Scottish Journal of Theology* for permission to use material already published by them. My greatest indebtedness, however, is to my wife. Not only did she undertake to type my (at times almost indecipherable) manuscript; it is only owing to her constant care that it has been at all possible for me to write this book in the midst of a busy parish ministry.

Edinburgh,
January 1965.   R. J. E.

8

ACKNOWLEDGEMENTS

I acknowledge with gratitude the permission given me by the undernoted publishers to quote extracts from the following works:

T. & T. Clark, Edinburgh—Karl Barth, *Church Dogmatics* (editors G. W. Bromiley and T. F. Torrance), Vols. I/1 and I/2, *The Doctrine of the Word of God*, 1936 and 1956, Vol. II/2, *The Doctrine of God*, 1957, Vols. IV/1 and IV/2, *The Doctrine of Reconciliation*, 1956 and 1958.

Concordia Publishing House, Saint Louis, Missouri—*Luther's Works*, American edition (editor Jaroslav Pelikan), Vol. 12, *Selected Psalms, I*, 1955, Vol. 23, *Sermons on the Gospel of St. John, Chapters 6-8*, 1959, Vol. 26, *Lectures on Galatians, 1535, Chapters 1-4*, 1963.

Fortress Press, Philadelphia, Pennsylvania—*Luther's Works*, American edition (editor Helmut T. Lehmann), Vol. 31, *Career of the Reformer, I*, 1957; Vol. 36, *Word and Sacrament, II*, 1959; Vol. 40, *Church and Ministry, II*, 1958.

M. H. Gill & Son, Dublin—Otto Semmelroth, S.J., *Mary, Archetype of the Church*, 1963.

Harvill Press, London—Louis Bouyer, *The Spirit and Forms of Protestantism*, 1963 (Fontana Library).

Johannes Verlag, Einsiedeln—Hans Küng, *Rechtfertigung. Die Lehre Karl Barths und eine katholische Besinnung. Mit einem Geleitbrief von Karl Barth*, 1957.

Darton, Longman & Todd, London and Helicon Press, Baltimore, Maryland, Karl Rahner, S.J., *Theological Investigations*, Vol. I, *God, Christ, Mary and Grace*, 1961.

J. C. B. Mohr (Paul Siebeck), Tübingen—Joseph Klein, *Skandalon um das Wesen des Katholizismus*, 1958.

Oliver & Boyd, Edinburgh and London—T. F. Torrance, *Kingdom and Church. A Study in the Theology of the Reformation*, 1956.

Sheed & Ward, London and New York—Hans Küng,

The Council and Reunion, 1961 and *The Living Church. Reflections on the Second Vatican Council*, 1963, E. Schillebeeckx, O.P., *Christ The Sacrament of encounter with God*, 1963.

Verlag Herder, Freiburg im Breisgau—Henricus Denzinger-Adolfus Schönmetzer, S.I., *Enchiridion Symbolorum Definitionum et Declarationum De Rebus Fidei Et Morum, Editio XXXII*, 1963, Josef Rupert Geiselmann, *Die Heilige Schrift Und Die Traditionen. Zu den neueren Kontroversen über das Verhältnis der heiligen Schrift zu den nichtgeschriebenen Traditionen*, 1962, Hans Küng, *Strukturen der Kirche*, 1962.

Westminster Press, Philadelphia, Pennsylvania and S.C.M. Press, London—Calvin, *Institutes of the Christian Religion* in two volumes, ed. by John T. McNeill, trans. by Ford Lewis Battles, 1960, copyright W. L. Jenkins (Library of Christian Classics, Vols. XX and XXI).

R. J. E.

ABBREVIATIONS

A.A.S.	*Acta Apostolicae Sedis.*
A.E.	*Luther's Works*, ed. by Jaroslav Pelikan and Helmut T. Lehmann, Saint Louis and Philadelphia, 1955– (*American Edition*).
C.D.	Karl Barth, *Church Dogmatics*, ed. by G. W. Bromiley and T. F. Torrance, Edinburgh, 1936–.
C.R.	*Corpus Reformatorum, Ioannis Calvini Opera*, Brunswick, 1863–1900.
Denz.	Henricus Denzinger—Adolfus Schönmetzer, *Enchiridion Symbolorum Definitionum et Declarationum de Rebus Fidei et Morum*, 32nd Edition, Barcelona, Freiburg, Rome, etc., 1963 (numbers in brackets refer to earlier editions).
Institutes	*Institutionis Christianae religionis* 1559 in O.S., III–V. John Calvin, *Institutes of the Christian Religion*, 2 Vols., ed. by John T. McNeill and trans. by Ford Lewis Battles, Philadelphia and London, 1960.
O.S.	*Joannis Calvini Opera Selecta*, ed. by Peter Barth and Wilhelm Niesel, München, 1926–52.
S.B.	J. T. Müller (Editor), *Die Symbolischen Bücher der evangelisch-lutherischen Kirche*, 12th edition, Gütersloh, 1928.
Schaff II	Philip Schaff, *The Creeds of Christendom*, Vol. II, *The Creeds of the Greek and Latin Churches. With Translations*, London, 1877.
Schaff III	Philip Schaff, *The Creeds of Christendom*, Vol. III, *The Creeds of the Evangelical Protestant Churches. With Translations*, London, 1877.
S.F.P.	Louis Bouyer, *The Spirit and Forms of Protestantism*, trans. by A. V. Littledale, London and Glasgow, 1963 (Fontana Library).
R.	Hans Küng, *Rechtfertigung. Die Lehre Karl Barths und eine katholische Besinnung. Mit einem Geleitbrief von Karl Barth*, 3rd Edition, Einsiedeln, 1957.
W.A.	*D. Martin Luthers Werke, Kritische Gesamtausgabe*, Weimar, 1883– (*Weimar Ausgabe*).

INTRODUCTION

INTRODUCTION

THE CHANGE OF CLIMATE

ONE OF THE most hopeful and encouraging signs of the times is the change that has taken place in the climate of relationship between the Church of Rome and the Churches of the Reformation. Following as it does upon more than 400 years of bitterness and recrimination this change is remarkable enough in itself, but even more dramatic is its recent progress.

In 1864 Pope Pius IX published his *Syllabus Errorum* in which he listed as one of "the principal errors of our time"[1] the idea that "Protestantism is nothing more than another form of the same true Christian religion, in which it is possible to be equally pleasing to God as in the [Roman] Catholic Church".[2]

The same icy wind of disapproval still blew from Rome in 1928 when, in his Encyclical *Mortalium animos*, Pius XI reiterated the reasons why the Apostolic See had never allowed the Roman Communion or clergy to take part in the conferences and meetings of non-Catholics: "There is but one way in which the unity of Christians may be fostered, and that is by furthering the return to the one true Church of Christ [i.e. the Church of Rome] of those who are separated from it; for from that one true Church they have in the past fallen away."[3]

In 1948 the Holy See was obviously alarmed at the gathering momentum of the Ecumenical Movement: Roman and non-Roman theologians were having another look at their respective positions and in different places mixed gatherings had taken place. Therefore Rome decided to take steps for the protection of the faithful. The *Monitum* of the Holy Office, *Cum compertum*, reminded Roman Catholics that unless prior permission was obtained from the Holy See they were forbidden by Canon Law to participate in, and still less to organize, meetings, especially "ecumenical" gatherings, with non-Roman Catholics at which matters of faith and morals were to be discussed.[4]

The Instruction of the Holy Office *De motione oecumenica*, issued in 1949, though officially taking note of the existence of the Ecumenical Movement, reiterated the refusal of the Roman Church to take part in ecumenical congresses. The Holy Office acknowledged, however, that the Ecumenical Movement was the result of the common prayers of the faithful and of the action of the Holy Spirit. A limited participation of Roman Catholics in ecumenical work was now to be permitted, though only under the strictest supervision of the competent ecclesiastical authorities, i.e. the diocesan bishops. But the Holy Office, whose duty it is to keep intact and to protect the *depositum fidei*, made it abundantly clear to those inside and outside the Roman Church that the only way to true unity of faith was the return of the separated Christians to Rome and also that if these returned they would not bring with them anything essential which the Church of Rome is now lacking.[5]

It is, therefore, all the more significant that when John XXIII announced in 1959 his intention to hold an "Ecumenical" Council, he set up in the following year the *Secretariat for the Promotion of Christian Unity*. In 1961 this Secretariat appointed official Roman Catholic observers to the Meeting of the World Council of Churches in New Delhi. This practice has since then been repeated: Roman Catholic observers were present, for instance, at the 4th World Conference on Faith and Order in Montreal (1963), the 19th General Council of the World Alliance of Reformed Churches in Frankfurt-am-Main (1964), the 4th Nyborg Conference of European Churches (1964), etc. Even more remarkable is the fact that since 1962, by invitation of the Vatican, representatives of the World Council of Churches, the World Alliance of Reformed Churches, the Lutheran World Federation, the Anglican Communion, etc., have been present as official observers at the successive sessions of Vatican II and were specially welcomed and received by John XXIII and Paul VI.

What had happened in the period between 1864 and 1964? What had brought about that amelioration of climate which started the thaw and at least opened the way towards the development of some sort of ecumenical relationship between the Church of Rome and the Churches of the Reformation? Time may mend many wounds, but not the wound inflicted by schism in the Body of Christ. The best that time can do is to deaden the pain and make it tolerable. Protestants and Roman Catholics alike had become resigned to their situation and insensitive to the scandal of schism. They had come to tolerate the disgrace of division. But in this matter Almighty God is neither tolerant nor resigned and He has been at work making His Church sensitive again through His Holy Spirit. That is why Christians, as members of the Body of Christ, are once more aware of the open sore caused by schism and are conscious of its pain.

The very division of the Church has become a point of contact among Christians who, realizing that through Baptism they have been incorporated into the same Body of Christ, can no longer regard the disunity of the Church with complacency or indifference. The reasons for disunity and its continuance are therefore being re-examined. In this re-appraisal, theologians, Protestant and Roman Catholic alike, have found a new approach to the questions at issue. This is the dialogue. The old polemical approach was based on the assumption that the opponent was not really worth listening to since his viewpoint was already disposed of; the dialogue, on the other hand, presupposes that Protestants and Roman Catholics have something to say to one another; it is the conversation of two partners who, though they are not in agreement, are nevertheless each willing to listen to what the other has to say and to answer him so that the debate may be carried on responsively and responsibly in the light of mutual knowledge and understanding. It is the willingness of Protestant and Roman Catholic theologians to enter into this dialogue that has brought about the change of climate in inter-church relations.

Theological discussions between Protestant and Roman

17

Catholic scholars, meetings of clergy and laymen of both Communions, joint publications in the field of theology, have become everyday occurrences. Even in countries where the Protestant Church is greatly outnumbered by the Church of Rome a new spirit of mutual understanding makes the dialogue possible. In Italy, ministers of the Waldensian Church and Roman priests have been meeting together for Bible study. While on March 1, 1562, Protestants were massacred by Roman Catholics at Vassy in France, exactly 400 years later to the day in the same place members of both Churches met to commemorate the event of 1562 and a Protestant service was held and a Roman Catholic mass offered in intercession for unity. It may seem incredible that this point has been reached in so short a time—for the theological dialogue of today had its first tentative beginnings less than fifty years ago. Such has been the speed of the thaw—such the progress of the new venture upon which a courageous vanguard in both Communions has bravely embarked in this age when the world's sore and clamant need is Christian unity in Christian witness.

An historical examination of the contemporary Protestant–Roman Catholic dialogue would probably show that its causes were many and varied, theological and non-theological. There were, for example, the experiences of persecution and suffering shared by many Continental Protestants and Roman Catholics during the Church Struggle in National Socialist Germany and the occupation of Europe during World War II. In this period both Communions, confronted and attacked by a régime whose avowed aim was the "liquidation" of the whole Christian Church, discovered not only that they held much in common but also that their division weakened them in the defence of what was common to them. It is not our intention to trace here the history of the dialogue but merely to indicate what we believe to be *one* of the theological factors in its inception.

In 1927 Karl Barth was invited by the university association of the Roman Catholic Centre Party in Münster i.W. to deliver a lecture on *The Concept of the Church*. His very first word sounded a warning: "We must be quite clear in our minds and not deceive ourselves for a moment: our meeting here today signifies a very daring undertaking. I have shouldered only half of the responsibility by accepting this most kindly proffered invitation and I must admit I am glad of that."[6] But why was it "a very daring undertaking" for a professor of Protestant Theology to lecture to Roman Catholics and for Roman Catholics to listen to him? What made this undertaking "a daring venture"[7] was not that a Protestant was meeting with Roman Catholics (no unusual event in a German university town); it was that Protestant lecturer and Roman Catholic audience had chosen a theological topic for discussion. The choice of subject, of this particular subject, was so "daring" in 1927 that Karl Barth asked himself and his listeners whether it was "at all possible for [Roman] Catholics and Protestants to enter into a theological conversation which concerns itself seriously with a *substantial* question, which concerns itself with a concept of Christian *dogmatics* and not merely with a historical or practical subject. . . ."[8] Protestants and Roman Catholics alike must admit, and face up to, the appalling truth that as recently as 1927, less than half a century ago, they had nothing "substantial", i.e. theological, to say to each other.

When the German Church historian, Karl von Hase, published his *Handbook to the Controversy with Rome* he himself said that in spite of its irenic intentions his book was "an incursion into the enemy's country".[9] This is a perfect description of the situation in which the Church of Rome and the Churches of the Reformation found themselves in the nineteenth century and at the beginning of the twentieth. Roman Catholics and Protestants were facing each other as "enemies". Their respective doctrine, theology and history were hostile "country" into which an occasional "incursion" was made with a view to finding some weakness in the opponent's defences which might be used to his discredit.

When the dogma of Papal Infallibility was promulgated in 1870 Karl von Hase rejected it (as a Protestant he had no alternative) but he also sought to use it to discredit the

Church of Rome. He attributed to the doctrine of Papal Infallibility a meaning which, as it is defined by the First Vatican Council, it neither explicitly nor implicitly contains: von Hase asserted that the Council had made the Pope the "new God-man"[10] and had thus erected an "idol"[11] in Rome; in other words, that the Pope was a reincarnation of Christ. However objectionable and unbiblical Roman Catholic dogmas may be from a Protestant point of view, if the rejection of these is based on a misinterpretation no dialogue can ever be possible.

Heinrich Denifle, the erudite Dominican scholar, used the great authority conferred on him by his prodigious learning and expert knowledge of medieval thought, not to discover the true Luther as opposed to the Luther of popular legends (Protestant and Roman Catholic alike), but to produce a caricature inspired by hatred and designed to discredit the Reformer and the Reformation: Luther was a gutter-snipe, a drunkard, sensual and ignorant, who invented the doctrine of justification to excuse his own scandalous living.[12] However unpleasant Luther's personality may be in Roman Catholic eyes, no dialogue is possible if he and his teaching are judged and condemned on the evidence of a hideous and repulsive caricature produced by a self-appointed judge.

When we consider Barth's lecture on *The Concept of the Church* against the background of the ecclesiastical scene in 1927 we realize just how daring a venture both Protestant lecturer and Roman Catholic audience had undertaken.

The "daring venture" of 1927, however, was not destined to remain an isolated event. Subsequent developments show that Barth's initial misgivings about the possibility of a theological conversation between Roman Catholics and Protestants were unfounded. As the massive volumes of his *Church Dogmatics* began to appear from 1932 onward (and even before they appeared) his theology found an echo and a measure of interest and even of sympathy in a quarter where Barth himself had least expected it: among Roman Catholic theologians, such as Gottlieb Söhngen, Hans Urs von Balthasar, Henri Bouillard, Louis Bouyer, Hans Küng, etc.

But why should Roman Catholic theologians have chosen Barth as their interlocutor in the dialogue with the Churches of the Reformation? His criticism of the Church of Rome is so trenchant and pungent that it seems quite impossible to find even an inch of common ground for discussion and debate; his reservations regarding the policy and aims of the Ecumenical Movement, even within non-Roman Christendom, are so numerous that to use his theology as the material with which to build a bridge across the abyss separating the Church of Rome from the Churches of the Reformation seems to be a quite hopeless venture; above all, the rejection of his theology as modernistic by right-wing and as reactionary by left-wing Protestantism seems to make him a most unrepresentative champion of the Protestant viewpoint in the dialogue with Roman Catholic theology.

Hans Urs von Balthasar (whose searching examination of Barthian theology is one of the most outstanding contributions to the Roman Catholic encounter with Protestantism) explains in his book *Karl Barth, Darstellung und Deutung seiner Theologie* (*Karl Barth, Exposition and Interpretation of his Theology*) why Roman Catholic theologians had to choose Barth as their partner in their dialogue with Protestantism. It was not that other equally worthy representatives of Protestantism were lacking. On the contrary, there were some with whom—because they were closer to the Roman position—a conversation would have been easier from a Roman Catholic point of view. Nor would it be true to say that Roman Catholics were influenced in their choice of Barth by the fact that he initiated a new and powerful movement within Protestantism. Movements, after all, have their day and disappear. What determined Roman Catholic theologians to make Barth their *vis-à-vis* in the encounter with the Churches of the Reformation was not the structure but the substance of his theology and the question raised by it.[13] "We [Roman Catholics] must choose Karl Barth as our partner because in him genuine Protestantism has found *for the first time* . . . its completely consistent expression. This expression was attained not only by the radical return to the sources, to Calvin and Luther, cutting right across all the 'developments', deformations and dilutions of Neo-Protestantism, but, what is more important, by the purification and radicalization of the sources themselves."[14] In other words, since in the Roman view Barth is the true heir of the Reformers, calling the Church of Rome even more in question than the Reformation of the sixteenth century, Roman Catholic theology felt itself, at least indirectly, addressed and challenged by him and therefore compelled to answer him.

Here, we believe, is one of the sources of the contemporary dialogue: the theology of Karl Barth which as "a completely consistent expression" of the Reformation once again addressed and challenged the Church of Rome and questioned the validity of its theology and doctrinal teaching. In claiming that Barth's theology is one of the sources of the contemporary Protestant–Roman Catholic dialogue we do not deny but rather affirm the work of the Holy Spirit, for it is surely agreed that without the Spirit theology ceases to be Christian.

Barth's attack on Rome was recognized by Roman theologians as a true challenge, i.e. a challenge for the sake of the Truth, which could not be ignored or shrugged off as irrelevant but had to be answered. Roman theologians in their turn called in question the theology of Barth and as a corollary (since they see in him the true heir of the Reformers) the theology of the Reformation too. In this process of asking and answering questions, of giving and countering answers, both sides—not only Barth and, for instance, von Balthasar personally, but Protestant and Roman theologians generally—discovered, and are still discovering, to their mutual enrichment that disagreement so long as it springs from the love of the Truth and not of self-glory can and in fact does lead to a partnership—a partnership in the common examination of what divides the Churches and the common search for what will heal these divisions. This discovery led to the contemporary dialogue.

Before we embark upon our own inquiry and examine and

assess theologically the beginning and progress of the contemporary dialogue and what we believe still remains the
barrier to Christian unity we must try to indicate to Protestant and Roman Catholic reader alike where we ourselves
stand. Honesty demands this clarification!

In his inaugural address to the second session of Vatican
II (1963) Paul VI spoke these weighty words concerning the
schism of the Christian Church: "If any guilt for this separation is to be ascribed to us, we humbly ask God for forgiveness and also the brethren for pardon should they feel themselves injured by us. As far as we are concerned we are ready
to pardon the wrong done to the [Roman] Catholic Church
and to forget the sorrow to which she has been subjected by
reason of the long dissension and separation"—*Si quae culpa ob
huiusmodi separationem in nos admittenda sit, veniam humili rogatu a
Deo petimus, ab ipsisque Fratribus veniam petimus, si iniuriam a nobis
se accepisse putent. Ad nos quod attinet, animo parati sumus
ad condonandas iniurias catholicae Ecclesiae illatas, et ad relin-
quendum moerorem, quo confecta est, diuturnarum dissentionum atque
separationum causa.*[15]

This papal statement is, unfortunately, not an unambiguous admission that the Church of Rome shares in the
guilt of schism. The Latin text is capable of being interpreted
as meaning that the Roman Church is not guilty: "if any
guilt . . . is to be ascribed to us"—but none can be. . . ! But
while this interpretation of the Latin text is possible, it is not
necessary. What the Pope said may be accepted as an
admission that the Church of Rome too shares in the guilt of
schism and as a prayer for forgiveness.

There cannot be any doubt that the Council of the
Evangelical Church in Germany understands that papal
statement in a positive sense. In a *Pastoral Letter* (1964) to its
twenty-seven member-Churches and their congregations, the
Council recognizes that Paul VI was concerned in his
allocution with "mutual forgiveness between the Communions for insults and injustices".[16] The Council calls on
Evangelical Christians to remember in inter-confessional
conversations and contacts the fifth petition of the Lord's

23

Prayer: "Forgive us our debts as we forgive our debtors". Those who gladly call themselves "evangelical" Christians can and must do this and so admit the inadequacy of their own Church. The Reformation learned from Scripture that "the Church of Jesus Christ is not pure in herself but lives from the justifying grace of her Lord. Self-righteousness and self-justification would be the worst perversion of her nature."[17] The Pastoral Letter envisages the relationship between the Church of the Reformation and Rome thus: "In the striving-together (*Wetteifer*) of faith, love and hope we will co-operate with our Roman Catholic fellow-Christians to remove the stumbling-blocks (*Ärgernise*) which in the common life of Christians today call in question the Christian witness before the world."[18]

We are in full agreement with this statement which also says: "We thank God anew for the gift of the Reformation, in which the Gospel of Jesus Christ as the message of the peace with God emerged again clearly."[19] We are most certainly not ashamed of the Reformation but see in it the work of God for the re-formation and preservation of His Church.

But while we give thanks to God for the Reformation, we also remember one of its fundamental principles: *ecclesia reformata semper reformanda est*. Has the Reformed Church kept the Gospel of Jesus Christ intact? As Reformed Churchmen we know only too well that our Roman brethren have every right to ask us "whether we ourselves have not despised the riches of the grace of God".[20] Since "in the history of the Church too God acts in such a way that no flesh should glory in His presence",[21] we realize that there is no room for complacency but that we have once more much to learn before "the Gospel of Jesus Christ as the message of the peace with God emerges again clearly". Some of this learning can and must be done through the relationship with other Communions. We are, therefore, not only willing to engage in a dialogue with the Church of Rome but believe that it is our bounden duty to our common Lord, laid on us by Himself.

24

The Report of the Standing Committee on Roman Catholicism adopted by the 19th General Council of the World Alliance of Reformed Churches in Frankfurt-am-Main expresses our own viewpoint: "As we welcome the new openness of many of our Roman Catholic brethren to new apprehension of truth and new relationship, so we too must cultivate minds and hearts that will be hospitable to new convictions and the wider opportunities opening before us.

"We must therefore ask ourselves whether we are ready to engage in helpful dialogue with our Roman Catholic brethren. Do we know and can we communicate that for which we stand? Have we the will to engage in fruitful discussion? Have we the skills required to engage in such discussions and to mediate them to our Churches? Have we the firmness to maintain the truth we have already received while being receptive to new understanding?

"Likewise, if we ask searching questions of the Roman Catholic Church, and hope for reforms within the life of that Church, we must expect equally searching questions to be asked concerning the Reformed Churches. We must not fear the dialogue, and must be true successors of the Reformation by making it a continuing process within our own Churches."[22]

NOTES ON INTRODUCTION

1. Schaff II, p. 213.
2. Para. III, 18; Denz. 2918 (1718); Schaff II, pp. 217–18.
3. A.A.S., 20; 10.1.1928; Nr. 1, p. 14; cf. also G. K. A. Bell (Editor), *Documents on Christian Unity*, 2nd Series, London, 1930, p. 61.
4. Cf. A.A.S., 40; 15.6–10.7. 1948; Nr. 6–7, p. 257.
5. Cf. A.A.S., 42; 31.1.1950; Nr. 2, pp. 142–4.
6. Karl Barth, *The Concept of the Church* in *Christianity Divided, Protestant and Roman Catholic Theological Issues*, ed. by Daniel J. Callahan,

Heiko A. Obermann, Daniel J. O'Hanlon, S.J., London and New York, 1961, p. 153 (hereafter referred to as K. Barth, *The Concept of the Church.*)
7. *Ibid.*, p. 153.
8. *Ibid.*, p. 153.
9. Karl von Hase, *Handbook to the Controversy with Rome*, trans. (from the 7th German edition) by A. W. Streane, Vol. I (2nd revised edition), London, 1909, p. ix. (Preface to the first German edition published in 1862.)
10. *Ibid.*, p. 328.
11. *Ibid.*, p. 328.

12. Cf. Heinrich Denifle, *Luther und Luthertum*, Mainz, 1904–9.

13. Hans Urs von Balthasar, *Karl Barth, Darstellung und Deutung seiner Theologie*, Köln, 2nd Edition, 1962, pp. 30–31 (hereafter referred to as H. U. von Balthasar, *Karl Barth*).

14. *Ibid.*, pp. 31–32.

15. A.A.S., 55; 15.11.1963, Nr. 15, p. 853.

16. *Zur interkonfessionellen Lage, Wort des Rates der Evangelischen Kirche in Deutschland an die Glied-*kirchen *und ihre Gemeinden* in *Die Zeichen der Zeit, Evangelische Monatsschrift für Mitarbeiter der Kirche*, Leipzig, Nr. 5, 1964, p. 161.

17. *Ibid.*, p. 161.

18. *Ibid.*, p. 161.

19. *Ibid.*, p. 161.

20. *Ibid.*, p. 161.

21. *Ibid.*, p. 161.

22. Part III, 4 and 5 in *Reports from Frankfurt, World Alliance of Reformed Churches, 19th General Council Frankfurt-am-Main, August 3–13, 1964, Germany*, p. 45.

PART I

THE BEGINNING OF THE CONTEMPORARY DIALOGUE

LOUIS BOUYER

As we have noted, the present situation is that the rigid positions behind which the Church of Rome and the Church of the Reformation have been entrenched for so long have again become fluid and that today it is an indisputable fact that, in the realm of theology, at least, the two Communions stand no longer disengaged, side by side, but are once more engaged in conversations, in a dialogue dedicated to a common search for the Truth.

Whether this dialogue will ever reach the stage of that common search leading to a common understanding of Truth is unpredictable. Here, as elsewhere, Protestant and Roman Catholic partner alike must trust their common Lord who, since He is the Truth, will make them free—free from those errors, prejudices and false presuppositions which prevent them from accepting the Truth itself as the criterion to which their understanding of it ought to be subjected.

But while the dialogue has not yet resulted in a common understanding, the common search for the Truth has at least taught the partners, Protestant as well as Roman Catholic, that charity is the prerequisite of their dialogical inter-relationship and "charity . . . thinketh no evil" (1 Cor. 13:5). It is for neither partner to compromise the Truth, but charity, the refusal to think evil of the other, makes it possible to see his point of view and to admit that he too is at least concerned about the Truth.

It is in this sense above all that there has been an advance in the Protestant–Roman Catholic dialogue. The writings of two Roman Catholic theologians, Louis Bouyer and Hans Küng, have been taken to illustrate the beginning of the contemporary dialogue and its progress. The choice of these two scholars has not been arbitrary—it has been made for several very good reasons. Both Bouyer and Küng have been active in the dialogue between their own Church and the Church of the Reformation; both have a world-wide reputation as scholars and theologians; and both have a first-hand and practical knowledge of Protestantism, not only as a doctrinal system, but as a living Communion. Those of their writings that are to be discussed form part of a debate and dialogue with that true Reformation theology which is represented by Luther, Calvin and Barth. And finally, the work of these scholars shows that Roman theology has not stood still but is moving in certain respects towards a more evangelical, i.e. biblical, position. Küng, for instance, who, holding views on grace which are rejected by Bouyer as Protestant aberrations, has moved closer than any other Roman theologian to the Reformation standpoint. In this section we shall discuss Bouyer's appreciation of the "positive" elements of Protestantism and then his rejection of its "negative" elements; this will entail an examination of Luther's and Calvin's teaching on grace, union with Christ, justification, sanctification, faith, Baptism and the Lord's Supper, and Bouyer's criticism of those Reformed doctrines. Küng's views will be examined in the light of his own debate with Barth in the next section.

I

Bouyer's Recognition of the "Positive" Elements of Protestantism

Louis Bouyer, a convert to Roman Catholicism, rejects Protestantism as schismatic and heretical. For him there is but one Church, the Church of Rome. There is, consequently only one way for Protestantism towards the fulfilment of what is genuinely Christian in the Reformation movement: the way back to Rome! His book *The Spirit and Forms of Protestantism* is thus "a personal witness, a plain account of the way in which a Protestant came to feel himself obliged in conscience to give his adherence to the [Roman] Catholic Church".[1] The original French title of Bouyer's work

Du Protestantisme à l'Église reflects better than its English adaptation the author's outlook and conviction, since it implies that he travelled a road which led him from partial to the full truth, from a sect into the reality of the Church. He assures his readers, however, that "no sentiment of revulsion turned him from the religion fostered in him by a Protestant upbringing, followed by several years in the [Protestant] ministry. The fact is, he has never rejected it."[2] But, in exploring the "depths" and the "full scope" of the Reformation and its results, he discovered "the absolute incompatibility between Protestantism as a genuinely spiritual movement stemming from the teachings of the Gospel, and Protestantism as an institution, or rather complexus of institutions, hostile to one another as well as to the [Roman] Catholic Church."[3] Thus "he saw the necessity of returning to that Church—not in order to reject any of the positive Christian elements of his religious life, but to enable them, at last, to develop without hindrance".[4]

Protestants will find it quite impossible to emulate Bouyer and seek the unhindered development of "the positive Christian elements" of their faith within the Church of Rome. Just because these very elements were not permitted to develop without hindrance, but were repressed and stifled in the sixteenth-century Roman Church, the Reformation took place. Although Protestants cannot deny that their forefathers were often hostile, not only to the Roman Church but to one another, this was not the source of what Bouyer calls "the fatal error which drove the spiritual movement of Protestantism out of the one Church",[5] i.e. the Church of Rome. In actual fact the anathemas of the Council of Trent (1545–63) rent the one Church of Christ in the West asunder. The Tridentine decrees as understood by Roman Catholics and Protestants at the time of their promulgation—whatever their present-day interpretation may be—finally compelled Rome to deny the name of Church to Protestant Communions and to brand them as heretical sects; it also led Protestants to label Rome as an un-reformed, false, or even apostate Church.

Yet, in spite of Bouyer's inability to convince Protestants that his own way back to Rome is the right way towards Christian unity, and that the positive Christian elements of the Reformation are all contained within Roman Catholicism, dialogue with him is possible and even necessary.

This possibility and necessity are based on the fact that Bouyer acknowledges the *sola gratia* of the Reformation—justification by grace alone—not only to be the vital principle of Protestantism but also genuinely Christian and "fully in accord . . . with [Roman] Catholic tradition properly understood".[6] He is convinced that "if both Protestants and [Roman] Catholics could be persuaded of it [i.e. that the *sola gratia* is in accordance with the teaching of the Apostles and Roman Catholic tradition] the object of the basic antagonism of Protestants to the Church [i.e. the Church of Rome] would cease to exist".[7]

What is true of the formula *sola gratia* is equally true of the *sola fide* of the Reformation—justification by faith alone. In his relevant chapter Bouyer is able to say:

> What is more, it is certainly true that the "protestation" of the Reformers on this point, whenever it has been made, besides conforming . . . to the strictest orthodoxy, has been no less amply justified by the circumstances. For a religion that had come to be identified with the observances of a community and which was in so advanced a state of religious and moral decay as was the Christian community at the end of the Middle Ages, nothing was more urgent than to insist on the inescapable necessity for a personal and, as we say now, "engaged" response to what God exacts. At that period there was no more serious threat to the survival of real Christianity than man's acquiescence in a façade of religion, and his being satisfied with a respect, often wholly external, for the religious framework acknowledged by society.[8]

Bouyer freely grants that Luther's discovery

> "the just man lives by faith" . . . abolished, once and for all, his Pelagian or semi-Pelagian idea of salvation, replacing it by one which gave the initiative to God alone.[9]

32

The Reformation doctrine of justification by faith alone therefore merely expresses that

> the essential, for salvation, is to realize that God is its author, that it depends, not on one's own strength, but on God's.[10] "What we could not do, God, in Christ, has done for us."[11]

Bouyer readily agrees that

> the insight of Luther, preserved in the type of Protestantism most faithful to its origins and most truly Christian, is that *all* is grace, and that, consequently, *all* in our salvation comes to us by faith. If this *all* is compromised, the very heart of Protestant spirituality is wounded mortally.[12]

As clearly as any Protestant this author sees that

> either we are not saved by divine grace, acknowledged and accepted by faith, or this grace, which is in God, is the sole cause of our salvation, and faith, which is in us, the sole means of access to it. For if there is something needed for salvation which has a source other than grace received by faith, we are confronted again with the impossible task of the salvation of man by man. The Gospel, however, is the good news that someone else—God in Christ—has done for us what we could not do.[13]

The material principle of the Reformation—*sola gratia, sola fide*—and its formal principle—*sola scriptura* (Bouyer does not use the term *sola scriptura* but speaks of "the supreme authority of Scripture") Bouyer assesses as follows:

> . . . if the various revivals in Protestantism are invariably due to a return to the first Reformers, this is due to the positive values which lie at the root of Luther's insight, formulated into an axiom [i.e. *sola gratia* and *sola fide*]. Apart from these values, and their presence in that first principle [i.e. *sola gratia* and *sola fide*], the fact is unaccountable. There lies the sole reason for the possession by Protestants of the kind of spiritual life . . . [which] exists, not in spite of their Protestant principles, but because of them—whatever objections may be raised against other features to be found in the origin of the Reformation.[14]

To the material principle of the Reformation there was added, as a necessary presupposition, the formal principle of

Protestantism: the supreme authority of Scripture. Bouyer says that these two

> are closely united, both on the plane of fact and on that of ideas. For if, as Luther found at Erfurt, salvation is a grace, a pure gift to be received by faith, neither our reason nor any human endeavour can attain in the realm of thought what our will is powerless to reach in reality. Divine revelation alone can make known to us the divine action; both are equally gratuitous gifts.[15]

In Bouyer's view, Luther made his great discovery

> through meditation on Scripture, always looked on by Christians as the Word of God. . . . Herein lies the positive value contained . . . in the second Protestant principle: the supreme authority of the Bible. It signifies, primarily, a return to the essential. We can be saved because God has acted. We can believe in His action because He has spoken to us. It follows, easily and naturally, that the first impulse of the religious man should be to seek to know God's Word, to render it, not just an undefined respect, but the active worship due to it. Of this Word the Church is the guardian, set down in a book inspired, unvarying, yet impregnated with the life of its writers and its divine subject. No other source has such an imperative claim.
>
> Again, as in the case of the gratuitousness of salvation by faith, the original basis of this principle, so strongly felt, is undeniably positive. In the same way . . . the fact remains that the living Protestantism of our time sees here another link with its origins. And just as the expression *sola gratia, sola fide*, in the sense expounded, is nowise inconsistent with [Roman] Catholic tradition, the assertion that Scripture, the Word of God, is invested with the authority of the Holy Ghost is quite in keeping with the status of the teaching Church [i.e., the Church of Rome]; that, again, is one of the elementary doctrines of the [Roman] Church.[16]

Although *sola gratia* was the watch-word of Lutheranism, Bouyer believes that the more specifically Calvinist contribution to the Reformation was *soli Deo gloria*—to God alone be the glory. In Bouyer's opinion here again there is basic agreement between Protestantism and Roman Catholicism.

Here, without any doubt, we enter on territory where prejudice and misconceptions on both sides [Protestant and Roman Catholic] have played a much more extended and serious part than in the *sola gratia*.[17]

But Bouyer believes that

here equally (perhaps even more) the [Roman] Catholic should have no hesitation in acknowledging the true Christian character of the Protestant assertion [i.e. *soli Deo gloria*], provided it is reduced to what is primary and essential in it. The sense of God, so finely expressed by Calvin, which Barth raised perhaps to a still higher plane, and which makes every Protestant, true to the best in his religion, recognize his affinity to them, however remote he be from entire agreement —this sense of God so distinctive of Protestantism is, in certain of its aspects, undoubtedly part of the content of Scripture, and so cannot be called in question; nor can we dispute that it is in fact something supreme and final.[18]

Bouyer warns Roman Catholics that his own account of Calvin and the Genevan Reformer's various followers can only be fully understood by those

who recognize in their teaching [i.e. in that of Calvin and his followers] a true echo of the revelation of Moses, of the great Hebrew prophets, and, in no less degree, of the Gospels.[19]

Bouyer agrees even further with Calvin's line of thought on the *soli Deo gloria*. He holds that Barth's teaching in this respect is

the exact echo of the final teachings of the New Testament; all that the divine Word wished not only to tell us, but to accomplish in us at the same time, is that God, and He alone, in Christ, is the Lord.[20]

Surely this is a far cry from Heinrich Denifle, who claimed that the doctrine of justification had been invented by Luther to excuse his own scandalous way of life. How could it possibly be denied that the Protestant–Roman Catholic dialogue has in fact made progress, when in their theological conversations both partners can and do reach a measure of agreement—unthinkable half a century ago?

The undoubted progress of the dialogue, however, by no

means suggests that full and final agreement between the Church of Rome and the Church of the Reformation will be reached in the foreseeable future. The partners are learning only too quickly that, as their conversations progress, new disagreements hitherto concealed or ignored are brought to light. Thus their very dialogue, designed to make them one in the Truth, lays bare, not only what they have in common, but also what divides them, and what, humanly speaking, may always do so.

2

Bouyer's Criticism of the "Negative" Elements of Protestantism

Bouyer's book shows admirably how many disagreements still remain, in spite of what has already been achieved, before real *rapprochement* between the Church of Rome and the Church of the Reformation will be possible.

Bouyer's central question is this:

> How was it that, starting from positive, orthodox, traditional principles [i.e. "justification by faith alone in divine grace alone, and the supreme authority of the Scriptures divinely inspired"] . . . the Reformation became something individualistic, heretical, and negative?[21]

This question reveals the whole magnitude of the difficulties with which the Protestant–Roman Catholic dialogue continues to be confronted; for Protestants will and must strenuously deny what Bouyer affirms about the development of the Reformation.

Bouyer holds that what was true in the Reformation was not new, and what was new was not true. In his opinion the positive elements in the Reformers' teaching were merely the necessary re-emphasis of orthodox and traditional principles that had become somewhat obscured owing to the decadence of the theology prevailing in the sixteenth century. He believes that

> Protestantism, reduced to what Protestants themselves regard as its essence, was under no necessity to embody itself in schism

36

and heresy. On the contrary, by the very logic of its nature, it should have initiated in the Church itself [i.e. the Church of Rome] a powerful movement of regeneration, one of those returns to its own origins and rediscoveries of its own spiritual wealth, which from time to time renew its vitality.[22]

Here is one of the problems the Protestant–Roman Catholic debate is called upon, if not to solve, at least to clarify. The Reformers never claimed that what they taught was new, but expressly maintained that their teaching was true, because it constituted a return to Apostolic doctrine and Catholic, though not Roman, tradition. The unresolved problem is whether "Protestantism" or "Romanism" is the embodiment of schism and heresy; whether it was the Protestant attitude or the Roman which brought about division and separation. Is it possible to solve this problem while each partner continues to blame the other for the schism in the sixteenth century, takes hardened and "crystallized" views, and thinks of their respective Communions in categories of pure black and white?

In his *Reply to Sadolet* (1539) John Calvin vindicates the necessity of the Reformation and cogently says:

As to the charge of forsaking the Church, which they were wont to bring against me, there is nothing of which my conscience accuses me, unless, indeed, he is to be considered a deserter, who, seeing the soldiers routed and scattered, and abandoning the ranks, raises the leader's standard, and recalls them to their posts. For thus, O Lord, were all thy servants dispersed, so that they could not, by any possibility, hear the command, but had almost forgotten their leader, and their service, and their military oath. In order to bring them together, when thus scattered, I raised not a foreign standard, but that noble banner of thine which we must follow, if we would be classed among *thy* people.

Then I was assailed by those who, when they ought to have kept others in their ranks, had led them astray, and when I determined not to desist, opposed me with violence. On this grievous tumults arose, and the contest blazed and issued in disruption. With whom the blame rests it is for thee, O Lord, to decide. Always, both by word and deed, have I protested how eager I was for unity. Mine, however, was a unity of the Church

37

which should begin with thee and end in thee. For as oft as thou didst recommend to us peace and concord, thou, at the same time, didst show that thou wert the only bond for preserving it.[23]

Here Calvin is speaking for all the Reformers. Everyone of them was anxious for "unity". When the Roman Church rejected the *Augsburg Confession* (1530), the Reformers—especially Melanchthon and Calvin—tried again for a settlement of outstanding difficulties. Witness the Colloquies of Hagenau (1540), Worms (1540/41), and, above all, Ratisbon (1541). Ratisbon marked a compromise on the doctrine of justification—uneasy it is true, but nevertheless a working agreement. Calvin saw its dangers, but, in spite of his misgivings, defended it for the sake of the peace of the Church. Luther called it a "patched up thing",[24] but was willing to accept it on condition that Rome admitted to having previously taught another doctrine. Rome, however, rejected it out of hand.

Since the Colloquy of Ratisbon there have been no official conferences to work out doctrinal formulae acceptable to both Communions. Rome has barred the way—the Council of Trent would have no dealings with the Protestants but pronounced them "anathema". Granted that the *vera ecclesia*—the true Church—is justified in wielding its anathema as a weapon against the *falsa ecclesia*—the false Church. But who anathematized whom at Trent? Did the true Church separate itself from the *falsa ecclesia* or did the false Church say to the *vera ecclesia: anathema sis*?

This leads us directly to the question: Can the dialogue, the colloquy of today, cause both partners to seek the solution of the problem of the true and false Church by penitently re-thinking all their theological concepts; can such re-thinking, grounded in common obedience and subjection to Christ alone, produce new and better formulations of the faith than the old, and do so to the honest satisfaction of each and without compromising the truth, which would enable both Churches to manifest themselves visibly as the true Church?

The re-thinking and re-formulation of theological concepts, especially those that separate the Church of the Reformation from the Church of Rome, obviously demand clarification. Not only must the partners in the dialogue understand the theological concepts of their respective Communions, but they must also appreciate the reasons why one Church objects to the other's doctrine.

The central theme of the Reformation, and consequently the basic cause of controversy with Rome, was *justification*. This is variously expressed as justification by faith alone, or by grace alone, or by Christ alone.

The *Augsburg Confession* lists justification among the *Articuli Fidei Praecipui*—the chief articles of faith.[25] In his *Lectures on Galatians* (1531, published 1535) Luther, in commenting on chapter 3: 5, declares:

> Therefore the Papacy is collapsing and tumbling down today, not by the tumult of the sectarians but by the proclamation of the doctrine of justification. This doctrine has not only weakened the kingdom of the Antichrist, but until now it has also sustained and defended us against his violence.[26]

Again, in the *Schmalkald Articles* (1537) he writes:

> Here is the first and chief article: . . . it is clear and certain that such faith alone justifies us, as St. Paul says in Rom. 3: 28: "Therefore we conclude that a man is justified by faith without the deeds of the law"; and in verse 26 he says ". . . that He might be just and the justifier of him who believeth in Jesus." Nothing of this article may be yielded or conceded, though heaven and earth and what will not abide, fall to ruin, for "there is none other name under heaven given among men whereby we must be saved", says St. Peter (Acts 4:12); "and with His stripes we are healed" (Is. 53: 5). And on this article all that we teach and practise is based, against the Pope, the devil, and the world. That is why we must be very certain of this doctrine and not doubt; otherwise all is lost, and the Pope and the devil and all things gain the victory over us and are adjudged right.[27]

John Calvin is no less certain of the centrality of justification by grace and faith alone. In his *Reply to Sadolet* he calls it "the first and keenest subject of controversy"[28] between himself and Rome. "Wherever the knowledge of [justification] is taken away", he informs Sadolet, "the glory of Christ is extinguished, religion abolished, the Church destroyed, and the hope of salvation utterly overthrown."[29] Again in his *Institutes* (1559) he accuses "the schools of the Sorbonne, mothers of all errors, [of having] taken away from us justification by faith, which is the sum of all piety".[30]

Now, if Bouyer's view is to be accepted, it would appear that the Reformers rightly stressed the centrality of justification by grace or faith alone, but were wrong in accusing the Church of Rome as such of having rejected it.

Bouyer summarizes the "positive" elements of the Reformation as follows:

> Salvation as the pure gift of God in Christ, communicated by faith alone, in the sense that no other way can be thought of apart from faith or even along with faith; justification by faith in its subjective aspect, which means that there is no real religion where it is not living and personal; the absolute sovereignty of God, more particularly of His Word as contained in the inspired writings—all these principles are the heart of Protestantism as a reforming movement.[31]

Up to this point Protestants—and the Reformers themselves may be included here—fully agree with Bouyer. But is it possible still to agree with him when he says:

> . . . if we go to the root of them all [i.e. all the principles listed above], to what the Reformers considered most essential, to what is retained by living Protestantism, today and always, we are bound to say that they are all corroborated by [Roman] Catholic tradition, and maintained absolutely by what is authoritative, in the present, for all [Roman] Catholics.[32]

If the Reformers' teaching on *sola fide* and *sola gratia*, and therefore on justification, is corroborated and borne out by Scripture and the tradition of the Roman Church, we are bound to ask: why did the schism of the sixteenth century nevertheless happen? Bouyer regards the reasons as clear and says:

if . . . the Protestant Reformers were undeniably expelled from communion with the Church [of Rome], it was obviously not on account of their positive principles.[33]

Therefore in his view one must simply say "that with these principles were associated others that the Church [of Rome] could not accept".[34]

In his total view of Protestantism, its assertions, formulations and "systematizations", Bouyer makes an important "discovery" which explains to his own satisfaction why the Church of Rome, then and now, must reject the Reformation. He holds that

it is not that other principles appear side by side with those which we have already stated and developed in all their positive implications; it is that within Protestantism these very principles seem drawn by a mysterious fatality to adopt a negative significance.[35]

Bouyer's contention seems to be that the Reformers made positive assertions—*sola gratia, sola fide, sola scriptura*—but then misinterpreted them. They thus acquired a meaning and significance which is neither biblical nor traditional. A typical example of such a misinterpretation perpetrated by the Reformers is justification grounded in *sola gratia*. Since this is "the first and keenest subject of controversy", Bouyer ought to produce evidence to convict the Reformers of his indictment that their positive assertion was "drawn by a mysterious fatality to adopt a negative significance".

3

Bouyer's Criticism of Luther

His charge against Protestantism and its representative theologians from Luther and Calvin to Barth is that their conception of grace is neither ontological nor substantial.

Luther is thus supposed to identify

his affirmation about *sola gratia* with a particular theory, known as extrinsic justification . . . he himself unites two statements so closely that they become inseparable—one an

41

affirmation: grace alone saves us; the second a negation, it changes nothing in us in so doing. . . . The sinner, after receiving grace and so saved, is no less a sinner than before.[36]

Bouyer considers that Protestant theoreticians then seized upon this and came to say

that grace saves us independently of any change effected in us, that no change is effected, that it could not be effected, that it ought not to be effected, that the contrary assertion is scandalous, destructive of all true Christianity, and so forth.[37]

Bouyer observes that for Protestant theology it is apparently impossible "to agree that God could put something in man that became in fact his own, and that at the same time the gift remained the possession of the giver".[38] Summing up his charge against Protestantism Bouyer says:

If the grace of God is such, only on condition that it gives nothing real; if man who believes, by saving faith, is in no way changed from what he was before believing; if justification by faith has to empty of all super-natural reality the Church, her sacraments, her dogmas; if God can only be affirmed by silencing His creature, if He acts only in annihilating it, if His very Word is doomed to be never really heard—what is condemned [by Protestant theology] is not man's presumptuous way to God, but God's way of mercy to man.[39]

Bouyer thus takes issue here with Luther (and the Reformation) for two reasons: (1) the Reformer's denial that God could put "something" in man, and (2) his assertion that the grace of God is such only on condition that it gives "nothing real". To some extent Bouyer errs through obviously misunderstanding the Reformation theology of grace. He maintains that "something" is put into man; Luther, however, believes that not "something" but "someone" is given and united by God to man: Christ Himself. Luther, in fact, realizes that Christ can only be possessed by man as one person is possessed by another, i.e. Christ is not transmuted into the believer's own being. Christ is given to man and so possessed by him, yet the Lord and the believer remain two distinct persons without confusion. But, though Christ is not "possessed" by man in the same way as man possesses his own inherent capacities, He is not less "real". Therefore, in attributing to Luther a doctrine which makes grace only such on condition that it gives "nothing real", is Bouyer not misunderstanding and confusing the "real" with the "physical"? Once we remember that Reformation theology holds that what grace gives is *"real"* though not "physical", Bouyer's objections are seen to be inapplicable to the statements of Luther, Calvin and Barth.

Luther is supposed to believe that the grace which alone saves man changes nothing in him in the process. It is impossible to deny that Luther sometimes spoke recklessly; nevertheless in this connection he is referring to a very definite change brought about in believing man. He says in his *Thesis against the Antinomians* of 1538:

> In Christ who is arisen there is certainly no sin, no death, no law, to which He was subjected so long as He lived. But the very same Christ is not yet fully resurrected in His believers; rather has He only begun in them as a first-fruit, to be resurrected from the dead. . . . So far as Christ is risen in us, we are without law, sin and death. But so far as He is not arisen in us, we are under law, sin and death.[40]

In his *Third Disputation against the Antinomians* Luther elaborates this thought:

> A Christian is a person who is buried with Christ in His death, he has died to sin, the law and death, and every other such tyrant. But we do not see that, for it is hidden from the world; it does not appear, does not strike us in the eye [1 Pet. 3: 4 and Jn. 3:8 are then quoted]. For the Christian is not in this world. He does not live, he is dead. He stands in another life, the heavenly, which is far beyond that which we have here. And yet what troubles and work and what plagues we shall have to experience before we reach there. . . . But the Christian lives here as there through God's imputation, righteous and holy under the wings which like a hen He spreads over us. And yet, so far as the Christian is a fighter and is engaged on military service, he is still under the law here and under sin, for he is still in this life. Daily he feels and experiences the struggle with his flesh and lives only too close to it [Rom. 7: 23, 25 is then quoted]. . . . A man who believes in Christ is through divine

imputation righteous and holy; he already lives in heaven for he is surrounded with the heaven of mercy. But here while we are embraced in the Father's arms, clothed with the best robe, our feet stick out from below the mantle, and Satan tries to bite them if he can. Then the child whimpers and cries and feels that it still has flesh and blood, and the devil is still there. . . . Thus we are holy and free in the Spirit, not in the flesh. . . . For the feet have still to be washed, for they are unclean and so Satan bites and attacks them until they are clean. You must pull your feet under your cloak else you will have no peace.[41]

Bouyer maintains that according to Luther the grace that saves man does not change him. Bouyer forgets that the change which takes place by grace in man is in his relation to God, for it is in that relation that man has his being. The changed relation brought about by grace also affects man's being, since it brings him into a new ontological relation to Christ as Creator and Redeemer. The changed relation to God brought about by grace affects the whole being of man, i.e. his body and soul, since it is only in the unity of soul and body that he is man. In speaking of renewal and re-creation, Luther is thinking in terms of man in his totality of that unity of body and soul. Thus commenting on John 3: 6, "That which is born of the flesh is flesh", Luther says:

Because flesh and blood cannot enter into the Kingdom of God it must cease, die and pass away and rise in a new spiritual being in order to reach heaven. Therefore He [Christ] warns them as Christians that they must become new men, so that on that day they may not be found as flesh and blood.[42]

They are not found "as flesh and blood" because Christ is risen in them having thus begun their resurrection to be completed in the life to come. A man who is buried with Christ in His death, who has died to sin, the law and death, who has already risen to a new life in Christ, is he not changed? And, if grace alone has wrought this change in him, can it be maintained that Luther holds that a man is "saved", but not "changed", by grace?

Bouyer seems to overlook the fact that it is the whole of

man, man in his unity of body and soul, who is renewed and recreated. This change, however, is not truly "seen"—except by faith—until the body, too, is *seen* to be changed. This change, however, can only be spoken and thought of eschatologically—for the believer walks by faith and not by sight and still waits for the redemption of the body at the *parousia* of Christ.

Protestants will not object to Bouyer's view that "the very condition of existence of the 'new creature' is the loving recognition of his actual and necessary dependence for everything upon God".[43] Nor will they contend that such dependence means that the new creature "has to remain in the state where sin has placed him".[44] They will agree that "he must bear the image of the heavenly Adam as He did that of the earthly one".[45] Again Protestants are at one with Bouyer when he says that "God reveals Himself as Sovereign and alone Holy, not by leaving sinners to their powerlessness and sinfulness, but by rescuing them from it".[46] But what more can Luther do than acknowledge Christ's resurrection in man? Does Christ's rising from the dead, in which man participates through grace and faith, not constitute a rescue from powerlessness and sinfulness?

What Bouyer fails to understand is that, in referring to the change brought about in man through grace, Luther is speaking of its being effected theologically, i.e. through faith, and not metaphysically or physically, i.e. by speculation or sight. What Luther (and the other Reformers) has to say about the change in man must therefore also be understood theologically, i.e. from the point of view of a centre in God rather than in man. To speak thus of this change in man and to understand it in this way by no means affects its reality.

Bouyer's main criticism is directed against Luther's *Lectures on Galatians.* In these, Bouyer holds, extrinsic justification is identified with the *sola gratia, sola fide* by the Reformer excluding "from the sphere of justification, not only . . . works in general but even . . . the love of God in 'faith informed by charity' . . .".[47] Luther teaches that grace changes nothing in man. Luther, however, is himself aware of this possible objection; he observes that reason, being offended by his doctrine, says:

> When you teach men to do nothing at all to obtain such an immense gift [i.e. forgiveness of sins, Christ and the Holy Spirit] except to listen to the Word, this seems to verge on a great contempt for grace and to make men smug, lazy and sleepy, so that they loose their grip and do not do any good works at all. Therefore it is not good to preach this; nor is it true. Men must be urged to labour, sweat and exert themselves toward righteousness; then they will obtain this gift. [48]

The Reformer counters this argument by pointing out that what we must learn is this:

> Forgiveness of sins, Christ, and the Holy Spirit are granted— and granted freely—only when we hear with faith. Even our huge sins and demerits do not stand in the way. We must not consider how great the thing is that is being given and how unworthy we are; otherwise the greatness both of the thing and of our unworthiness will frighten us away. But we must bear in mind that it pleases God to grant this inexpressible gift to us freely—to us who are unworthy. [49]

When this gift is granted

> a Christian man is righteous and a sinner at the same time [*simul iustus et peccator*], holy and profane, an enemy of God and a child of God. [50]

Yet

> righteousness is not in us in a formal sense, as Aristotle maintains, but is outside us, solely in the grace of God and in His imputation. In us there is nothing of the form or of the righteousness except that weak faith or the first fruits of faith by which we have begun to take hold of Christ. Meanwhile sin truly remains within us. But the fact itself is not easy or trivial; it is serious and important, because the Christ who is given to us has not done something meagre for us and has not been playing. But, as Paul said earlier (Gal. 2: 20), He "loved us and gave Himself for us"; and (Gal. 3: 13) "He became a curse for us". It is not an idle speculation that Christ was given for my sins and was made accursed for me in order that I might be rescued from eternal death. To take hold of the Son and to believe in Him with the heart as the gift of God causes God to

reckon that faith, however imperfect it may be, as perfect righteousness.[51]

Bouyer is, of course, correct in saying that for Luther justification is a declaration of God's: God declares man to be righteous. This righteousness is not intrinsic but extrinsic to man; it is the righteousness of Christ. But it is imputed to man and is therefore, because of God's declaration, also the righteousness of the man to whom it is imputed. In Bouyer's opinion

all Protestant exegetes, anxious to safeguard the expressions used by Luther and Calvin, set out to show that [δικαιοῦν, to justify] can only mean "to declare just", not "to make just"; that is, it applies merely to extrinsic justice, which has nothing real to correspond with it in the person justified. Nevertheless, modern scientific exegesis unanimously acknowledges that the word can only mean "to declare officially just someone who is so in reality".[52]

Protestant exegesis does in no way deny that, when God justifies a man, that man, because he is declared to be just by God, also is just, since God makes him so. Bouyer himself gives an excellent summary of the Protestant position:

. . . the idea of the Word of God creating what He says by the act of saying it—so well drawn out by Barth from the entire Bible—would be enough to show that God makes just whom He "declares just", even if he were not so beforehand, by the very fact of His declaration.[53]

The opposition between "to declare" and "to make" just set up by the Reformers is, therefore, in Bouyer's opinion, "without meaning".[54] There is of course no opposition! God makes just whom He justifies, i.e. whom He declares just, for what He declares to be comes to pass. The opposition is not between "to declare" and "to make" just, but between what the Reformation and the Roman Church understand by making just. The Reformers understand justification as the declaration of God whereby the sinner, having been declared righteous, is made righteous with the righteousness of Christ. The man who is *totus peccator* is at the same time by God's declaration *totus iustus* but he is only so in Christ.

Justification, in the Roman view as represented by Bouyer at least, is quite different. Justification is not only a process initiated by God, but also a divine act whereby "we are not only reputed, but are truly called, and are, just—*non modo reputamur, sed vere iusti nominamur et sumus*".[55] But the efficacy of this divine act is jointly determined by man's prior disposition and preparation, together with his active co-operation with the grace of God: We "are just, receiving justice within us, each one according to his own measure, 'which the Holy Ghost distributes to every one as He wills' [1 Cor. 12:2] and according to each one's proper disposition and co-operation."[56]

This disposition prior to justification and this co-operation on the part of man are essential according to the Council of Trent, for "if any one saith, that men are justified, *vel sola imputatione iustitiae Christi, vel sola peccatorum remissione*, to the exclusion of the grace and the charity which is poured forth in their hearts by the Holy Ghost and is inherent in them; or even that the grace whereby we are justified is only the favour of God: let him be anathema."[57]

Unjust man is made just "through the voluntary reception of grace, and of the gifts"—*per voluntariam susceptionem gratiae et donorum, unde homo ex iniusto fit iustus.*[58] Justification, in the Roman view as represented by Bouyer, is thus the act of God whereby grace is infused into man—properly disposed and co-operative—which brings about in him a new state—a new *habitus*.

Since justification in the Roman view comes not solely from the imputation of Christ's righteousness, or solely from the remission of sins, but from the infusion of habitual or sanctifying grace, it is not surprising that such justification received by man can be augmented and increased. The act of justification, depending on a process which prepares man for its reception, and which determines the degree of its effectiveness once it has taken place, is followed by a further process: growth in justification. This is what the Council of Trent has to say of the justified:

Having, therefore, been thus justified . . . they, through the observance of the commandments of God and of the Church, faith co-operating with good works, increase in that justice which they have received through the grace of Christ, and are still further justified . . . [*crescunt atque magis iustificantur*].[59]

Growth in justification, then, is possible: but the commission of mortal sin may entail its loss. Yet

as regards those who, by sin, have fallen from the received grace of justification, they may be again justified when, God exciting them, through the sacrament of Penance they shall have attained to the recovery, by the merit of Christ, of the grace lost.[60]

What then is the difference between the Reformation and Roman conceptions of δικαιοῦν, to justify? The Reformers hold that justification is a creative act. When God spoke and declared: "Let there be light", then without any preparation, disposition and co-operation on the part of His creation, "there was light". In justification God once more speaks creatively and does so through His Word. By His declaration man is made righteous without his prior disposition or co-operation; the divine declaration becomes an actual event; the believer is made righteous because the righteousness of Christ becomes his.

In the view of Rome justification is not a creative act making man through grace and in Christ *totus iustus*. Rather it is conceived of as the culmination of a process in which man himself co-operates with God, and which began before, and continues after, his justification.

If the Bible sets God's holiness, His sovereign greatness, in an "inaccessible light", [says Bouyer], it does not at all intend to deny Him the act of creating, or re-creating anything real or of value outside Himself. Rather, it does so to emphasize how much the first creation, still more the second, attest by their intrinsic reality and goodness the incomparable reality and goodness of Him they manifest.[61]

Bouyer can rest assured that Protestants are in full agreement with him here; they, too, read in the book of Genesis: God saw that "it [His creation] was good"! They, too, glory in the wonder of His recreation for they believe that through the miracle of His grace alone the *totus peccator* is declared to be and, by virtue of that declaration, becomes *totus iustus* but he is *iustus* in Christ. Bouyer complains that "the God of Calvinism and Barthism . . . keeps all His greatness only if His creatures return to nothingness".[62] But do God's creatures return to nothingness when their righteousness is made real in Christ? Does God remain great by reducing man to nothing, when the Reformers teach on biblical grounds that the grace through which the sinner is declared, and so made, righteous is *God Himself in Christ*? Grace, the gift of God, is identical with God the Giver, who gives Himself to man in Jesus Christ. Jesus Christ is the grace of God; grace and Jesus Christ are one and the same. Man, in his fallen state is no longer in relation to God, and is indeed nothing. But he is nothing only if he is without grace, without the gift which is God Himself in Christ. Having the gift, the grace which is Jesus Christ, man is no longer nothing; he is everything. He is everything, however, in his own place and station, and on his own level. In Christ he is really righteous since he is once more in relation to God.

But what reality has grace as it is understood by Bouyer? He agrees that man is justified by grace. But what sort of grace justifies him? Is it uncreated or created? Is it *gratia increata* which Rome holds is God Himself, who as the divine will of love is the ground of all grace, or is it *gratia creata*, the finite product of the former, "but which is essentially different from God Himself, a created good"?[63] Justification is, in fact, to be regarded as the "finite product" of uncreated grace, which as *gratia actualis* prepares and as *gratia habitualis* accomplishes, justification. Actual grace given for a time to do one or more acts prepares man for the reception of habitual grace which justifies man by making him righteous. *Gratia habitualis*, however, is not God Himself in Christ, it is not a gift identical with the Giver. Habitual grace is "an inner supernatural life-energy which the Holy Ghost effects in us by baptism".[64] On scriptural grounds, Reformed theology from Luther and Calvin to Barth maintains that the divine reality itself comes concretely to man as *tota gratia*, which is *totus Christus*, always one, undivided, and indivisible, justifying man once and for all, i.e. judging and acquitting, condemning and vindicating, exposing him as guilty and making him righteous in Christ.

What has Bouyer to offer? A grace which is not God Himself in Christ but a created good which is an inner supernatural life-energy. Man receives, not the one grace, which is Christ, but many graces. He is the recipient, not of *tota gratia* which is *totus Christus*, but only of portions of grace which may increase or decrease. Bouyer truly states that "the God of the Bible . . . shows His greatness in snatching [men] from [nothingness] not only, as St. John says, 'that we are *called* but really *are*, the sons of God' (1 Jn. 3: 1)".[65] But is this any argument against what Bouyer calls "the God of Calvinism and Barthism"? That God, the God who gives Himself in Christ, justifies man, and so makes him righteous in Christ once and for all? What "intrinsic reality and goodness" is displayed by the "second creation" of man as understood by Bouyer? Today we really are the sons of God, but will we be so tomorrow? It is possible that mortal sin might make us fall from the received grace of justification, so that, in order to return to a state of grace, we should have to be justified all over again. The God of Bouyer, it seems, "keeps all His greatness" only if the threat of "nothingness", of the loss of the state of grace, continually hangs over his creatures' heads.

Again Bouyer fails to see that, while justification is God's act of declaring man righteous on the sole ground of Christ's righteousness which is extrinsic to him, that grace does yet not only save but also changes him. Luther shows this in his *Lectures on Galatians* where he deals with the relationship between faith and works. Here again Luther is speaking theologically. "A new and theological grammar"[66] is in his view required to understand the relationship between faith and works. The trouble with his opponents is that they "confuse philosophy and theology and make theological works into moral works. A theological work is a work done in faith; thus a theological man is a man of faith. In like manner, a right reason and a good will are a reason and will in faith. Thus faith is . . . the one and only cause of justification; afterwards this is attributed to the matter on account of the form, to the work on account of the faith."[67]

Luther can speak of the relationship between faith and works in this way on account of the christological analogy he applies to it. Faith must be understood sometimes

apart from the work and sometimes with the work . . . the Holy Spirit speaks about faith in different ways in Scripture: sometimes . . . about an abstract or an absolute faith and sometimes about a concrete, composite, or incarnate faith. Thus if Christ is looked at on the basis of outward appearance, He seems to be a mere man. And yet Scripture sometimes speaks of Christ as God, and sometimes it speaks of Him as composite and incarnate. Faith is absolute or abstract when Scripture speaks absolutely about justification or about those who are justified. . . . But when Scripture speaks about rewards and works, then it is speaking about faith as something compound, concrete, or incarnate. [Gal. 5: 6; Titus 1: 15; Matt. 19: 17; Gal. 3: 12 and Ps. 37: 27 are then cited.] In these and similar passages... where mention is made of "doing", Scripture is always speaking of doing in faith. . . . It is no wonder, then, if merits and rewards are promised to this incarnate faith, that is, to this working faith. . . . And why should Holy Scripture not speak in these different ways about faith when it speaks in different ways about Christ as God and man? That is, sometimes, it speaks about His whole Person, sometimes about His two natures separately, either the divine or the human nature. If it speaks about the natures separately, it is speaking of Him absolutely; but if it speaks about the divine nature united with the human in one Person, then it is speaking of Christ as composite and incarnate. . . . Thus justification belongs to faith alone, just as creation belongs to the divinity; nevertheless, just as it is true to say about Christ the man that He created all things, so justification is attributed to incarnate faith or to faithful "doing". . . . Therefore faith is the "do-all" [*fac totum*] in works. . . .[68]

Bouyer then asserts that in the Protestant view grace is regarded as saving man without changing him. But the present writer would stress that the two aspects of faith—

faith apart from work and faith with the work; absolute or abstract and compound, concrete, or incarnate faith can and must be distinguished, but they cannot be separated. Faith alone justifies without works, but faith is also the *fac totum*, the sole agent in works, it is a "new doing".[69] But if one of the two aspects of faith, the gift of God, is a "new doing", can it still be maintained that grace saves man without changing him since anyone who is justified by faith is also involved in a "new doing"?

Bouyer seems to be unaware that Luther says the change into the new man, the man in Christ, takes place *sub contraria specie*.[70] But though it takes place in this way, it really does take place and is therefore an actual event. If Bouyer rejects this view, he must needs repudiate the Roman doctrine of transubstantiation too. For this doctrine is based on the postulate that the substance is really, but not visibly, changed even though to all appearances the *species* remains unchanged. Luther teaches that the sinner is really changed, though he appears to remain a sinner still; the reason being that his outward aspect, the *species*, is still awaiting the resurrection of the body. Bouyer seems to confound and confuse the outward appearance of man, who remains a part of the world under the divine judgement and awaiting renewal, with that inner reality already renewed in Christ. As far as outward appearance is concerned the change effected by grace is still hid with Christ; nevertheless that change has actually taken place and been consummated in Him. The reality and finality of the change in Christ are such that for Luther and the other Reformers further portions of grace were unnecessary to augment or complete it.

Luther's teaching on Christ's union with the believer gives yet more evidence of how unwarranted Bouyer's contention is that in the Protestant view grace saves man without changing him. As early as 1520 Luther maintains in his treatise, *The Freedom of a Christian*, that one of the benefits

> of faith is that it unites the soul with Christ as a bride is united with her bridegroom. By this mystery, as the Apostle teaches, Christ and the soul become one flesh [Eph. 5: 31–32]. And if

they are one flesh and there is between them a true marriage, indeed the most perfect of all marriages, since human marriages are but poor examples of this one true marriage—it follows that everything they have they hold in common, the good as well as the evil. Accordingly the believing soul can boast of and glory in, whatever Christ has as though it were its own, and whatever the soul has Christ claims as His own. Let us compare these and we shall see inestimable benefits. Christ is full of grace, life, and salvation. The soul is full of sins, death and damnation. Now let faith come between them and sins, death and damnation will be Christ's, while grace, life, and salvation will be the soul's; for if Christ is a bridegroom, He must take upon Himself the things which are His bride's and bestow upon her the things that are His. If He gives her His body and very self how shall He not give her all that is His? And if He takes the body of the bride, how shall He not take all that is hers?[71]

If, in uniting Himself to the soul, Christ "bestows . . . the things that are His" and "gives . . . His body and very self", on what ground can it be said that this grace saves without changing a man?

In the same treatise Luther makes the (so easily misunderstood) statement that

as our heavenly Father has in Christ freely come to our aid, we also ought freely to help our neighbour through our body and its works, and *each one should become as it were a Christ to the other* that we may be Christs to one another and Christ may be the same in all, that is, that we may be truly Christians.[72]

If, in Luther's opinion, to be Christians involves our being "Christs to one another", the grace that saves our neighbour must surely change us too.

In his *Lectures on Galatians*, in which Luther deals more particularly with the justification of the sinner, union with Christ is shown to be a decisive factor in that justification.

Works or love are not the ornament or perfection of faith; but faith itself is a gift of God, a work of God in our hearts, which justifies us because it takes hold of Christ as the Saviour. . . . Faith in its proper function has no other object than Jesus Christ, the Son of God, who was put to death for the sins of the world. It does not look at its love and say: "What have I done?

54

Where have I sinned? What have I deserved?" But it says: "What has Christ done? What has He deserved?" And here the truth of the Gospel gives you the answer: "He has redeemed you from sin, from the devil, and from eternal death." Therefore faith acknowledges that in this one Person, Jesus Christ, it has the forgiveness of sins and eternal life. Whoever diverts his gaze from this object does not have true faith; he has a fantasy and a vain opinion.[73]

The idea, therefore, of a justifying faith formed by charity (*fides caritate formata*) is "an empty dream". The "jewel" contained in justifying faith is not love but Christ Himself whom the Christian possesses in faith.[74]

Paraphrasing and commenting on Gal. 2: 20 ". . . nevertheless I live; yet not I, but Christ liveth in me", Luther shows the essential connection between union with Christ and justification.

. . . who is this "I" of whom he [Paul] says: "Yet not I"? It is the one that has the Law and is obliged to do works, the one that is a person separate from Christ. This "I" Paul rejects; for "I", as a person distinct from Christ, belongs to death and hell. This is why he says: "Not I, but Christ lives in me". Christ is my "form" [i.e. Christ, not charity, is the *forma* of faith], which adorns my faith as colour or light adorns a wall. (. . . Christ clings and dwells in us as closely and intimately as light or whiteness clings to a wall.) "Christ", he says, "is fixed and cemented to me and abides in me. The life that I now live, He lives in me. Indeed, Christ Himself is the life that I now live. In this way, therefore, Christ and I are one."[75]

Since the presence of Christ in the believer means the disappearance of law, sin and death, union with Him

causes me to be . . . pulled out of my skin, and to be transferred into [Him] and into His kingdom, which is a kingdom of grace, righteousness, peace, joy, life, salvation, and eternal glory.[76]

Unless Christ counts for nothing and His righteousness is unreal, it cannot be argued as Bouyer does that Luther holds that man is not changed by saving grace. Does Luther suppose that the believer remains unchanged, when he says that by faith you are so cemented to Christ that He and you are as one person, which cannot be separated but remains attached to Him forever and [which] declares: "I am as Christ". And Christ, in turn, says: "I am as that sinner who is attached to Me, and I to him. For by faith we are joined together into one flesh and one bone".[77]

4
Bouyer's Criticism of Calvin

Rome repudiates and rejects Protestantism, and according to Bouyer does so because "in virtue of the divine Word"[78] the Church of Rome must and does teach that

the Word of God categorically proclaims a grace that is a real gift; a justification by faith that makes man really just; a faith that does not give itself, but receives, its content, proclaimed by the κήρυγμα of the apostolic Church, in the celebration of the Eucharist; a God who puts His greatness in giving, giving Himself, by a fully effective gift, where there is no question of docetism or legalism, for His Incarnation is no more a pretence or a legal fiction than was the Creation—He is the living God who gives life.[79]

And so Bouyer holds that Luther departs

not only from the tradition of the Church, but from the Gospel and St. Paul himself, in creating the chimera of a salvation which should save us, without drawing us in the least from the state of sin.[80]

He is nevertheless willing to admit that Calvin ". . . applied himself with some success to correcting Luther"[81] with regard to the doctrine of extrinsic justification. (Extrinsic justification according to Bouyer is "a justification independent of any interior change, of any new capability given to man to perform acts pleasing of themselves to God. . . .")[82] Yet Calvin, too, is condemned because

the clear-cut distinction he tried to draw between justification and sanctification, while willingly admitting that they are inseparable in fact, cannot be maintained in a scientific exegesis.[83]

The gravamen of Bouyer's objection to Calvin and his followers is that they misunderstand the sovereignty of God. He remarks that the Reformed teaching on the sovereignty of God may be summed up by saying:

> In the light of numerous Protestant accounts, from the sixteenth century to the present day . . . it is impossible to affirm and uphold the sovereignty of God without a corresponding annihilation of the creature, especially man. To recognize any worth at all in man, whether in his external acts, in the innermost workings of his mind, even in his being, while maintaining his close dependence on God, would seem an infringement of the divine majesty, by the very fact of this dependence. In particular, to suppose that man as the result of God's grace has the power to do acts good in themselves, even granted his total dependence on God, would be to destroy the gratuitousness of grace, and so to deny the sovereign freedom of God's action. And to say that man, as the recipient of saving grace, could be himself pleasing to God, is to be guilty of blasphemy. Finally, it would be a relapse into idolatry to suppose that man, even when regenerated and recreated, in St. Paul's words, in holiness and justice, could possess any value, and still worse to attribute to him the power to "merit" anything, in any sense of the word.[84]

In all this there is nothing about Calvin's teaching (so vitally important for the understanding of his whole theology) on the Christian's union with Christ. For Calvin the *unio cum Christo* is, if anything, an even more decisive factor in *causa iustificationis* than it is for Luther. It is somewhat surprising to find that, in spite of his genuine appreciation of Calvin's work, Bouyer is among those who persist in reviving and perpetuating the ancient legend that the Genevan Reformer is the advocate of notions and conceptions which make the gulf between God and man unbridgeable. Bouyer does not explain how it is that Calvin (who seems to find it "impossible to affirm and uphold the sovereignty of God without a corresponding annihilation of the creature") can and does teach the believer's union with Christ, which so obviously bridges the gulf between the Creator and the creature, without thereby infringing on the divinity of the former or annihilating the humanity of the latter.

Calvin's definition of justification makes it clear that he understands it in the same way as Luther does:

He is said to be justified in God's sight who is both reckoned righteous in God's judgement and has been accepted on account of his righteousness. Indeed, as iniquity is abominable to God, so no sinner can find favour in His eyes in so far as he is a sinner and so long as he is reckoned as such. Accordingly, wherever there is sin, there also the wrath and vengeance of God show themselves. Now he is justified who is reckoned in the condition not of a sinner, but of a righteous man; and for that reason, he stands firm before God's judgement seat while all sinners fall. If an innocent accused person be summoned before the judgement seat of a fair judge, where he will be judged according to his innocence, he is said to be "justified" before the judge. Thus, justified before God is the man who, freed from the company of sinners, has God to witness and affirm his righteousness. In the same way, therefore, he in whose life that purity and holiness will be found which deserves a testimony of righteousness before God's throne will be said to be justified by works, or else he who, by the wholeness of his works, can meet and satisfy God's judgement. On the contrary, justified by faith is he who, excluded from the righteousness of works, grasps the righteousness of Christ through faith, and clothed in it, appears in God's sight not as a sinner but as a righteous man.[85]

On this ground Calvin bases his concept of justification as follows:

Therefore, we explain justification simply as the acceptance with which God receives us into His favour as righteous men. And we say that it consists in the remission of sins and the imputation of Christ's righteousness.[86]

In Christ the innocence of man is confirmed and established as a concrete reality. Calvin holds that

"to justify" means nothing else than to acquit of guilt him who was accused, as if his innocence were confirmed. Therefore, since God justifies us by the intercession of Christ, He absolves us not by the confirmation of our own innocence but by the imputation of righteousness, so that we who are not righteous in ourselves may be reckoned as such in Christ.[87]

It is just here that without essentially differing from Luther, Calvin has a wider vision of God's great deed of salvation in Christ.

Luther continually engages in controversy with his Roman Catholic opponents and, intent on upholding the righteousness of Christ, extrinsic to man, as the sole ground of his justification, does not see quite so clearly as Calvin does that "to declare or to reckon" man righteous, meaning to justify him, and "to make" man righteous, which signifies to regenerate or sanctify him, in Christ, are only two aspects of one and the same salvation-event in Christ.

Luther, especially in his *Lectures on Galatians*, is almost exclusively concerned with justification; Calvin, however, takes a more comprehensive view of what is involved in man's salvation. In commenting on Gal. 2: 19–20 (1548) Calvin refers first of all to justification:

> . . . let us remember that we are delivered from the yoke of the Law, only by becoming one with Christ, as the twig draws its sap from the root, only by growing into one nature.[88]

Because man believes he exists outside himself in a "real and substantial communication" (*vera et substantialia communicatio*)[89] with Christ, the believer's life is a life lived together with Christ "in virtue of union"[90] with Him and received into man's consciousness by "the power of the Spirit".[91]

Calvin differs from Luther in stressing (as early as 1548 in his *Commentary on Galatians*) that union with Christ has two sides—justification and regeneration or sanctification.

> Christ lives in us in two ways. The one life consists in governing us by His Spirit, and directing all our actions; the other, in making us partakers of His righteousness; so that, while we can do nothing of ourselves, we are accepted in the sight of God. The first relates to regeneration, the second to justification by free grace.[92]

In the final edition of his *Institutes* (1559) Calvin's teaching on union with Christ is fully developed.

> . . . that joining together of Head and members, that indwelling

. of Christ in our hearts—in short, that mystical union [*mystica unio*]—are accorded by us [Calvin] the highest degree of importance, so that Christ, having been made ours, makes us sharers with Him in the gifts with which He has been endowed. We do not, therefore, contemplate Him outside ourselves from afar in order that His righteousness may be imputed to us but because we put on Christ and are engrafted into His Body—in short, because He deigns to make us one with Him.[93]

Thus it is by union with Christ that man obtains all His benefits and appropriates His salvation to himself. The benefits or gifts received by man are two: forgiveness of sins and regeneration, i.e. justification and sanctification.

Christ was given to us by God's generosity, to be grasped and possessed by us in faith. By partaking of Him we principally receive a double grace [*duplicem gratiam*]: namely, that being reconciled to God through Christ's blamelessness, we may have in heaven instead of a Judge a gracious Father; and secondly, that sanctified by Christ's Spirit we may cultivate blamelessness and purity of life.[94]

But how is this union with Christ effected? How do the gifts of justification and sanctification become man's? For "as long as Christ remains outside of us, and we are separated from Him, all that He has suffered and done for the salvation of the human race remains useless and of no value for us".[95]

Calvin's answer to this question is that "we grow into one body with Him . . . by faith".[96] But since not everyone embraces that communion with Christ offered through the Gospel "reason itself teaches us to climb higher and to examine into the secret energy of the Spirit [*de arcana Spiritus efficacia*], by which we come to enjoy Christ and all His benefits."[97]

It is Christ Himself who acts through the Holy Spirit and so unites Himself to man. Without the Holy Spirit, i.e. without Christ Himself acting through the Spirit, "Christ, so to speak, lies idle"[98] and men can only indulge in idle speculations about Him. Union with Him takes place through the Spirit by whom "we are made His [Christ's] members, to keep us under Himself and in turn to possess

Him".[99] The union of Christ with the believer and of the believer with Christ, wrought by Christ Himself through the Holy Spirit, is a "sacred wedlock [*sacrum coniugium*] through which we are made flesh of His flesh and bone of His bone [Eph. 5: 30]."[100]

The gravamen of Bouyer's charge against Calvin is that his idea of the sovereignty of God is false. In summing up the Reformed teaching from the sixteenth century to the present day, Bouyer, as we have already pointed out, concludes that for the Reformers it is impossible to affirm and maintain the sovereignty of God without thereby annihilating man. One can only hope that Bouyer is unaware of or overlooks Calvin's teaching on union with Christ—unless Bouyer is prepared to say that Calvin's view of union as a *sacrum coniugium*, through which we are made flesh of His flesh and bone of His bone, is one instance of the annihilation of man apparently taught in the Reformed Church since the sixteenth century.

Bouyer's specific charge against Calvin is that while admitting that justification and sanctification are inseparable, he definitely distinguishes between them. In other words Calvin, too, is accused of teaching that man is saved, but not really changed, by grace.

It is interesting (and important) to note that Calvin, in his treatment of justification and sanctification, departs from the method and procedure adopted by most of the other Protestant theologians and Confessions. For example, in the *Augsburg Confession*, Part I, Article iii, "*on the Son of God*" and His work, is immediately followed by the Article on "*Justification*". "*The New Obedience*" is dealt with in Article vi, "*Repentance*" in Article xii and "*Good Works*" in Article xx.[101]

Calvin, however, in dealing with the question of man's appropriation of the salvation achieved and revealed in Christ, begins with the source of "the double grace" received by man. Its source is union with Christ, accomplished through the secret operation of the Holy Spirit, and received through faith, the gift of God. The "double grace" derived from union with Christ is justification and sanctification (i.e. regeneration). But, since union with Christ is impossible without the Christian's participation in Christ, in His death and resurrection, so that he dies with Christ to sin and rises with Him to newness of life, Calvin gives in his exposition of the double grace pride of place to sanctification. By becoming one with Christ the believer is born again and is continually recreated in the likeness of His Lord. In a word, by his sharing in Christ's death and resurrection the believer is sanctified, i.e. he is holy with Christ's own holiness.

> ... if we truly partake in His death, "our old man is crucified by His power, and the body of sin perishes" [Rom. 6: 6], that the corruption of original nature may no longer thrive. If we share in His resurrection, through it we are raised up into newness of life to correspond with the righteousness of God. [102]

The sole end of regeneration is thus "to restore in us the image of God", [103] i.e. to restore holiness in man by changing him into the likeness of Christ.

But why does Calvin depart from normal procedure of Protestant theologians and Confessions and deal first with sanctification rather than with justification? As will be seen later, there is no question that for Calvin justification is the effect, the consequence or the fruit of sanctification—nor does the one in his opinion precede the other in time or importance.

Calvin gives priority in his exposition to sanctification because of his desire to anticipate the objections of his Roman critics, whose arguments 400 years ago were identical with Bouyer's in our day—grace as understood by the Reformers saves man without changing him. [104] Then as now Roman theology interpreted the Reformation doctrine of justification by grace and faith alone as implying that there is no need for any change in man himself. Calvin's opponents charged him "with abolishing good works, and with seducing men from the pursuit of them" and "with making the path to righteousness too easy". [105] Since he taught that justification lies in free remission of sins they charged him "with luring into sin men who are already too much inclined to it of their own accord". [106] This is practically identical with Bouyer's argument that according to Reformed theology the idea that "to suppose that man as the result of God's grace has the power to do acts good in themselves . . . would be to destroy the gratuitousness of grace".[107]

Now, if "acts good in themselves" means meritorious works which can contribute to man's salvation, Bouyer's assessment of Reformation theology is correct: the works of the regenerated do not "merit" him salvation because, even when man is recreated in holiness and justice, he is still an unprofitable servant. Calvin says: "Whatever is praiseworthy in works is God's grace."[108] But, though even the works of recreated man "are always spattered with much uncleanness", God "examines our works according to His tenderness, not His supreme right" and "therefore accepts them as if they were perfectly pure; and for that reason, although unmerited, they are rewarded with infinite benefits, both of the present life and also of the life to come".[109]

Throughout the ages God's acceptance of their works "as if they were perfectly pure" has been a source of great comfort to Christian men and women, who, instead of fearing God's judgement on their imperfect works, have rejoiced in that mercy which accepts them as if they were perfect. Bouyer, of course, is free to deprive himself of this source of comfort. Is he, however, entitled to say that according to Reformed teaching man, even after the reception of grace which is Jesus Christ, has no power to do acts good in themselves? Is an act, accepted by God as good, not good? Is the grace, present and active in the works of recreated man, not praiseworthy? In short, does Calvin really teach that nothing is changed in man, even when he is united to Christ in faith through the operation of the Holy Spirit?

It is precisely in anticipation of the Roman argument—grace in the Protestant view saves man without changing him—that Calvin expounds sanctification before he discusses justification. On the one hand, the possibility of regarding justification as pious opinion or theoretical speculation on the relationship between God and man is thus excluded, and, on the other, the Roman argument that the Reformation view of grace means that man, though saved, remains unchanged is made pointless.

After his detailed exposition of sanctification as the actualization of the risen life of Christ in the believer, and so as "the continual unfolding and maintaining", as "the continual renewing and re-enacting in the believer of a justification that is made once and for all",[110] Calvin goes on to discuss that justification itself. Justification is described by Calvin in christological terms on the analogy of Christ's death and resurrection—since it entails substantially the same as sanctification does: participation by the believer in Christ's death and resurrection. Calvin therefore says:

> . . . by His death we are redeemed from the condemnation of death and freed from ruin [cf. Col. 1: 14, 20]; . . . we have been adopted unto Him as sons and heirs by our Heavenly Father [cf. Rom. 8: 17; Gal. 4: 5–7]; . . . we have been reconciled through His blood [Rom. 5: 9–10]; . . . given into His protection, we are released from the danger of perishing and falling [Jn. 10: 28]; . . . thus ingrafted into Him [cf. Rom. 11: 19] we are already, in a manner, partakers of eternal life, having entered in the Kingdom of God through hope. Yet more: we experience such participation in Him that, although we are still foolish in ourselves, He is our wisdom before God; while we are sinners, He is our righteousness; while we are unclean, He is our purity; while we are weak, while we are unarmed and exposed to Satan, yet ours is that power which has been given Him in heaven and on earth [Matt. 28: 18], by which to crush Satan for us and shatter the gates of hell; while we still bear about with us the body of death, He is yet our life. In brief, because all His things are ours and we have all things in Him, in us there is nothing. Upon this foundation . . . we must be built if we would grow into a holy temple to the Lord [cf. Eph. 2: 21].[111]

Thus to be justified by the grace of Christ means that

> believers have Christ abiding in them (1 Jn. 3: 24], through whom they may cleave to God; sharers in His life, they sit with Him in heavenly places [Eph. 2: 6]; "they are translated into the Kingdom of God" [Col. 1: 13], and attain salvation. . . .[112]

The biblical passages cited by Calvin do not mean that "by faith in Christ there comes to us the capacity either to procure righteousness or only to acquire salvation, but that both are given to us".[113] In the light of the scriptural message Calvin is thus able to say that

> as soon as you become engrafted into Christ through faith, you are made a son of God, and heir of heaven, a partaker in righteousness, a possessor of life; and . . . you obtain not the opportunity to gain merit but all the merits of Christ, for they are communicated to you.[114]

Calvin, in speaking of a "double grace" or in stating that "there are two principal graces which we receive through Jesus Christ",[115] i.e. justification and sanctification, runs some risk of being misunderstood. Strictly speaking there is only the one gift or grace—Jesus Christ received in faith by man. Calvin therefore holds that there is no question of God imparting two graces to man,—one of justification and another of sanctification. God imparts to man the one gift or grace: Himself in Jesus Christ from whom the benefits of justification and sanctification are solely derived. "Those benefits would not come to us unless Christ first made Himself ours."[116] Christ becomes ours when He unites Himself to man through the bond of the Holy Spirit, and so enables him to give the response of faith. In faith, engendered in his heart by the living exalted Lord Himself through the Holy Spirit, man receives, not a part or parts of that Lord, but always the whole of Christ and all His benefits, i.e. justification and sanctification, and so these are inseparable.

"Why, then, are we justified by faith?" asks Calvin. His answer is: "Because by faith we grasp Christ's righteousness, by which alone we are reconciled to God. Yet you could not grasp this without at the same time grasping sanctification also."[117] Since Christ "is given unto us for righteousness, wisdom, sanctification, and redemption [1 Cor. 1: 30]"[118] justification and sanctification are inseparable and together and at the same time. ". . . Christ justifies no one", insists Calvin, "whom He does not at the same time sanctify. These benefits are joined together by an everlasting and indissoluble bond, so that those whom He illumines by His wisdom, He redeems; those whom He redeems, He justifies; those whom He justifies, He sanctifies."[119]

Were justification and sanctification to be separated from each other, Christ would be divided. But this is impossible since He "contains both of them [righteousness and sanctification] inseparably in Himself."[120] "Do you wish . . . to attain righteousness in Christ?" asks Calvin. If so, "You must first possess Christ; but you cannot possess Him without being made partaker in His sanctification, because He cannot be divided into pieces [1 Cor. 1 : 13]." Since both in justification and in sanctification it is Christ who expends Himself, "He bestows both of them at the same time, the one never without the other."[121]

Is there then any ground for Bouyer's argument that Calvin believes that man is saved but not changed? Calvin catagorically states that "we are justified not without works yet not through works, since in our sharing in Christ, which justifies us, sanctification is just as much included as righteousness".[122] Bouyer, to be sure, admits that Calvin regards justification and sanctification as inseparable. What he finds unacceptable is the clear-cut distinction between them.

We now turn to Calvin's reason for making such a distinction. Calvin makes a "clear-cut distinction" between sanctification and justification for a very simple reason: ". . . Scripture, even though it joins them [sanctification and justification], still lists them separately in order that God's manifold grace may better appear to us . . . [Paul thus] clearly indicates that to be justified means something different from being made new creatures."[123] Since "both repentance and forgiveness of sins—that is, newness of life and free reconciliation—are conferred on us by Christ and both are attained by us through faith . . . actual holiness of life . . . is not separated from free imputation of righteousness."[124] Nevertheless not sanctification but justification is "the main hinge on which religion turns".[125]

In the life of the Christian, justification and sanctification cannot be divorced from each other, for both are experienced simultaneously and conjointly by him in their indivisible unity in the person of Christ, who is both man's justification and sanctification.[126] In thought, however, the distinction must be made.

It is for pastoral reasons that Calvin insists on the biblical distinction between justification and sanctification. If the distinction is not made, and there is any confusion between the righteousness of Christ imputed to man and the righteousness achieved by man himself, then man is faced with the possibility of annihilation by his own despair and despondency. Wilhelm Niesel rightly observes that "the recollection of the fact that in Christ we are truly born again and in this life make progress in holiness does not help us at all in regard to the question how we can stand before God".[127]

If no clear-cut distinction between justification and sanctification were made (not even in thought), the Christian would be deprived of any kind of assurance with regard to his salvation. His progress in holiness discloses itself paradoxically in the realization of the sheer impossibility of attaining the end of holiness, which is perfect renewal. Yet God requires that perfect obedience and holiness which alone would enable man to appear righteous before Him. The Christian, however, does not despair when his very progress in holiness reveals to him the utter impossibility of reaching the goal of perfect renewal in this life. He neither contemplates nor numbers his own achievements but, resolutely turning his back on them, flees to Christ on whose perfect obedience and righteousness he relies—and in Christ, through union with Him, that obedience and righteousness becomes his own.

In Calvin's own day, Andreas Osiander thought it would be contrary to God's nature were He to justify those who in fact remain wicked.[128] Bouyer follows the same line when he says:

> Extrinsic justification, a justification independent of any interior change, of any new capability given to man to perform acts pleasing of themselves to God, is so far from being a

Pauline doctrine that it is quite irreconcilable with the whole body of his teaching.[129]

Calvin's answer to Osiander also applies to Bouyer:

> ... we must bear in mind ... that the grace of justification is not separated from regeneration, although they are things distinct.[130]

Since justification is never separated from sanctification, there is for Calvin no question of God justifying those who actually remain wicked in the sense that they do not make progress in holiness. The moment the Christian is justified he is also sanctified: justification and santification are two aspects of one and the same gift which is Jesus Christ. Bouyer describes extrinsic justification as a justification unconditioned by an inner change in man. Does he mean by this that, whereas, in the Reformation view, justification is for its validity and effectiveness independent of any change in man, in the Roman view, on the contrary, it depends on such a change to become valid and effective? Or does he use the term "independent" in the sense of "detached" or "separate"?

If he uses the word "independent" in the first sense, his definition of extrinsic justification is correct: man's justification is indeed independent of any interior change or new capability in him, but it does depend solely on a righteousness outside man, i.e. on the righteousness of Christ.

But if Bouyer uses "independent" in the second sense, his criticism of Calvin is as unfounded as was Osiander's 400 years ago. Bouyer himself admits that Calvin does not separate justification and sanctification. If both occur simultaneously and conjointly, so that both are aspects of one and the same gift, why then does Bouyer object so strongly to their distinction in thought? Does he ascribe salvation partly to man's co-operation with God? He would deny this! Or does he want to deprive the Christian of his assurance of salvation and so of his peace?

The distinction—and it is a biblical distinction in spite of what Bouyer may say—must be made because experience teaches us that, since "traces of sin always remain in the righteous, their justification must be very different from reformation into newness of life [cf. Rom. 6: 4]. For God so begins this second point in His elect, and progresses in it gradually, and sometimes slowly, throughout life, that they are always liable to the judgement of death before His tribunal."[131]

Were the distinction between justification and sanctification not made, and had man to look in any way to his own works—Bouyer calls it the interior change and the new capability—for his justification, there could be neither peace nor assurance for the Christian: "our consciences [would] never be pacified; for we are very far from being perfectly renewed".[132] But here is the evangelical assurance which Calvin can, and Bouyer cannot, give: God "does not justify in part but liberally, so that they [His elect] may appear in heaven as if endowed with the purity of Christ. No portion of righteousness sets our consciences at peace until it has been determined that we are pleasing to God, because we are entirely righteous before Him."[133]

The necessity of distinguishing between justification and sanctification without ever separating the one from the other may be further illustrated by Calvin's doctrine of the Sacraments.

In the fourth book of his *Institutes* he expounds his teaching on union with Christ in terms of the Sacraments of Baptism and the Lord's Supper. These are the sacramental counterparts of justification and sanctification. They are therefore connected with, but also distinct from, each other.

Both sacraments—and this is the indissoluble connection between them—testify to, and assist in effecting, man's union with Christ, that same union which is the source of his justification and sanctification. Yet the two sacraments are distinct, for, as Calvin observes,

Baptism should be, as it were, an entry into the Church, and an initiation into faith; but the Supper should be a sort of continual food on which Christ spiritually feeds the household of His believers. Therefore, as there is but one God, one faith, one Christ, and one Church, His Body; so Baptism is but one

69

[Eph. 4: 4–6], and is not a thing oft-repeated. But the Supper is repeatedly distributed, that those who have once been drawn into the Church may realize that they continually feed upon Christ.[134]

Baptism, witnessing to the entry into the Church, the incorporation into the Body of Christ, the initiation into faith, is administered and received once for all. Thus, as the visible sign with which God seals us as His own, it testifies to the one aspect of the gift appropriated by us through union with Christ: our "once-and-for-all" justification by Christ, never to be repeated, for God does not revoke a declaration He has made once for all.

The Lord's Supper, on the other hand, is a continual feeding on Christ, on His Body and Blood. It is the sign and seal that testifies to the other aspect of the gift received by us through union with Christ: our sanctification, which entails our progress and growth in holiness, so that we may become that which we already are in Christ: righteous.

"The chief point of Baptism" is that like a sealed document it confirms to us "that all our sins are so abolished, remitted, and effaced that they can never come to His sight, be recalled, or charged against us."[135] Calvin says:

> We are not to think that Baptism was conferred upon us only for past time, so that for newly committed sins into which we fall after Baptism we must seek new remedies of expiation in some other sacraments, as if the force of the former one were spent.[136]

On the contrary,

> we must realize that at whatever time we are baptized, we are once for all washed and purged for our whole life. Therefore, as often as we fall away, we ought to recall the memory of our Baptism and fortify our mind with it, that we may always be sure and confident of the forgiveness of sins. For, though Baptism, administered only once, seemed to have passed, it was still not destroyed by subsequent sins. For Christ's purity has been offered us in it; His purity ever flourishes; it is defiled by no spots, but buries and cleanses away all our defilements.[137]

Baptism assures us of the forgiveness of sins, which are buried and cleansed away once for all; so it signifies and promises, not a part but the whole, of our salvation, and is thus essentially the counterpart of justification. Justification by Christ takes place once for all! Even the holiest and most sublime works of man can add nothing to his justification; even his vilest and most obnoxious sins can take nothing away from it.

> ... our Lord came forth as true man and took the person and the name of Adam in order to take Adam's place in obeying the Father, to present our flesh as the price of satisfaction to God's righteous judgement, and, in the same flesh, to pay the penalty that we had deserved.[138]

The Son of God, who rendered perfect obedience in His human nature to the will of His Father, has done all, and therefore all of God's salvation is man's who, being justified by Christ, is righteous in Him.

While Baptism confirms to us that all our sins are forgiven, the Lord's Supper testifies to the other aspect of our salvation: sanctification. Calvin has this to say:

> God has received us, once for all, into His family, to hold us not only as servants but as sons. Thereafter, to fulfil the duties of a most excellent Father concerned for His offspring, He undertakes also to nourish us throughout the course of our life. And not content with this alone, He has willed, by giving His pledge, to assure us of this continuing liberality. To this end, therefore, He has, through the hand of His only-begotten Son, given to His Church another sacrament, that is, a spiritual banquet, wherein Christ attests Himself to be the life-giving bread, upon which our souls feed unto true and blessed immortality [Jn. 6: 51].[139]

In their sacramental counterparts—in Baptism and the Lord's Supper—the indissoluble connection on the one hand, and the necessary distinction on the other, between justification and sanctification becomes obvious. Using the New Testament's sacramental mode of speaking, whereby the thing signified is transferred to the sign, Calvin says that "in Baptism, God, regenerating us [regeneration is used here in the sense of adoption into the family and household of God] engrafts us into the society of His Church and makes us His own by adoption".[140] This happens once for all, and so Baptism corresponds to justification by Christ.

Although we are incorporated into Christ once for all, we must yet be continually nourished and maintained in His Body. The Lord's Supper testifies to our growth into the Body of Christ, and our being sustained therein.

According to Calvin, God "discharges the function of provident householder in continually supplying to us the food to sustain and preserve us in that life into which He has begotten us by His Word".[141] In the Lord's Supper God invites us to Christ, the only food of our soul, that, "refreshed by partaking of Him, we may repeatedly gather strength until we shall have reached heavenly immortality".[142] Since this is necessary throughout our earthly lives, the Lord's Supper is administered and received frequently, and so corresponds to sanctification, which continues throughout the Christian's life.

It is thus clear that the two sacraments, while distinct from each other, cannot be separated from each other. Baptism is the sign and seal of our entrance into union with Christ through participation in His death and resurrection. The Lord's Supper is the sign and seal of the maintenance and deepening of our union with Christ through participation in His death and resurrection. Anyone who is sacramentally engrafted into the Body of Christ through Baptism is, and must be continually, maintained in that Body, which God does by feeding him through Christ in the Holy Supper. The grafting of the bud into the stock and the process of development that follows, are two different things but cannot be separated.

A careful examination of Calvin's teaching on union with Christ, on the one hand, and on the sacraments on the other, shows, as we have seen, that Baptism and the Eucharist are essentially the sacramental counterparts of justification and sanctification. Just as Baptism and the Lord's Supper must be distinguished, but not separated, from each other in the

life of the Church and the individual believer, so justification
and sanctification are distinct and yet conjoint. Thomas F.
Torrance demonstrates their inter-connection and differ-
entiation in his *Kingdom and Church*:

> As he who is sacramentally incorporated into the Body of
> Christ is in Holy Communion continually nourished and
> maintained in the Body of Christ, so sanctification is the
> continual unfolding and maintaining of our justification.
> Sanctification is not a response of man that must be added to
> justification, but the continual renewing and re-enacting in the
> believer of a justification that is made once and for all. The
> experience of sanctification is such an exercise in Word and
> Sacrament that the believer is ever being nourished with the
> new humanity of Christ, and being clothed with His divine–
> human righteousness, which is the fundamental reality of his
> Christian being.[143]

Baptism and the Lord's Supper confirm, and testify to, the
two aspects of one and the same reality: the salvation-event
manifested and accomplished in and through Jesus Christ.
God justifies us: He declares us to be righteous with the
righteousness of Christ which He imputes to us. God
sanctifies us: that which He declares us to be—new creatures
in Christ—is continually unfolded and maintained, renewed
and re-enacted through the Holy Spirit in our lives. Grace—
Jesus Christ—saves us, and in saving us maintains us in
what by God's declaration we have become, and already are,
in Christ.

In Bouyer's view the doctrine of extrinsic justification
compels the Reformers to assert, on the one hand, that "grace
alone saves us" but, on the other, that "it changes nothing
in us in so doing".[144] It is at this point that Protestants are
tempted to ask Bouyer whether the Roman doctrine of the
sacraments, and its implied notion of grace, does not compel
him to grant that, while grace changes man, it does not save
him; at least does not save him totally and once for all?

The Council of Trent affirms that

> by the grace of our Lord Jesus Christ, which is conferred in
> Baptism, the guilt of original sin is remitted

and

> the whole of that which has the true and proper nature of sin
> [*veram et propriam peccati rationem habet*] is . . . taken away . . . in
> those who are born again, there is nothing that God hates . . .
> [they] are made innocent, immaculate, pure, harmless, and
> beloved of God . . . so that there is nothing to retard their
> entrance into heaven.[145]

The instrumental cause of justification—for Trent not merely
the remission of sins but also the sanctification and renewal of
the inner man[146]—is "the Sacrament of Baptism, which is
the Sacrament of faith, without which [faith] no man was
ever justified".[147]

Grace indeed "changes" man, but does it really "save"
him? The Reformers teach that on the ground of his
Baptism, which signifies and seals the promise of Christ to
him, the believer, being justified once for all, is assured that
all his sins, past and future, are forgiven. This doctrine, however, is expressly condemned and anathematized by the
Council of Trent: "If any one saith, that by the sole remem-
brance [*recordatione*] and the faith of the Baptism which has
been received, all sins committed after Baptism are either
remitted, or made venial: let him be anathema."[148] It is
true that Baptism cannot be repeated, because according to
Roman doctrine there is imprinted by it "in the soul a
character, that is, a certain spiritual and indelible sign",[149]
which can never be lost, even through mortal sin. Baptism,
however, is not able to consummate the new life of sanctifying
grace. In all ordinary circumstances the Sacrament of
Confirmation is necessary "to increase sanctifying grace, to
give special sacramental grace and to imprint a lasting
character on the soul".[150] The indelible character conferred
by Baptism is that of a Christian and member of the Church;
the character conferred by Confirmation is that of a soldier of
Christ ready to profess and defend his faith.

In the Roman view more grace can thus be added by
Confirmation to what has already been received in Baptism.
In other words, in Confirmation the new life of grace received

74

in Baptism reaches its consummation. "Confirmation is the completion of Baptism."[151]

The Roman Catechism (1566) enjoins pastors to teach that

in common with the other sacraments, Confirmation, . . . confers new grace . . . and as we are not even permitted to imagine that grace can exist simultaneously with sin, it follows that [Confirmation] also pardons and remits sins. But in addition to this . . . it is peculiar to Confirmation first to perfect the grace of Baptism. For those who have been made Christians by Baptism still possess a certain tenderness and weakness, as it were, like new-born infants but afterwards, by the sacrament of Chrism they are made stronger to resist all the assaults of the flesh, the world and the devil, and their minds are altogether confirmed in faith to confess and glorify the name of our Lord Jesus Christ. Thus, as no one will doubt, originated the very name of Confirmation . . . by virtue of this sacrament God confirms in us the work He began by Baptism and leads us to the perfection of Christian firmness [soliditatis]. But not only does it [the sacrament of Confirmation] confirm; it also increases grace.[152]

The same *Roman Catechism* defines a sacrament as *invisibilitis gratiae visibile signum, ad nostram iustificationem institutum*—a visible sign of invisible grace instituted for our justification.[153] This justification is accomplished, not merely by the remission of sins, but by the infusion of sanctifying grace.

In *Christ The Sacrament*, E. Schillebeeckx, an outstanding modern representative of Roman sacramental theology, gives practically the same definition. ". . . a sacrament is a divine bestowal of salvation in an outwardly perceptible form which makes the bestowal manifest; a bestowal of salvation in historical visibility."[154] "Salvation" must be understood as the act of encounter between God (who takes the initiative) and man. On God's part this encounter involves a disclosure of Himself by revelation and on man's part devotion to His service. "This encounter itself, seen from man's side, is the reality of what is called sanctifying grace. . . ."[155] Schillebeeckx, defending Infant Baptism, says "the sacrament produces within the child the ontological foundation which makes the future response possible; the foundation of the

75

encounter with God is laid. In other words, sanctifying grace is now present as the positive possibility of an encounter with God when the child's psyche awakes. . . ."[156] Referring to Baptism and Confirmation Schillebeeckx says that "as sacraments they are both a sanctification of the person".[157]

Schillebeeckx explains the relationship between Baptism and Confirmation and the "perfecting" and "completing" of the one by the other thus:

> . . . a person receiving Baptism is incorporated into the Easter mystery of the visible Church and thus into the eternal passover of Christ. On the other hand, when a person is confirmed he begins to participate in that fullness of the Holy Spirit which the visible Church possesses, and in her activity of sending the Spirit; thus he is incorporated into the eternal Pentecost mystery of the glorified Lord. Consequently Baptism makes us members of the ecclesial People of God, the "child of the Father"; we become children of the Father, *filii in Filio*, in the power of the Spirit of sonship which Baptism gives us. Then in Confirmation, as members of the Church and so as children of God, we are "established in power"; within the visible Church, we receive a share in her fullness and bestowal of the Spirit, and thus in the Pentecost mystery of Christ Himself. Therefore Confirmation makes us adult members of the Church, incorporates us into the fullness of her mystery *filii Dei in virtute*. The *robur* or strength of which theological tradition has spoken since the Middle Ages undoubtedly reflects an essential aspect of Confirmation.[158]

Schillebeeckx, faithful to Tridentine theology, understands Baptism as requiring an addition to complete and perfect it: *robur*, strength, the establishment in power by the bestowal of the Spirit. St. Paul's saying "as many of you as have been baptized into Christ have put on Christ" (Gal. 3 : 27) was understood by the Reformers as meaning that *tota gratia, totus Christus*, was received. In Calvin's view the sacraments, i.e. Baptism and the Lord's Supper, are instituted by God to signify the whole Christ with all His gifts. The believer who participates in them is brought "into a fullness of grace in which he receives and enjoys more and more what has already been offered to him in Christ, so that the reality which will in the end be fulfilled is one that is already given in the beginning".[159]

The Roman Catholic conception of grace seems to ignore the *homoousion* of the Nicene Fathers, who regarded gift and giver as one, and to consider grace as a quality, infused in varying quantities into man, which changes his being by raising him from lower to higher ontological levels. Reformation theology on the other hand believes that through faith, grace—Jesus Christ—comes to dwell in the heart of man, who thus enters into a new ontological relation with Christ, who redeems and recreates his being in Himself.

If, as Schillebeeckx avers, Baptism "produces within the child the ontological foundation" that makes the future encounter with God possible, then Confirmation, in order to complete Baptism, presumably provides the ontological factor that establishes the baptized adult in power, and so raises him to a higher ontological level. The end product of this gradual process of elevation from lower to higher ontological planes is the deification of man.

In Schillebeeckx' view

> every bestowal of grace not only deifies but at the same time makes the forgiveness of sin take a more profound hold on a person. Although forgiveness can be realized instantaneously it nevertheless allows of a subsequent process through which holiness steadily takes possession of and re-forms the whole psychological make-up of the "convert". This also indicates that the different sacraments, however much they may be formally distinct from one another, make up one organic whole through which grace gradually completes its victory and man becomes wholly redeemed.[160]

In the light of this modern exposition of Roman sacramental theology by Schillebeeckx, we may ask whether Bouyer regards the grace which changes man as also saving him, totally and once for all. In the life of the Christian there seems to be not only increase, but also decrease, and indeed loss, of grace, and so of salvation.

The grace received in Baptism can not only be increased as in Confirmation; it can also be lost. The grace conferred in

Baptism raises those who are spiritually dead in original sin to life, and makes them "innocent, immaculate, pure, harmless, and beloved of God". But, since post-baptismal sins are not forgiven, man's first subsequent mortal sin deprives him of his state of grace, and so he is once more spiritually dead. The Sacrament of Penance helps the spiritually dead in mortal sin to rise again by restoring him to a state of grace. Baptism and Penance are therefore called *sacramenta mortuorum* as distinguished from the sacraments of the living (Confirmation, Eucharist, Extreme Unction, Holy Orders and Matrimony) so named "because they may be received worthily only by those persons who have the life of grace".[161]

The Sacrament of Penance is *secundam post naufragium deperditae gratiae tabulam*—"a second plank after the shipwreck of grace lost".[162] This post-baptismal justification—the Tridentine Fathers regarded sanctification and renewal as included in justification—achieved by the Sacrament of Penance, removes the obstacle, mortal sin, which prevents the influx of grace. Penance is thus *lapsi reparatio*—the restoration of the fallen.[163]

Since both Baptism and Penance confer the grace which justifies and sanctifies, both sacraments are necessary for salvation. The recipient of the Sacrament of Penance must, however, actively co-operate in his restoration to a state of grace. ". . . by Baptism putting on Christ, we are made therein entirely a new creature, obtaining a full and entire remission of all sins."[164] Unto this "newness and entireness, however, we are in no way able to arrive by the Sacrament of Penance, without many tears and great labours on our parts, the divine justice demanding this".[165] Penance is thus called *laboriosus quidam baptismus*—a laborious kind of Baptism.[166] The Sacrament of Penance which requires "three acts in the penitent . . . contrition, confession, and satisfaction"[167] was "instituted by Christ our Lord for reconciling the faithful unto God, as often as they fall into sin after Baptism".[168]

Penance again and again procures for the lapsed and the fallen the possibility of being justified, for "through [this] sacrament . . . they shall have attained to the recovery, by the merit of Christ, of the grace lost."[169] The Church exercises jurisdiction over "those who are of the household of faith, whom Christ our Lord has once, by the laver of Baptism, made the members of His own Body",[170] and so controls their restoration to the life of grace. "If they [the baptized] should afterwards [i.e. after Baptism] have defiled themselves by any crime, He would no longer have them cleansed by a repetition of Baptism . . . but be placed as criminals before this tribunal; that, by the sentence of the priests, they might be freed, not once, but as often as, being penitent, they should, from their sins committed, flee thereunto."[171]

The reality of grace, which according to Bouyer is only a "chimera" in Reformation teaching, is, however, in the Roman system so illusive that the salvation which today is might not exist tomorrow. Mortal sin can, and does, so supplant the benefits of Baptism, the "divine bestowal of salvation in an outwardly visible form", that another visible sign of invisible grace—the Sacrament of Penance—is required for the removal of the obstacle to grace and, by the same token, to salvation. When is the Christian, changed by Baptism into a new creature and established in power by Confirmation, yet deprived again and again by mortal sin of his state of grace, totally and once and for all saved? When can the Christian know that, though still continuing to progress in sanctification, he is yet justified once for all, and therefore saved and that his Baptism testifies to this fact? Confusing justification and sanctification, or rather including sanctification in justification and so making it too a process, Rome speaks of a beginning, an increase or decrease and indeed even a loss, of justification, which could surely mean that, while grace changes man, it does not save him, at least not totally once for all.

This is a fair question on the Protestant part, since even the new life of grace conferred in the Sacrament of Penance is not permanent. "We should receive the Sacrament of Penance often because, besides forgiving sin, the Sacrament also restores or increases sanctifying grace in the soul and helps us to resist temptation."[172] In other words sanctifying grace has to be continually reinfused and augmented so as to preserve the believer in a state of grace and to make his salvation possible.

Moreover, just as Baptism requires to be perfected by Confirmation, so the Sacrament of Penance has to be completed by Extreme Unction. Referring to the Sacrament of Extreme Unction, the Council of Trent states that the Fathers regarded it as "the completion not only of penance, but also of the whole Christian life, which ought to be a perpetual penance".[173] Extreme Unction is thus still another salutary remedy provided by Christ for His servants against the weapons of their enemies. "As, in the other sacraments, He [Christ] prepared the greatest aids, whereby, during life, Christians may preserve themselves whole from every more grievous spiritual evil, so did He guard the close of life, by the Sacrament of Extreme Unction, as with a most firm defence."[174]

The Sacrament of Extreme Unction strengthens the soul of the Christian, remits his sin, its punishment and its consequences, so that, in spite of the attempts of the adversary to ruin him at the end of his life, he does not fall from trust in the mercy of God.[175]

The grace which so often has restored the Christian to the new life without ever being able to save him totally once for all, intervenes once again at the end of his days to remit his sin and its punishment.

Moreover the thing signified, and the effect of this sacrament [Extreme Unction], are explained in those words: "and the prayer of faith shall save the sick man, and the Lord shall raise him up, and if he be in sins they shall be forgiven him [James 5: 15]. For the thing here signified is the grace of the Holy Ghost; whose anointing cleanses away sins, if there be any still to be expiated, as also the remains of sins; and raises up and strengthens the soul of the sick person, by exciting in him a great confidence in the divine mercy; whereby the sick being supported, bears more easily the inconveniences and pains of his sickness; and more readily resists the temptations of the devil who "lies in wait for his heel" [Gen. 3: 15]; and at times obtains bodily health, when expedient for the welfare of the soul.[176]

But does the grace conferred in Extreme Unction really save the Christian who receives it? Since in the Roman view the believer is at no time justified once for all, even the Sacrament of Extreme Unction does not necessarily complete the process of his salvation.

A soul in the state of grace enters heaven immediately after the particular judgement [judgement on the individual immediately after death] if it is fully purified from the effects of sin; otherwise it goes to purgatory.[177]

If here on earth grace effects the full purification of the soul, the perfect sanctification of the believer, he enters heaven and is saved. But, if he has not reached perfection, his soul goes to purgatory. Explicitly rejecting the Reformation teaching of a justification accomplished once for all by Christ, the Council of Trent declares:

If any one saith, that after the grace of justification has been received, to every penitent sinner the guilt is remitted, and the debt of eternal punishment is blotted out in such wise that there remains not any debt of temporal punishment to be discharged either in this world, or in the next in purgatory, before the entrance to the Kingdom of Heaven can be opened [to him] let him be anathema.[178]

A grace that remits the guilt and the debt of eternal punishment, but cannot do so with any debt of temporal punishment, seems to Protestants rather ineffective and impotent in comparison with the *tota gratia* rediscovered by the Reformers, which saves men once for all and in so doing changes them into what they already are in Christ. All the Roman Church has to offer seems to be salvation only at the time of the particular judgement to those who are fully purified—how does the Christian know whether he is wholly sanctified?—and salvation *in spe* to those whose debt of temporal punishment is not yet paid. The process of their sanctification is to be completed in purgatory, where they await the consummation of their salvation.

Is Bouyer sure that it was the Reformation that created "the chimera of a salvation which should save us, without drawing us in the least from the state of sin"?[179] Is it not rather Roman doctrine which, despite grace which draws man again and again from the state of sin, yet makes salvation so illusive that some souls at least will have to wait for its consummation until the Last Judgement, when purgatory shall be no more?

5

Bouyer's Defence of "Fides Caritate Formata"

The relationship between faith and works has already been discussed. Since Bouyer bases his rejection of Protestantism to a large extent on the Reformers' supposed misconception of how faith and love are related one to another, their relationship must now be further examined.

Bouyer is convinced that in the elaboration of its own principles Protestantism is involved in an *aporia*: Protestantism must either maintain its unwarranted opposition to the *fides caritate formata* and so be unfaithful to the express teaching of the New Testament or it must admit the invalidity of its position and so cease to be Protestant.[180]

For Bouyer

the real truth is that the love of God by which God loves is the cause of everything in justification considered objectively, whereas "faith" is its only principle in the subjective aspect. But "faith", in St. Paul's sense, being the fruit of "the charity of God poured forth in our hearts by the Holy Spirit", supposes the total abandonment of man to the gift of God. For this reason, as Luther himself says in a passage we have quoted, one where he forgets his polemical systematization, either the "faith" which justifies is wholly penetrated with charity, or else it is the principle of the charity restored in our hearts, both to God and to everything He loves. To suppose, on the one hand, that the person justified by faith, who calls to God, in the Spirit, "Abba, Father", does not love God, or has not to love Him in order to be justified, is certainly to maintain, not only a false deduction, from a premise absurd in itself, but one not even conceivable apart from supposing, what goes against the whole of St. Paul, that grace passes through man without affecting him at all, without changing his heart, without creating in him a new human nature in the image of that of the Son of God.[181]

Protestants will take no exception to Bouyer's statement that "the love of God by which God loves is the cause of everything in justification considered objectively". What else could be its cause but the love of God in Christ? Which of the Reformers denies it? Nor will any objection be raised on the part of Protestants against his definition of faith as the only principle of justification "in the subjective aspect", as long as it is clearly understood that faith being the work and gift of the Holy Spirit "embraces Christ, as offered to us by the Father".[182]

But can Protestants agree with the statement that "the faith which justifies is wholly penetrated with charity", or that it is, in a certain sense, "the principle of the charity (i.e. love) restored, in our hearts, both to God and to everything He loves"?

Bouyer refers to his own quotations from Luther[183] where the Reformer is supposed to forget "his controversial systematization" and to see the proper connection between faith and love. The first text cited by Bouyer is from *The Freedom of a Christian* where Luther says:

Now when a man has learned through the commandments to recognize his helplessness and is distressed about how he might satisfy the law—since the law must be fulfilled so that not a jot or tittle shall be lost, otherwise man will be condemned without hope—then, being truly humbled and reduced to nothing in his own eyes, he finds in himself nothing whereby he may be justified and saved. Here the second part of Scripture comes to our aid, namely, the promises of God which declare the glory of God, saying, "If you wish to fulfil the law and not covet, as the law demands, come, believe in Christ in whom grace, righteousness, peace, liberty, and all things are promised you. If you believe, you shall have all things; if you do not believe, you shall lack all things." That which is impossible for you to accomplish by trying to fulfil all the works of the law—many and useless as they all are—you will accomplish quickly and easily through faith. God our Father has made all things depend on faith so that whoever has faith will have everything, and whoever does not have faith will have nothing. "For God has consigned all men to disobedience, that He may have mercy upon all", as it is stated in Rom. 11[: 32]. Thus the promises of God give what the commandments of God demand and fulfil what the law prescribes so that all things may be God's alone, both the commandments and the fulfilling of the commandments. He alone commands, He alone fulfils. Therefore the promises of God belong to the New Testament. Indeed, they are the New Testament.[184]

Bouyer rightly points out that in Luther's view the believer is not exempt from the obligation of the law, for when the promises of the New Testament are mentioned in contrast to the precepts of the Old Testament, there occurs the phrase: "If you wish to fulfil the law and not covet, as the law demands, come, believe in Christ. . . ." Bouyer does not allow any Roman Catholic misinterpretation of the cited passage, in the sense that the function of faith here is merely to silence the scruples of those who wish to fulfil the law—not by enabling them to do so, but by dispensing them from the necessity. God does not dispense the believer from the obligations of the law but enables him to fulfil them for, as Luther puts it, "all things [are] God's alone, both the commandments and the fulfilling of the commandments. He alone commands; He alone fulfils."[185]

The second passage cited by Bouyer is taken from Luther's *Large Catechism* (1529):

Until now we have heard of the first part of Christian doctrine [the Ten Commandments] and there have seen what God wills us to do and not to do. This is now rightly followed by "the faith" [the second part of Christian doctrine, i.e. the Apostles' Creed] which sets before us all that we ought to expect and receive from God; in short it teaches us to know Him perfectly.[186]

Luther then gives what Bouyer calls "the capital definition of salvation by faith":[187]

84

The purpose to be achieved is that we are able to do what according to the Ten Commandments we should do. For they are (as we said before) so high and lifted up that men's ability is much too weak and feeble to keep them. Consequently, it is as necessary to learn this part [of Christian doctrine, i.e. "the faith"] as the other [i.e. the Ten Commandments] so that we may know how we can succeed in obtaining such power [i.e. to keep the commandments]. For, if in our own strength, we could keep the Ten Commandments as they are to be kept, we should need nothing else, neither "faith" [as expressed in the Apostles' Creed] nor the Lord's Prayer.[188]

Bouyer claims that Luther, forgetting "his polemical systematization", teaches the same as the Church of Rome:

Knowledge of God's demands; experience, confirmed by the words of Scripture, of our powerlessness to meet them *of our own strength;* acknowledgement by faith, of the gift of God— that is to say, the discovery that *the force needed to effect what we could not do of ourselves is given to us in Christ.*[189]

It should be added that in a writing in which, Bouyer would agree, Calvin does anything but forget "his polemical systematization", i.e. in the *Institutes*, the Genevan Reformer says exactly the same as Luther. Calvin too teaches what apparently has always been taught by the Roman Church:

Since faith embraces Christ, as offered to us by the Father [cf. Jn. 6: 29]—that is, since He is offered not only for right-eousness, forgiveness of sins, and peace, but also for sanctification [cf. 1 Cor. 1: 30] and the fountain of the water of life [Jn. 7: 38] —without a doubt, no one can duly know Him without at the same time apprehending the sanctification of the Spirit. Or, if anyone desires some plainer statement, faith rests upon the knowledge of Christ. And Christ cannot be known apart from the sanctification of His Spirit. It follows that faith can in no wise be separated from a devout disposition.[190]

Calvin, too, believes that, in embracing Christ through faith, the gift of God, man obtains not only the forgiveness of his sins—Christ having been made sin for him—but at the same time, being in Christ whose righteousness has become his, the ability—however prone to failure—to obey the law

whose basic and ultimate demand is love: "Thou shalt love
the Lord thy God . . . and thy neighbour as thyself" (Lk.
10: 27).

Neither Luther nor Calvin, then, separates love from faith.
"Behold," says Luther, "from faith . . . flow forth love and
joy in the Lord. . . ."[191] Calvin is no less explicit:

> But how can the mind be aroused to taste the divine goodness
> without at the same time being wholly kindled to love God in
> return? For truly, that abundant sweetness which God has
> stored up for those who fear Him cannot be known without at
> the same time powerfully moving us. And once anyone has
> been moved by it, it utterly ravishes him and draws him to
> itself. Therefore, it is no wonder if a perverse and wicked heart
> never experiences that emotion by which, borne up to heaven
> itself, we are admitted to the most hidden treasures of God and
> to the most hallowed precincts of His Kingdom, which should
> not be defiled by the entrance of an impure heart. For the
> teaching of the schoolmen, that love is prior to faith and hope,
> is mere madness; for it is faith alone that first engenders love
> in us.[192]

The Reformers make a distinction, but no separation,
between faith and love. In the experience of the believer these
are co-present and conjoint. One cannot separate the
moment in time when faith is planted in the believer by the
Holy Spirit and the moment when his heart is filled with
love. Priority in thought, however, must be given to faith,
which engenders love.

Luther holds that love flows forth from faith; Calvin that
faith engenders love. Both Reformers are thus agreed that
faith cannot be separated from love but works through it
(Gal. 5: 6). Which comes first—faith or love? Is our love for
God and our neighbour the *cause* or the *effect* of our faith?
Quoting Rom. 5: 5 "the charity, i.e. the love, of God is
poured out in our hearts by the Holy Spirit", Bouyer says
that faith is the fruit of this love of God. As long as it is understood that Paul speaks here, not of our love for God, but of
His love in Christ, the statement that the gift of faith is the
fruit of the divine love is unexceptionable. God in Christ
reconciling the world unto Himself provides the instrument

whereby man may take hold of Christ and in doing so is able to love God and his neighbour.

It must, however, be pointed out that the clause "because the love of God poured out in our hearts by the Holy Spirit" refers not to faith but to hope—"hope which maketh not ashamed", because it is continually confirmed by the love of God.

> . . . wherever this faith is alive [Calvin observes], it must have along with it the hope of eternal salvation as its inseparable companion. Or rather, it engenders and brings forth hope from itself.[193]

In spite of tribulations the hope of our eternal salvation is not disappointed because God's love for us in Christ floods our hearts through the Holy Spirit, and continually confirms the promises of God on which our hope is based.

But what do Luther and especially Calvin mean when they say that the faith which justifies engenders love, and what does Roman Catholic theology understand by *fides caritate formata*?

The Reformers are quite sure that faith engenders love in us, and that therefore a faith from which no love flows forth is not the kind of faith through which justification is received. The Reformers, however, are equally certain that "as regards justification, faith is something merely passive, bringing nothing of ours to the recovering of God's favour [*Dei gratiam*] but receiving from Christ that which we lack".[194] Faith thus contributes nothing to justification.

> We are . . . said to be "justified by faith" (Rom. 3: 28; 5: 1) not because faith infuses into us a *habitus* or a quality [*non quia fides habitum aut qualitatem in nos transfundat*], but because we are accepted by God . . . we receive by faith what God freely gives.[195]

In a sermon on Gen. 15 Calvin says:

> . . . faith does not justify us by its virtue and here is the reason why one must have no regard for its perfection in order to say that our salvation is perfect . . . it [faith] does not justify . . . because of any excellence it may have in itself but in the measure that it derives of Jesus Christ what we lack . . . we are

justified by faith, that is, the means by which we make ourselves pleasing to God is that we give an opening to our Lord Jesus and that He applies to us His justice . . . when God justifies us by the means of faith, the grace He confers on us is included in that justice in the same measure in which He closes His eyes to the feebleness which is in our faith. Faith therefore justifies in such a way that what it lacks is the measure in which it justifies . . . it [faith] simply receives what is given to it by God.[196]

Faith, in the Reformation view, though the source from which love inevitably flows forth, justifies only in the sense that it is the instrument whereby the mercy of God is received. Faith is indeed man's response in love to the love of God. Yet it is not his response to the divine love or even his ability to respond to it that justifies him; it is God's mercy alone which, prior to any human response to it, is received through faith, the work of the Holy Spirit in the heart of man.

What lies behind Bouyer's statement that "either the faith which justifies is wholly penetrated with charity, or else it is the principle of the charity restored in our hearts . . ."[197] to which the "non-polemical" Luther would apparently have agreed? In other words what do Roman Catholic theologians mean when they speak of justifying faith as *fides caritate formata*?

The refusal by Roman theology to make a proper distinction between justification and sanctification has led to an equally serious confusion with regard to faith and love. In his *Symbolism*, Johann Adam Möhler asserts that justification "consists in a total change of the whole inward man".[198] This being the case

we can understand why the [Roman] Catholic Church should so urgently insist that faith alone doth not justify before God; that it is rather only the first subjective, indispensable condition to be justified; the root from which God's approval must spring; the first title whereon we can establish our claim of divine filiation . . . (to make use of the expression of Seripando's at the Council of Trent), if love is enkindled out of faith, as fire out of brimstone, then, only after faith and love doth regeneration or justification ensue. Hence, the schools of the Middle

Ages recognized, likewise, a faith, whereof they said, that it alone justified; it is known by the designation of the *fides formata*, under which the schoolmen understood a faith, that had love in itself as its vivifying, its plastic [*gestaltendes*] principle (*forma*); and on this account it was called *fides caritate formata*, *animata*, *fides viva*, *vivida*. This is that higher faith, which brings man into real, vital communion with Christ, fills him with an infinite devotion to God, with the strongest confidence in Him, with the deepest humility and inmost love towards Him; liberates him from sin, and causes all creatures to be viewed and loved in God.[199]

Of course faith alone does not justify—"justifying faith" is a most misleading term. What justifies is the object, the content and formative norm of faith which, however, is not love—if it were, love would be the cause of justification—but Jesus Christ. Faith as such is a vacuum—it "justifies" because this vacuum is filled with Jesus Christ and, being filled with Him, it produces love; for, where Jesus Christ is, there is love also. Faith does not "justify" because it is penetrated with our love of God and man, but it is penetrated with love because it "justifies", i.e. because its content is Jesus Christ, who, in justifying us, gives us the ability to respond to His love with love. "Justifying" faith is *fides a Christo formata*, and, since Christ is its *forma*, it produces love and works by it.

The Reformers do not believe that "grace passes through man without affecting him at all. . . ." They maintain most definitely that grace, changing the heart of man, creates in him "a new human nature in the image of that of the Son of God". The Reformers never affirm that "the person justified by faith . . . does not love God." Of course the justified sinner loves God. But they utterly reject the Roman view that the person justified by faith has to love God in order to be justified. Christ and Christ alone justifies—not love; not even the most sublime love of man can obtain for him the forgiveness of sins—only grace, which is Christ, can do it and does it. Man does not love so as to be justified, he loves because he is justified.

As faith and love are closely connected with justification and sanctification, their relationship with one another is in many respects analogous to that between justification and sanctification themselves. Karl Barth's description of the relationship between justification and sanctification can therefore also be applied to that between faith and love. Barth's argument at the same time completely refutes Bouyer's charge that the Reformation teaches that grace saves man without changing him:

> It remains only to ask whether there is perhaps an *ordo* (*salutis*) in the relationship of justification and sanctification and therefore a superiority and subordination, a *prius* and *posterius*, in the one event of grace and salvation. We presuppose that there is no such order in the temporal sense. The *simul* of the one redemptive act of God in Jesus Christ cannot be split up into a temporal sequence, and in this way psychologized. The justification and sanctification of man, manifest in the resurrection of Jesus Christ and effective in the Holy Spirit, are an event in this *simul*, and not therefore in such a way that his justification first takes place separately (as though it could be his justification by God if it did not also include his santification), and then his sanctification takes place separately (as though it could be his sanctification by God if at all its stages and in all its forms it were not based upon and borne by the event of his justification). No, they both take place simultaneously and together, just as the living Jesus Christ, in whom they both take place and are effective, is simultaneously and together true God and true man, the Humiliated and the Exalted. Yet this does not mean that we can lay aside the question of their order. . . .
>
> [In a very definite sense] justification has to be understood as the first and basic and to that extent superior moment and aspect of the one event of salvation, and sanctification as the second and derivative and to that extent inferior. It is indeed in virtue of the condescension of God in which the eternal Word assumed our flesh that there takes place the exaltation of man in the existence of the royal man Jesus. It is in virtue of the forgiveness of his sins and his establishment as a child of God, both fulfilled in the gracious judgement and sentence of God, that man is called and given a readiness and willingness for discipleship, for conversion, for the doing of good works, for the bearing of his cross. It is in virtue of the fact that he is justified in the presence of God by God that he is sanctified by Him. Surely it is obvious that if we ask concerning the structure of this

occurrence justification must be given the priority over sanctification.

Yet is this the end of the matter? Do we not have to recognize that the existence of the royal man Jesus, and therefore the true answering of the question of obedience, the summoning and preparing of man for the service of God, have a radiance and importance in the Bible which are not in any way secondary to those of justifying grace? Is the first the only possible answer? In the question of the material order of this whole event do we not have to take into account—irrespective of the question of its inner movement—its meaning and purpose and goal? And does it not seem that that which is second in execution (*executione posterius*), i.e. sanctification, is first in intention (*intentione prius*)? What is it that God wills and effects in the reconciliation of man with Himself? By the incarnation of His Word does He not will and effect the existence of the royal man Jesus and His lordship over all His brothers and the whole world? By His humiliation to be the Judge judged for us, and therefore by the justification of man before Him, does He not will and effect the existence of a loyal and courageous people of this King in covenant with Himself, and therefore the sanctification of man? And even this may not be the ultimate, or penultimate, word concerning the *telos* of the event of atonement. Yet in relation to the relationship between justification and sanctification are we not forced to say that teleologically sanctification is superior to justification and not the reverse? It is obvious that we cannot help putting and answering the question in this form too.

Yet there are still good reasons for the first answer; and it is not without its significance. This being the case, is it really necessary or wise to choose between them at all? In so doing, might we not be encroaching on the actuality of the one grace of the one Jesus Christ? And this is something which cannot be permitted merely out of a desire to systematize. In any case, are we not asking concerning the divine order of the divine will and action revealed and effective in Jesus Christ? Might it not be that in this—in this particular function and respect—the *prius* is also the *posterius* and *vice versa*? This would mean that both answers have to be given with the same seriousness in view of the distinctive truth in both—intersecting but not cancelling one another. In the *simul* of the one divine will and action justification is first as the basis and second as presupposition, sanctification first as aim and second as consequence;

and therefore both are superior and both subordinate. Embracing the distinctness and unity of the two moments and aspects, the one grace of the one Jesus Christ is at work, and it is both justifying and sanctifying grace, and both to the glory of God and the salvation of man. Where else does God (the God known in Jesus Christ) seek and create His glory but in the salvation of man? And yet who can say that the glory of God to the salvation of man is greater or smaller in man's justification or sanctification? Again, where is the salvation of man (the man known in Jesus Christ) to be found but in the glory which God prepares for Himself in His action to and with man? Yet who is to say that the salvation of man to the glory of God is greater or smaller in the fact that man is justified by God or sanctified by Him? If we start at this point, and therefore at the grace of the covenant effective and revealed in Jesus Christ, we have the freedom, but we are also bound, to give to the question of the order of the relationship between justification and sanctification this twofold answer. There is no contradiction. As a twofold answer, it corresponds to the substance of the matter.[200]

It seems to us that here Karl Barth is speaking as the true heir of the Reformation. His statement about the relationship between justification and sanctification—and by analogy about the relationship between faith and love—is the Protestant answer to Romanism. But this is an answer which goes beyond what Calvin and especially Luther would have said, since it is even more strictly christological than the teaching of the sixteenth-century Reformers. Since the one grace of the one Jesus Christ justifies and sanctifies man, justification and sanctification can only be two aspects of the one event of salvation, and faith and love can only be two moments of man's one response through the Holy Spirit to the one grace of the one Jesus Christ. Therefore the grace that saves man also changes him. This was Reformed doctrine at the beginning; it is still the teaching of the Reformed Church. And it is based on Scripture.

6

The Reformation and "Scholasticism in its Decadence"

There is one more question to be answered. While in Bouyer's view the "positive" elements of the Reformation were taken from Scripture and (Roman) Catholic tradition, where did the "negative" elements propounded by the Reformers have their origin?

> To the historian [Bouyer observes], the reply is obvious. The Reformers no more invented this strange and despairing universe than they found it in Scripture. It is simply the universe of the philosophy they had been brought up in, scholasticism in its decadence. If the Reformers unintentionally became heretics, the fault does not consist in the radical nature of their reform, but in its hesitation, its timidity, its imperfect vision. The structure they raised on their own principles is unacceptable only because they used uncritically material drawn from the decaying [Roman] Catholicism they desired to elude, but whose prisoners they remained to a degree they never suspected. No phrase reveals so clearly the hidden evil that was to spoil the fruit of the Reformation than Luther's saying that Occam was the only scholastic who was any good.[201]

> [Bouyer's] conclusion . . . is that the negative, "heretical" aspect of the Reformation neither follows from its positive principles, nor is it a necessary consequence of their development or vindication, but appears simply as a survival, within Protestantism, of what was most vitiated and corrupt in the [Roman] Catholic thought at the close of the Middle Ages.[202]

Nominalism and its influence on mediaeval thought and theology would be a rewarding field of research, but goes beyond the scope of this work. We must therefore confine ourselves to a few remarks.

If Nominalism, and especially Occamism, is the philosophical and theological expression of everything that was most vitiated and corrupt in Roman Catholic thought at the time of the Reformation, it is rather surprising to learn on the authority of Joseph Lortz that the "dogmatic" Occam and the corresponding Occamism were not wholly condemned by the Church of Rome. Occam's theological work was censured, but the extent of the censure was never published. "Formally therefore he [Occam] remained uncondemned and the extent of the censure obscure (*unklar*)."[203]

Could this mean that the Church of Rome has never formally condemned its own decadence and vitiation, or that the extent of its censures is still obscure?

Nominalism had certainly a positive influence on the Reformers. In insisting on the distinction between intuitive and abstractive knowledge, and consequently between empiricism and formalism, Nominalism enabled the Reformers to see that the Word of God is operating in history, and to take seriously the relation of eternal Truth to historical fact. But, while Nominalism pursued this empirical and intuitive mode of inquiry within nature, it refused to do so within theology. The Reformers, operating with the positive elements of Nominalism within the realm of theology, could and did insist on the necessity and possibility of obtaining objective knowledge of God through His Word and Spirit. Nominalism replaced this objectivity by the objectivization of the Church's authority. It is due to the negative influence of Nominalism on Romanism that the Church's definitions of the truth are as authoritative as the Truth itself.

The Reformation doctrine of grace is not grounded in the acceptance of Nominalism on the part of the Reformers, but is the result of its rejection by them. Since the definition of the truth is not identical with the truth in the view of the Reformers, they were able to reject the idea of a grace that becomes effective by the Church acting in accordance with its own formulations of, and enactments concerning, it.

God is therefore precisely not in the Reformation view as Bouyer believes, "a Protean figure impossible to apprehend".[204] God, on the contrary, is He who, uncontrolled and uncontrollable by definitions and formulations of Him and His grace, gives Himself to man in Jesus Christ, thus saving and changing man and so creating His Church, where He reveals Himself through the Holy Spirit as the God who in Jesus Christ is reconciled to man.

If Bouyer is looking for the evils of Nominalism he must do so, not in the Church of the Reformation, but in his own Church.[205]

NOTES ON PART 1

1. S.F.P., p. 13.
2. S.F.P., p. 13.
3. S.F.P., p. 13.
4. S.F.P., p. 13.
5. S.F.P., p. 13.
6. S.F.P., p. 62.
7. S.F.P., p. 62.
8. S.F.P., p. 141.
9. S.F.P., p. 26.
10. S.F.P., p. 27.
11. S.F.P., p. 27.
12. S.F.P., p. 28.
13. S.F.P., p. 28.
14. S.F.P., pp. 29–30.
15. S.F.P., p. 30.
16. S.F.P., pp. 30–1.
17. S.F.P., p. 114.
18. S.F.P., p. 114.
19. S.F.P., p. 115.
20. S.F.P., p. 117.
21. S.F.P., p. 31.
22. S.F.P., p. 62.
23. O.S., I, p. 482; also John Calvin, *Tracts relating to the Reformation*, translated by Henry Beveridge, Vol. I, Edinburgh, 1860, pp. 52–53 (hereafter referred to as *Tracts I*).
24. Cf. Johannes von Walter, *Die Geschichte des Christentums*, II/1, Die Reformation, Gütersloh, 1935, p. 313.
25. Part I, Article 4. Cf. S.B., pp. 38–39; Schaff III, p. 7 and p. 10. (Where the original text required it, Schaff's translation has been altered.)
26. A.E., 26, p. 223.
27. Part II, Article I; S.B., p. 300, also E. M. Plass (Compiler) *What Luther Says*, An Anthology, Vol. II, Saint Louis, Missouri, 1959, p. 718.
28. O.S., I, p. 469; also *Tracts I*, p. 37.
29. O.S., I, p. 469; also *Tracts I*, p. 37.
30. *Institutes*, III, 15. 7.
31. S.F.P., p. 169.
32. S.F.P., p. 169.
33. S.F.P., p. 168.
34. S.F.P., p. 168.
35. S.F.P., pp. 169–70.
36. S.F.P., p. 170.
37. S.F.P., p. 171.
38. S.F.P., p. 184.
39. S.F.P., p. 185.
40. W.A., 39/1, p. 356. English translation taken from T. F. Torrance, *Kingdom and Church. A Study in the Theology of the Reformation*, Edinburgh and London, 1956, pp. 48–49 (hereafter referred to as T. F. Torrance, *Kingdom and Church*).
41. W.A., 39/1, pp. 519–22. English translation taken from T. F. Torrance, *Kingdom and Church*, p. 49.
42. Sermon on 1 Cor. 15 (1533). W.A., 36, p. 673. English translation taken from T. F. Torrance, *Kingdom and Church*, p. 50.
43. S.F.P., p. 180.
44. S.F.P., p. 180.
45. S.F.P., p. 180.
46. S.F.P., p. 180.
47. S.F.P., p. 173.
48. Commentary on Gal.; A.E., 26, p. 214.
49. *Ibid.*, p. 214.

50. Commentary on Gal.; A.E., 26, p. 232.
51. *Ibid.*, p. 234.
52. S.F.P., pp. 180–1.
53. S.F.P., p. 181.
54. S.F.P., p. 181.
55. Trent, Session 6, Chapter 7; Denz. 1529 (799); Schaff II, p. 95.
56. *Ibid.*
57. Trent, Session 6, Canon 11; Denz. 1561 (821); Schaff II, pp. 112–13.
58. Trent, Session 6, Chapter 7; Denz. 1528 (799); Schaff II, p. 94.
59. Session 6, Chapter 10; Denz. 1535 (803); Schaff II, p. 99.
60. Trent, Session 6, Chapter 14; Denz. 1542 (807); Schaff II, p. 104.
61. S.F.P., p. 181.
62. S.F.P., p. 181.
63. B. Bartmann, *Lehrbuch der Dogmatik*, Vol. 2, Freiburg, 1911, p. 113.
64. *Ibid.*, p. 96.
65. S.F.P., p. 181.
66. A.E., 26, p. 267.
67. *Ibid.*, p. 26.
68. *Ibid.*, pp. 264–6.
69. *Ibid.*, p. 264.
70. Cf. *De Servo Arbitrio*, W.A., 18, p. 633.
71. A.E., 31, p. 351.
72. *Ibid.*, pp. 367–8.
73. A.E., 26, p. 88.
74. Cf. *ibid.*, pp. 88–89.
75. *Ibid.*, p. 167.
76. *Ibid.*, p. 167.
77. *Ibid.*, p. 168.
78. S.F.P., p. 185.
79. S.F.P., pp. 185–6.
80. S.F.P., p. 190.
81. S.F.P., p. 176.
82. S.F.P., pp. 175–6.
83. S.F.P., p. 176.
84. S.F.P., p. 178.
85. *Institutes*, III, 11. 2.
86. *Institutes*, III, 11. 2.
87. *Institutes*, III, 11. 3.
88. C.R. 50, 199; John Calvin, *Commentaries on the Epistles of Paul to the Galatians and Ephesians*, translated by William Pringle, Edinburgh, 1854, p. 74 (hereafter referred to as Calvin, *Galatians*).
89. C.R., 50, 199; cf. Calvin, *Galatians*, p. 74.
90. C.R., 50, 199; Calvin, *Galatians*, p. 75.
91. C.R., 50, 199; Calvin, *Galatians*, p. 75.
92. C.R., 50, 199; Calvin, *Galatians*, p. 74.
93. *Institutes*, III, 11. 10.
94. *Institutes*, III, 11. 1.
95. *Institutes*, III, 1. 1.
96. *Institutes*, III, 1. 1.
97. *Institutes*, III, 1. 1.
98. *Institutes*, III, 1. 3.
99. *Institutes*, III, 1. 3.
100. *Institutes*, III, 1. 3.
101. Cf. S.B., pp. 39–41 and 44–47; Schaff III, pp. 9–11; 14–15 and 20–26.
102. *Institutes*, III, 3. 9.
103. *Institutes*, III, 3. 9.
104. Cf. S.F.P., p. 170.
105. *Institutes*, III, 16. 1.
106. *Institutes*, III, 16. 1.
107. S.F.P., p. 178.
108. *Institutes*, III, 15. 3.
109. *Institutes*, III, 15. 4.
110. T. F. Torrance, *Kingdom and Church*, p. 101.
111. *Institutes*, III, 15. 5.
112. *Institutes*, III, 15. 6.
113. *Institutes*, III, 15. 6.
114. *Institutes*, III, 15. 6.
115. *Sermon on Gal. 2, 17–18*, C.R., 50, p. 437.
116. *Institutes*, IV, 17. 11.
117. *Institutes*, III, 16. 1.
118. *Institutes*, III, 16. 1.
119. *Institutes*, III, 16. 1.
120. *Institutes*, III, 16. 1.
121. *Institutes*, III, 16. 1.
122. *Institutes*, III, 16. 1.
123. *Institutes*, III, 11. 6.
124. *Institutes*, III, 3. 1.
125. *Institutes*, III, 11. 1.
126. Cf. Ronald S. Wallace, *Calvin's Doctrine of the Christian Life*, Edinburgh and London, 1959, p. 26.
127. Wilhelm Niesel, *The Theology of Calvin*, translated by Harold Knight, London, 1956, p. 132.

128. Cf. *Institutes*, III, 11. 11.
129. S.F.P., pp. 175–6.
130. *Institutes*, III, 11. 11.
131. *Institutes*, III, 11. 11.
132. Commentary on Is. 39:20; C.R., 37. 351 and John Calvin, *Commentary on the Book of the Prophet Isaiah*, translated by William Pringle, Vol. 4, Edinburgh, 1853, p. 269.
133. *Institutes*, III, 11. 11.
134. *Institutes*, IV, 18. 19.
135. *Institutes*, IV, 15. 1.
136. *Institutes*, IV, 15. 3.
137. *Institutes*, IV, 15. 3.
138. *Institutes*, II, 12. 3.
139. *Institutes*, IV, 17. 1.
140. *Institutes*, IV, 17. 1.
141. *Institutes*, IV, 17. 1.
142. *Institutes*, IV, 17. 1.
143. p. 101.
144. S.F.P., p. 170.
145. Session 5. 5; Denz. 1515 (792); Schaff II, pp. 87–88.
146. Cf. Session 6, Chapter 7; Denz. 1528 (799); Schaff II, p. 94.
147. *Ibid.*, Denz. 1529 (799); Schaff II, p. 95.
148. Session 7, *de Sacramento baptismi*, Canon 10; Denz. 1623 (866); Schaff II, p. 124.
149. *Ibid.*, *de Sacramentis in genere*, Canon 9; Denz. 1609 (852); Schaff II, p. 121.
150. *The Scottish Catechism of Christian Doctrine*, approved by the Archbishops and Bishops of Scotland, London and Glasgow, 1957, Q. 349 (hereafter referred to as *Scottish Catechism*).
151. *Katholischer Katechismus der Bistümer Deutschlands*, Ausgabe für das Bistum Limburg, Frankfurt am Main, 1961, p. 143.
152. *Catechismus ex Decreto Concilii Tridentini*, Romae, 1845, Pars. II, Cap. 3. 20 and 21 (hereafter referred to as *Roman Catechism* or *Catechismus Romanus*).
153. *Ibid.*, Pars. II, Cap. 1. 4.
154. E. Schillebeeckx, O.P., *Christ The Sacrament of Encounter with God*, London and New York,

1963, p. 15 (hereafter referred to as E. Schillebeeckx, *Christ The Sacrament*).
155. *Ibid.*, p. 3.
156. *Ibid.*, p. 135.
157. *Ibid.*, p. 202.
158. *Ibid.*, p. 200.
159. *The Church of Scotland Interim Report of the Special Commission on Baptism*, Edinburgh, May 1957, p. 30 (hereafter referred to as *Church of Scotland Report on Baptism*).
160. E. Schillebeeckx, *Christ The Sacrament*, pp. 167–8.
161. *Scottish Catechism*, Q. 320.
162. Trent, Session 6, Chapter 14; Denz. 1542 (807); Schaff II, p. 105.
163. *Ibid.*; Denz. 1542 (807); Schaff II, pp. 104–5.
164. Trent, Session 14, Chapter 2; Denz. 1672 (895); Schaff II, p. 142.
165. *Ibid.*; Denz. 1672 (895); Schaff II, pp. 142–3.
166. *Ibid.*; Denz. 1672 (895); Schaff II, p. 143.
167. *Ibid.*; Canon 4; Denz. 1704 (914); Schaff II, p. 164.
168. *Ibid.*; Canon 1; Denz. 1701 (911); Schaff II, pp. 163–4.
169. Trent, Session 6, Chapter 14; Denz. 1542 (807); Schaff II, p. 104.
170. Trent, Session 14, Chapter 2; Denz. 1671 (895); Schaff II, p. 142.
171. *Ibid.*, Denz. 1671 (895); Schaff II, p. 142.
172. *Scottish Catechism*, Q. 403.
173. Session 14, *Doctrina de sacramento extremae unctionis;* Denz. 1694 (907); Schaff II, p. 159.
174. *Ibid.*, Denz. 1694 (907); Schaff II, p. 159.
175. Cf. *ibid.*; Denz. 1694 (907); Schaff II, p. 159; (also *Scottish Catechism*, Q. 455).
176. *Ibid.*; *Doctrina de sacramento extremae unctionis;* Chapter 2; Denz. 1696 (909); Schaff II, p. 161.
177. *Scottish Catechism*, Q. 161.

178. Session 6, Canon 30; Denz. 1580 (840); Schaff II, p. 117.
179. S.F.P., p. 190.
180. Cf. S.F.P., p. 177.
181. S.F.P., pp. 177–8; In two instances the English translation has been slightly altered in accordance with the original French text: (a) *sa systématisation polémique* is rendered: "his polemical systematization" instead of "his controversial system". (b) *"le principe de l'amour . . ."* is translated: "the principle of the charity . . ." instead of "the source of the charity . . .". cf. Louis Bouyer, *Du Protestantisme à L'Eglise*, Paris, 1955, p. 155.
182. *Institutes*, III, 2. 8.
183. Cf. S.F.P., pp. 34–39.
184. A.E., 31; pp. 348–9.
185. Cf. S.F.P., pp. 36–37.
186. Part II, *Symbolum Fidei*; S.B., p. 449.
187. S.F.P., p. 37.
188. *Large Catechism*, Part II, S.B., p. 449,
189. S.F.P., p. 38.
190. *Institutes*, III, 2. 8.
191. *The Freedom of a Christian*, A.E., 31, p. 367.

192. *Institutes*, III, 2. 41.
193. *Institutes*, III, 2. 42.
194. *Institutes*, III, 13. 5.
195. Commentary on Gal. 3: 6; C.R., 50. 205; Calvin, *Galatians*, pp. 84–85.
196. C.R., 23. 722–5.
197. S.F.P. p. 177.
198. Johann Adam Möhler, *Symbolism or Exposition of the Doctrinal Differences between Catholics and Protestants as evinced by their Symbolical Writings*, translated by James Burton Robertson, London, 1906, p. 121 (hereafter referred to as J. A. Möhler, *Symbolism*).
199. *Ibid.*, pp. 121–2.
200. C.D., IV. 2, pp. 507–9.
201. S.F.P., p. 186.
202. S.F.P., p. 198.
203. Joseph Lortz, *Einheit der Christenheit, Unfehlbarkeit und lebendige Aussage*, Trier, 1959, p. 39, footnote 63.
204. S.F.P., p. 187.
205. Cf. T. F. Torrance, *The Roman Doctrine of Grace from the Point of View of Reformed Theology* in E.C.Q. an Ecumenical Catholic Quarterly, Vol. XVI, No. 4, 1964, pp. 290–312.

PART II

THE DEVELOPMENT OF THE
CONTEMPORARY DIALOGUE

HANS KÜNG

BOUYER'S EVALUATION OF Protestantism clearly shows how great a task the partners in the Protestant–Roman Catholic dialogue have undertaken. They are like mountaineers setting out to climb a hitherto unknown mountain peak. Using all their skill and patience they succeed in negotiating a particularly difficult corner only to find to their dismay that they cannot rest or even relax. New obstacles bar their way and threaten the success of their whole enterprise.

In Bouyer's *The Spirit and Forms of Protestantism* there are passages on *sola gratia, sola fide, soli Deo gloria* and even on the supreme authority of Scripture, which make the Protestant reader ask himself whether the Reformation was not after all a mistake. Did the schism in the sixteenth century perhaps happen because the Reformers were unable to distinguish properly between the authoritative and normative teaching of the Roman Church and the misinterpretation of its true doctrine by its own scholastic theology now admitted to have been decadent?

If—as Bouyer avers—salvation through grace and justification by faith are as much part and parcel of the Roman Catholic as they are of the Reformation teaching, the most dangerous and difficult corner which barred progress towards Christian unity seems to have been successfully negotiated. But, alas, as soon as the partners in the dialogue have overcome what they thought was the most difficult obstacle, they are brought to a halt by a new barrier as formidable as anything hitherto encountered. This is their different understanding of grace.

The foregoing debate with Bouyer has established that his concept of grace is quite different from that of the Reformers and of those who stand in the tradition of the Reformation.

This means that the agreement between Romanism as represented by Bouyer and the Protestantism of the true Reformation tradition extends merely to the use of the same terminology, but not to the signification of that terminology. *Sola gratia, sola fide,* justification, sanctification, etc., are terms used by both Bouyer and Protestants. The partners in the dialogue, however, must not blind themselves to the fact that the basic disagreement between their respective Communions (though concealed by the use of the same terms) remains because the signification of the respective terminology is different.

It is certainly true that Bouyer often speaks "the same language" as Protestants. It is, however, equally true that even though he uses the same words as Protestants he does not mean what they do by terms like *sola gratia, sola fide,* justification, sanctification, etc.

Is it possible that Protestants have now found in the person of Hans Küng a partner for the dialogue who, though not always speaking the same language, means—at least sometimes—what they do?

In 1957 Hans Küng, then a young Roman Catholic priest, now Professor of Theology at the Roman Catholic Faculty of Divinity in Tübingen, published his Doctorate Thesis *Rechtfertigung—Die Lehre Karl Barths und eine Katholische Besinnung*[1] (*Justification—The Teaching of Karl Barth and a Catholic Consideration*). The book deals with one of the central issues that divides the Church of Rome and the Church of the Reformation, and aroused great interest among Roman Catholic as well as Protestant theologians. There cannot be any doubt that Küng's work—his *Rechtfertigung* as well as his later publications—represents a theological orientation which may be regarded as a new phase in the encounter of the Church of Rome with the Church of the Reformation.

Küng's views have certainly not found universal acceptance within his own Communion. On the contrary, he has been severely criticized, and even attacked, by some of the best-known Roman Catholic theologians. An eminent Roman Catholic dogmatician is reputed to have referred to

Küng during the second session of Vatican II—Küng had by that time been made an official *peritus* of the Council—as a "theological teenager". This should not unduly perturb us (or Küng for that matter!) since we have it on good authority that God can use even the mouth of babes and sucklings to perfect His praise (cf. Matt. 21:16). Why then should He not use a "theological teenager" for the same purpose?

More important from the point of view of the Protestant–Roman Catholic dialogue is the fact that not even Küng's severest (Roman Catholic) critics have ever questioned his orthodoxy. Although his views may not have the official approval of the magisterium of his Church, they have not—at least not yet—been officially repudiated or condemned by the Holy Office. What Küng says, he can and does therefore say as a member and priest in good standing in his Church, which permits him—at least until now—to state its teaching as he does.

Most important from a Protestant point of view, however, is the unique testimonial Barth in his introductory letter to *Rechtfertigung* gives to Küng:

> If what you develop . . . as the doctrine of the Roman Catholic Church is actually its doctrine, then I must admit that my own doctrine of justification is indeed in agreement with that of the Church of Rome.[2]

Whether Küng's teaching on justification is in fact the teaching of his Church must in Barth's opinion be decided by biblical, historical and dogmatic experts on the Roman side.[3] If Küng is right, and there is no opposition between the Barthian and the Roman doctrines of justification, it would mean that in many instances the use of a different terminology has concealed the basic agreement between the Church of Rome and the Church of the Reformation. This would indeed be progress! But in the debate with Küng it is essential to heed Barth's warning with regard to any possible misunderstanding of his own or Küng's position:

> That I could possibly be a crypto-[Roman]Catholic or you a

crypto-Protestant is so foolish an alternative that I hope none of your readers will think of it.[4]

Protestants must therefore realize that Küng is not on their side, even secretly, but is frankly and openly opposed to them. Furthermore, Protestants would entirely misunderstand Küng if they thought he was trying to show that the Roman Church, having become aware of the truth of the Reformation teaching on justification and cognate matters, was now willing to incorporate Protestant concepts into its own doctrinal system. On the contrary, Küng's whole concern is to prove that the Reformation, and more particularly the Barthian, teaching on grace, on justification and on its actualization and ground in the death and resurrection of Christ, on *simul iustus et peccator*, on *sola fide*, etc.— if free from the exaggeration, bias and partiality of the Reformers—is and has always been the teaching of the Roman Church. It is Küng's avowed aim—and this indicates how irrevocably "Roman Catholic" he is—to show that, since the Protestant churches are basically right with regard to grace, faith, justification, etc., and so are in fundamental agreement with the Church of Rome, their "protest" is pointless. For him there is therefore now "no genuine ground for separation from the old [i.e. the Roman] Church".[5]

Although it would be a grave mistake to regard Küng as a "crypto-Protestant", or as a possible convert to Protestantism, there is not the shadow of a doubt that a dialogical relationship can be established with him. He is an advocate of the inter-confessional conversation in which he wants to take part. It took 400 years, he observes, to work out and exhibit clearly the differences between the two Communions.

> Should the era of antitheses now perhaps be succeeded by an era of irenic syntheses? Certainly not! But could the method not be altered? One would wish to speak to the partner instead of the mere opponent, one would wish to attempt the dialogue, the sympathetic conversation instead of mere dialectics.[6]

The dialogue with Küng is not only possible but desirable

because the conditions he lays down for it are unimpeachable. For Küng, the Alpha and Omega, the beginning and the end, of all Christian unity is Jesus Christ Himself.

> Grace, Jesus Christ, who "hath made both one" (Eph. 2: 14) will also do away with this terrible division [the division between Christians]. The one thing that matters is to submit to the impact of His Word, to keep His revelation continually in mind, and to carry out His command without circumspection.[7]

In the first part of his *Rechtfertigung* Küng gives a concise exposition of Barth's teaching on justification. Barth's verdict is:

> Not only have you made a complete collection of everything important to be gathered on the subject of "justification" from the ten volumes of the *Church Dogmatics* published up to now[8] and not only have you rendered it correctly, i.e. according to my own meaning, but you have cast a splendid light upon it by your detailed exposition which in spite of its great conciseness is accurate, as well as by your many apt references to the wider context. Your readers may therefore (until perhaps they read me too) be assured that you allow me to say what I do say and that my meaning is what you allow that I say.[9]

Küng believes that Barth's assessment of the infallible definitions and declarations of the magisterium collected in *Denzinger* is unhistorical and therefore incorrect. He holds that this misunderstanding is responsible for Barth's unjust judgement in his dealing with the teaching of the Roman Church in general and of the Fathers of Trent in particular.[10]

The second part of Küng's *Rechfertigung* answers the questions Barth puts to the Church of Rome.[11] They are easily recognized as the same questions the Reformers asked the Roman Church. Küng's answers, or rather the answers he thinks he can give on behalf of his Church, may therefore be regarded as answers aimed at the Church of the Reformation as a whole.

I

Karl Barth's Teaching on Grace

Before Küng's claim that the Barthian and Roman doctrines of justification are in basic agreement can be accepted or rejected, an outline of Barth's teaching on grace must be given. Since we have it on Barth's own authority that Küng has gathered from the *Church Dogmatics* everything that is important on the subject of justification, and has stated it correctly, we shall use as far as possible Küng's own summaries to describe the Barthian position.[12]

For Barth

one primary thing [is] that in reconciliation as the fulfilment of the covenant of grace, as in the covenant of grace itself, we have to do with a free act of the grace of God. God re-establishes the covenant, or, rather, He maintains and continues it, in order to lead to his goal the man whom He has brought into covenant with Him.[13]

Küng recognizes and underlines that Barth's real concern, reflected in every aspect of his doctrine of reconciliation, is to show that what is involved in reconciliation is "not some process or a condition in man but the majestic *supremacy of God*, which is yet not imperious at all. . . . The whole reconciliation-event as the fulfilment of the covenant, like the covenant itself, is [for Barth] the free and sovereign act of the grace of God."[14]

Küng then aptly quotes from the *Church Dogmatics*:

Whatever connections there may be before or behind, they do not alter the fact that in so doing God makes a completely new start as the freest possible subject. No one who really knows Him in this activity will ever be able to think of Him as bound by these connections or committed to this activity. He acts to maintain and defend His own glory. But no one and nothing outside Himself could ordain for Him that this should be a matter of His glory. He acts with a view to the goal to which He wills to bring man, but there is not really any necessity which constrains Him to do this. He acts as a Creator to a creature, but sin is the self-surrender of the creature to nothingness. If this is what man wanted, God might easily have allowed man to fall and perish. He had and has plenty of other creatures in whose presence man would not necessarily be missed. He acts with the faithfulness of a covenant-Lord, but He would not have been unfaithful to Himself if He had regarded the covenant which man had broken as invalidated and destroyed. He loved the world of men, but He did not need to continue to love the sinful world of men. We can only say that He has actually done so, and that this decision and act invalidate all questions whether He might not have acted otherwise.[15]

Küng correctly observes that Barth's concern here is to show that the faithfulness of God's choice of man must always be understood unequivocally as the utterly free grace of God, the triumphant act of His sovereignty. Since the man whom God confronts is always the sinful creature, God's election of him must never be seen as anything else than the election of grace, and His covenant with him as the covenant of grace. Küng agrees that

reconciliation is God's crossing the frontier to man: supremely legitimate and yet supremely inconceivable—or conceivable only in the fact of His act of power and love.[16]

Another equally important aspect of Barth's teaching in this connection has Küng's full approval. For Barth, the grace of God not only has been His grace—as if grace were a mere historical recollection—but it was, is and shall be His supremacy yesterday, today and for ever. His grace is and remains indivisibly His righteousness, His holiness and His truth, always new and strange to man. God's grace, which is His free condescension, always new and strange to man, requires of man to rely solely on it without considering what he himself can possibly give God.[17]

It is at this point that Barth attacks the Roman notion of grace, which in his opinion denies what characterizes the very nature of grace: its unity.

The heart and guiding principle of the Romanist doctrine of grace is the negation of the unity of grace as always God's grace to man, as His sovereign act which is everywhere new and strange and free. It is the negation of the unity of grace as His grace in Jesus Christ. It is the division of grace by which it is first of all His, but then—and this is where the emphasis falls—effected and empowered by His grace, it is also our grace. Against this view we must at once and quite definitely set our face (for what follows, cf. the survey given in B. Bartmann, *Dogm. Handb.*, Vol. 2, 1929, 113).[18]

The division of grace and so the negation of its unity referred to by Barth is the current Roman distinction between *gratia increata—creata, externa—interna, gratia gratiam faciens—gratia gratis data, gratia actualis—habitualis, medicilanis—elevans, praeveniens—concomitans, operans—cooperans, sufficiens—efficax, gratia Dei—gratia Christi, gratia supernaturalis—gratia naturalis.*[19]

This dichotomy of grace is uncompromisingly rejected by Barth:

How dare we split up the grace of Christ and the grace of God in this way? Is it not the case that as outward grace, for example (that which is described as the grace of the life and death of Christ, of the Gospel, etc.), it is wholly inward and proper to man, and conversely, that as inward grace which is proper to us it is altogether outward, the grace of the life and death of Christ and the grace of the Gospel? Similarly, is it not the case that actual grace is habitual, and habitual actual? That *gratia praeveniens* is *concomitans*, and *sufficiens efficax*, and *vice versa*? How can that which is described as the second and perfect be perfect except in the power of the first, which is regarded as so meagre and impotent as a purely enabling and preparatory grace? How can the first not have already in itself the perfection of the second? If there is one God, and one Mediator between God and man, and therefore, one grace—what place is there for all these abstractions? These are the questions which crowd in upon us as we face the final Roman Catholic distinction. But the Romanist doctrine of grace insists on these abstractions. Naturally it also maintains—rather more emphatically on the Thomist side and rather less emphatically on the Jesuit—that in the last resort there is only one grace. But it merely says this: it does not make any use of it. It simply commemorates the fact. It says it as a precaution, e.g. to ward off the kind of questions that we have been putting. When left to itself and following its own inclination it says something very different; it talks about the division of grace. It says the first thing as a bracket in which to say the second: but it does not abolish the parenthesis in order to say it.[20]

It is Küng's intention and aim to show and prove that Barth's indictment of, and polemics against, the Roman doctrine of grace are quite unjustified, being based on, and determined by, a misunderstanding of the authoritative teaching of the Church of Rome. Küng would therefore agree, it seems, with Barth that

> if it is a matter of the grace of the one God and the one Christ, there can be only one grace.[21]

It can thus be assumed that Küng, too, believes presumably that

> we cannot ... split it [grace] up into an objective grace which is not as such strong and effective for man but simply comes before him as a possibility, and a subjective grace which, occasioned and prepared by the former, is the corresponding reality as it actually comes to man.[22]

In Küng's opinion, therefore, the Church of Rome, too, teaches that

> the grace of the one God and the one Christ, and therefore the objective grace which never comes to man except from God, must always be understood as the one complete grace which is subjectively strong and effective in its divine objectivity, the grace which does actually reconcile man with God.[23]

For Barth, there is one vital criterion by which it can be determined whether the understanding of grace is right, i.e. biblical, or wrong, i.e. unbiblical: the state of man in relation to grace. It must be acknowledged as a state of absolute need:

> a state in which—with all that this involves—[man] is and remains always a recipient, a state in which he not only does not cease but can never do more than begin (and he will always be a beginner) to beg and to reach out for it [grace] in his poverty, in order that in that poverty he may be rich.[24]

Barth does not believe that the Roman doctrine of grace could survive this test. For the Roman teaching ascribes to man in grace an *exousia* in which he can look back to the grace of Christ as such as to an indispensable but preliminary stage which he has already passed. It furnishes him with a wealth in which he is no longer poor and needy and hungry and sick, in which, therefore, he cannot be the recipient of the one complete grace of God and of Christ. At the point where its true interest emerges, it definitely does not describe him as the being which has known and experienced and acknowledged the atonement as the sovereign act of God. As reflected in its description of man in grace, God has ceased to be the free subject of the atonement, the grace of the atonement has ceased to be His grace. And since this is so, there can be no peace between this and the Evangelical doctrine of grace.[25]

Küng is really undertaking a twofold task. On the one hand he is trying to show that Barth misunderstands the Roman doctrine of grace, and on the other that that doctrine, if rightly understood, agrees with Barth's own teaching on grace, etc. In other words, Küng sets out to prove that the Roman Church in its binding and authoritative statements takes grace seriously as grace, and that it not only asserts the unity of grace but actually believes and teaches it.[26]

Küng does not fall into the common Roman Catholic error of interpreting Barth's insistence on the supremacy of grace as resulting in the annihilation of man. He realizes that for Barth man in grace is as focal as the sovereign act of God's grace. In this connection Küng quotes a passage from the *Church Dogmatics* which shows in his opinion that it is impossible to dismiss Barth by having recourse to the theological commonplace—"dialectical theology".[27]

In this way God takes care for His own glory. And He does it by bringing man to glory. That is His sovereign act in the atonement. That is the grace of Jesus Christ. . . .

It is apparent at once that the formula "God everything and man nothing" as a description of grace is not merely a "shocking simplification" but complete nonsense. Man is nothing, i.e. he has fallen a prey to nothingness, without the grace of God. . . . This creating and grounding of a human subject which is new in relation to God and therefore in itself is, in fact, the event of the atonement made in Jesus Christ. . . . We cannot say and demand and expect too much or too great things of man when we see him as he really is in virtue of the giving of the Son of God, of the fact that God has reconciled the world to Himself in Christ.

We underline the fact that it is a matter of a being of man. . . . The old has indeed passed away, all things are become new, God was in Christ reconciling the world to Himself, and those who believe in Him do not perish but have everlasting life. . . . We are now looking at man. We are speaking of the being of man reconciled to God in Jesus Christ. For it is the meaning and reach of the atonement made in Jesus Christ, the power of the divine act of sovereignty in grace, that God willed not to keep to Himself His own true being, but to make it as such our human being and in that way to turn us back to Himself, to create the new man. . . .

Notice that . . . those that know this new being as their own . . . have always characterized and described it as the being which has met them as their own in Jesus Christ. . . .[28]

Every Roman Catholic—so Küng at least believes—would see that here "dialectical" and "Reformation" positions are left behind. Yet there remains for the Roman Catholic still some uncertainty regarding Barth's teaching. This uncertainty gives rise to, and is the basis of, the question Roman Catholics have to ask: "Does Karl Barth's teaching really take reconciliation and justification seriously as the reconciliation and justification of *man*?"[29] "Is the assertion that man is brought into grace [*die Begnadigung des Menschen*] more than a mere assertion?"[30]

This is nothing new. This is in fact the question Roman Catholics have always put to Protestants, who on their part always asked Barth's question: "Does the [Roman] Catholic teaching take justification seriously as the free and sovereign act of God's grace? Does it really take grace seriously as grace? Is its assertion that grace is one more than just an assertion?"[31]

Küng formulates Barth's doubts and his own about their respective positions in terms of question and counterquestion. Barth calls the Roman teaching in question by asking:

Do you not assert, secretly, yet in good faith, a dangerously unchristian autonomy of the human, creaturely and natural, which ultimately makes the incarnation of *God* vain?

Küng counters by asking Barth and the Reformation:

Do you not in the last resort assert a dangerously unchristian lack of grace (*Gnadenlosigkeit*] in man, a secret negation of the human, creaturely and natural which ultimately makes the *incarnation* of God vain?[32]

Küng's "Catholic Consideration" of the teaching of Barth is presumably designed to show that both questions are really unjustified: Neither party denies that in the incarnation He who became man was *truly God*, and that He who was God became *truly man*.

2

Grace as Graciousness

There is on the one hand Barth's uncompromising statement that there can be no peace between the Roman and the Evangelical doctrine of grace. There is on the other his candid admission that, if what Küng claims to be the Roman teaching on grace, justification, etc., is actually the doctrine of the Church of Rome, then he and Rome are really agreed. Küng's claim is as astounding as Barth's admission, and, if the former's contention is justified, there would indeed be peace between the Church of the Reformation and the Church of Rome on issues which caused the division of the sixteenth century and have kept the two Communions apart for over 400 years.

These issues—the understanding of grace, of justification, etc.—are so crucial and the problems connected with, and arising out of, them, so important, that Küng's proffered view of the teaching of his Church must be carefully examined. This, as in the case of Bouyer, will require constant reference to the 6th Session of the Council of Trent.

Küng begins his exposition of the Roman Catholic teaching on justification with an analysis of the biblical term "grace". He finds that the word "grace" is not used in the

Old Testament to designate "a created, supernatural, inner gift".[33] The Hebrew words *chen* and *chesed* signify above all else favour, pleasure and mercy. In the New Testament χάρις is seldom used to designate "the created inner quality of the soul".[34] The primary meaning of "grace" is the favour and kindness of God and of Christ.

Since "the perspectives of Holy Scripture must also be the perspectives of theology",[35] all theology of grace in using the term "grace" must always begin with its primary and original Scriptural meaning: the favour and graciousness of God. Grace therefore is not first of all "a physical entity in the human subject", but "it is something personal through and through, a being and attitude of the living God Himself".[36] To receive grace means to receive the favour of God, not simply "grace" but *His* grace. "To be in a state of grace [*im Stand der Gnade*] therefore signifies: I am in favour with God. . . . He is gracious to me. . . ."[37]

What is involved in grace is always and above all God Himself:

> . . . grace is not an intrusive third factor between God and man, but the gracious God Himself. What is involved is not *my-having*-grace but *His-being*-gracious. It is precisely the word *habitus* which easily leads to wrong notions. With regard to grace the first thing to be said is: I do not *have* God, God *has* me.[38]

Küng observes that, once grace is understood as favour and kindness, its unity can no longer be doubted. This unity is assured "by the one gracious God Himself, who gives us His whole kindness, His whole grace in the one Jesus Christ".[39] Küng states clearly and unambiguously that "Jesus Christ is *the* grace of God, *the* favour, the personified kindness of God towards us men."[40] "'All graces' given to us are nothing else but the rays of the one *'sol iustitiae Christus Iesus'*[41]."[42]

It is, however, significant that the New Testament never uses the plural of χάρις. Küng is of course aware of this, and indicates it by putting *graces* in inverted commas. It would be better still if he adhered to New Testament usage and

employed the word grace only in the singular, thus under-
lining and stressing the fact that, since grace is the one Jesus
Christ, it cannot but be one.

The grace of God in Jesus Christ, which works through the
Holy Spirit, is never "private" grace. It does not work in an
isolated way in the individual, but establishes through the
one Holy Spirit communion with Jesus Christ, so that there
may be oneness in the Body of Christ which is the Church.
The grace of God in Jesus Christ is given to us through the
Holy Spirit in the Church. The nature of grace is therefore
essentially ecclesiological: it radiates into the world and so
draws men into the Church. It is given for the growth of the
Church.[43]

The first result of understanding grace as the favour of God
is the recognition of the unity of grace. The other equally
important result is to acknowledge that grace as the kindness
of God is not aimed at a vacuum:

> Over against the sinner it [grace] is not impotent but omni-
> potent: *Verbum Dei efficax*. . . . Grace effects something in man, it
> changes man internally, it illuminates and vivifies him in his
> heart, in his centre. Man is really brought into grace. [*Sie
> (Gnade) begnadet tatsächlich den Menschen.*][44]

What does the bestowal of grace on man [*die Begnadung des
Menschen*] involve? Man is brought into grace by God
communicating Himself to man, for the truth communicated by Him is indeed His own being. In communicating
Himself to man God permits him to share in His divine life.
The favour of God, the bringing of man into grace, consists
in this, that the triune God dwells in the man who is in grace.
As the Father, through the Son, in the Holy Spirit, God
dwells in man, who may know and love the Father through
the Son, in the Holy Spirit.

If God is to show His favour to man, so that He may dwell
in him, man must be prepared for the reception of this gift.
It is God Himself who must prepare him for it. "God Himself does this through His indwelling, but in such a way that
in the creaturely realm something actually happens and
becomes reality."[45] This reality is referred to in Roman

Catholic tradition as *gratia creata*. Created grace can never be primary. The primacy always belongs to *gratia increata*, which is God Himself in His favour and kindness.

In the light of Küng's exposition of what he believes is the Roman Catholic understanding of grace—grace as the graciousness of God—the question of what are the points of agreement between the Barthian and the Roman doctrine must now be answered.

Both the Roman and the Barthian teaching agree according to Küng that grace has a theocentric and an anthropological "aspect".[46] The Roman teaching therefore raises no objection to the theocentric emphasis in Barth's doctrine of grace, but rather supports it:

> When grace is to be defined as the personal free favour, the mighty act of God's sovereignty, when as the grace of Jesus Christ its unity and undividedness are to be taught there cannot be any serious differences between it [the Roman teaching] and him [Barth].[47]

It is gratifying to learn that Küng gives no credence to the legend—a modern version of the older one about Calvin—that Barth in exalting God annihilates man. In Küng's opinion Barth, too, sees "that through grace something actually happens in man":[48] man is in grace, his being is changed. Küng thus recognizes that Barth does not neglect, as some Roman theologians think, the anthropological aspect of grace.

Küng blames Barth's lack of sympathetic understanding for not doing justice to the true teaching of the Roman Church. He concedes, however, that post-tridentine theology has often ignored the fact that the condemnation of *gratiam, qua iustificamur, esse tantum favorem Dei*—the grace, whereby we are justified, is only the favour of God[49]—was polemical in its intention. It was, however, not meant to deny that grace is also the favour of God. Bias and one-sidedness—Küng holds that they were historically conditioned—have often prevented Roman theology from taking this aspect of grace seriously enough. Küng also admits that Roman theology, reacting against the Reformation teaching, has been strongly concentrated in its doctrine of grace on man. By classifying grace it has not always been able to expound the unity of grace convincingly enough.

But, while Küng admits that post-tridentine theology has at times been biased and one-sided, and has occasionally overstressed its concern for man in its doctrine of grace, he defends it most emphatically against some of Barth's criticisms. He charges Barth not only with a lack of sympathetic understanding of Roman theology but with completely misinterpreting and misunderstanding it in several instances.

An example is Barth's apparent misapprehension of the Roman notion of *gratia creata*. If this is true, it would be of the utmost importance for the Protestant–Roman Catholic dialogue, for it is in no way an exaggeration to say that, of the many Roman notions to which Protestant theology takes exception, few are more troublesome than that of *gratia creata*.

It would be utterly impossible for a theology in the tradition of the Reformation to countenance the idea that grace could in any way be "created". If grace is the favour of God, i.e. the communication of His very being to man, in short, if grace is Jesus Christ Himself, the term *gratia creata* is not only suspect but actually reprehensible and objectionable. It could be taken as meaning that the being of God communicated to man is created, and consequently that there is such a thing as a created God.

Whatever divides Protestantism and Roman Catholicism it is not the question of whether the being of God or any part of it could be created. Such an idea is surely as repugnant to Roman Catholics as it is to Protestants. Yet the notion of *gratia creata*, in spite of its possible unfortunate implications, is still current in Roman theology.

Since it is not our intention to impute to Roman scholars and fellow-Christians the blasphemous view of a created being of God or of a created God, other explanations of *gratia creata* must be possible. There seem to be two ways of interpreting the term "created grace". Either Roman theology understands something different by grace, and it is not the favour of God, i.e. it is not Jesus Christ Himself, or, when using the term *gratia creata*, Roman theology does not refer to the being of God communicated to man in Jesus Christ, but to a created reality which, strictly speaking, should not be called "grace".

Since Küng defines grace as the graciousness of God in Jesus Christ, the second interpretation of *gratia creata* must be the right one in his case. We believe that he would agree. This can be deduced from his own criticism of Barth. Küng maintains that Barth's attack on the Roman teaching here is unjustified because it arises from a terminological misunderstanding on his part.

In Barth's view a created gift cannot be called "grace". Küng contends that Rom. 1: 5; 1 Cor. 16: 3; 2 Cor. 8: 4, 6, 19 and 12: 9 do not support Barth's refusal. But the really important point is that though Barth refuses to use the term "grace" in connection with created gifts he does not deny the reality represented by them. Roman theology calls this reality *gratia creata*, although Küng questions the wisdom of this particular definition.[50]

Küng illustrates his point by referring to Barth's teaching on faith and its connection with the reality of the Christian's new being, his re-creation and rebirth.

For Barth, faith is a human action "yet it is also true . . . that in this action there begins and takes place a new and particular being of man."[51] It is, however, essential that Barth should be understood correctly when he speaks of the connection between faith and the new being of man:

> As a human act it [faith] consists in a definite acknowledgement, recognition and confession. As this human act it has no creative but only a cognitive character. It does not alter anything. As a human act it is simply the confirmation of a change which has already taken place, the change in the whole human situation which took place in the death of Jesus Christ and was revealed in His resurrection and attested by the Christian community.[52]

But while faith as the human act of acknowledgement, recognition and confession has only a cognitive character, it also involves a new being, a new creation and a new birth of the man who believes:

> By their faithfulness (as the doers of this act of believing) they [Christians] simply confirm without knowing it—and it is to be hoped without boasting about it—that they are the subjects who in some astonishing way are capable of and willing and ready for this act and therefore for this acknowledgement, recognition and confession. How has this happened? How do they come to be qualified to do this? They obviously cannot be, and will not be, as the sinful men they are like all other men. If they are all the same, since the faith and therefore the acknowledgement, recognition and confession are their act, it is evident that the event of their faith (while it has no creative aspect as their act) is more than cognitive in character. From the point of view of the presupposition at work in their act, from the point of view of the men as its doers, it is clearly the positing of a new being, the occurrence of a new creation, a new birth of these men. In their act these sinful men confirm that they are the witnesses of the alteration of the human situation which has taken place in Jesus Christ: not the men who are altered in it— for as such they cannot so far be seen—but certainly, and this is the astonishing thing—as those for whom it has happened and not "not happened", as the witnesses of it. It belongs to the alteration of the human situation, as it has taken place in Jesus Christ, that it now has at least the confirmation of its witness in certain human subjects. Not because they believe, not in the power in which they do believe, but as they do actually believe (in strength or weakness), as they do it and are in a position to do it, they become and are Christians in the midst of all other men—men with this particular characteristic as men. To this extent we cannot deny to the event of their faith a certain creative [*kreatorisch*] character.[53]

In Küng's opinion it should not be overlooked—presumably by Barth's Roman critics—that Barth's teaching is quite plain and clear: the *iustus* in spite of the *simul peccator* is with regard to his being (*seinshaft*) different from the sinner.[54]

> New being, new creation (Gal. 6: 15; 2 Cor. 5: 17), new birth —they are all predicates which are ascribed only to the Christian, and they are all too strong to be taken only as

figurative expressions to describe the changed feelings and self-understanding of Christians. Christians do not lose their character as members of the race which God created good and which fell from Him. But in these predicates they are addressed as something other than those with whom in other respects they are still bound in the twofold solidarity of creatureliness and sin. . . . [The word πιστός] does, of course, speak of a being of those who are described in this way, of the being of which they are participants as they are πιστεύοντες, but of the being of which they are real and objective participants in the fulfilment of this act and as the subjects of it. Just as the sinful man is what he does as such, so he is what he does when as a sinful man he is awakened to faith and can live by it.[55]

Although Barth holds that a certain creative character cannot be denied to the event of faith, this can only be understood and explained if

we . . . try to think seriously of the object of faith and therefore of Jesus Christ as its starting point. Christian faith is both orientated and based on Him. . . . [The believer] owes it to Him that he can believe at all, and that he does believe. He believes as one who is confronted and apprehended by Him (Phil. 3: 12), as the one in face of whom He is the stronger and has proved Himself to be the stronger. In face of him He is the stronger in virtue of what He has done for all men and therefore for him in His death, and of the fact that God has manifested Him for all men and therefore for him as the One who has done this in His resurrection from the dead. And in face of him He proves Himself to be the stronger by the irresistible awakening power of His Holy Spirit. In this strength and in this proof He calls him to faith. And in so doing He creates the presupposition on the basis of which the sinful man can and actually does believe. He introduces him as a new subject which is capable of and willing and ready for this act, as a witness of His act and revelation, as a Christian. Because the faith of this sinful man is directed on Him and effected by Him, the event of his faith is not merely cognitive as a human act but is also creative in character. The new being effective and revealed in it, the new creation, the new birth—they are all the mystery of the One in whom he believes and whom he can acknowledge and recognize and confess in faith. When it is this One who closes the circle around him, a man can and must do that which he does in faith.[56]

A man can and must do that which he does in faith because Christ is *pro eo*. Because Christ is *pro eo*—this is the only reason for it—the Christian is a new subject, a new creation—he is born again. There can of course be no identification of God's act of salvation with faith as the free act of man. The true actualization and the real re-enactment of the history of salvation are accomplished in the Christian by Jesus Christ Himself through His Holy Spirit. It is done by Jesus Christ making Himself what He is and continues to be: the object and origin of faith. To this act of God man's act of faith is the response.[57]

In summarizing Barth's teaching in this connection Küng says that once this fundamental distinction between God's act of salvation and man's act of faith has been made and established, it is permissible to speak analogically of a representation of Christ's act of salvation in faith. This analogy is permitted because in faith a total change of the whole human situation is brought about, which is related in the closest possible way to the death and resurrection of Jesus Christ. In short, the Christian is "the man determined and stamped by Him and set in His light".[58]

Küng is referring here to Barth's teaching on what an older theology called the *mortificatio* and the *vivificatio* of the Christian with which he is in obvious agreement.[59]

Barth maintains in this respect that the nature of what determines, stamps and enlightens the believer in Jesus Christ has two distinguishable aspects:

> They correspond to the positive and negative character of the substitutionary being and activity of Jesus Christ Himself (as the *analogans*), and they mark the beginning and end of the way on which the life of the Christian . . . will become and be the *analogatum*, the parallel, the likeness—no more but no less—of His justifying being and activity.[60]

As a result of the substitutionary being and activity of Jesus Christ on its negative side the pride and fall of the Christian is overcome; the man of sin is vanquished, i.e. removed, destroyed, put to death. "That is what He has done for [the Christian] in His death, and what, again for

[him], is shown to be done in His resurrection."[61] The whole self-understanding and self-apprehension of the Christian, his whole attitude towards himself, is necessarily and directly affected by what has happened to him in Christ.

Barth now proceeds with caution. Too much would be said if it were tried to "deduce from the overcoming which has come to [the Christian] in Jesus Christ that it has taken place in [him]. . . . For although that removing and destruction and putting to death has come to [the Christian] it has not taken place in [him]". . . .[62] While the believer sees "what has come to [him] in [Jesus Christ], [he] still find[s] in [himself his] pride and fall".[63] In this respect his history does not coincide with that of Jesus Christ. He has "overcome in Him, but not in [himself], not even remotely."[64]

On the other hand, too little would be said "if we allow and accept the overcoming of [the believer's] pride and fall which has taken place in Him, but are then acquiescent and content that it should not take place in [the Christian] . . . that [the old Adam] should be permitted to carry on just as before, [the Christian's] consolation being that he is overcome in Jesus Christ. . . ."[65]

The right alternative to "saying too much" or "too little" in this respect is *mortificatio*. The result of the recognition by the Christian that his pride and fall are vanquished in the death of Jesus Christ, and that this is manifest in His resurrection, is "that [he] can think of [himself] and [his] acts only with remorse and penitence".[66] Mortification which must be continually effected is "the Christian attitude on its negative side".[67] The remorse and penitence of the Christian which will accompany and penetrate his thoughts, words and works and disturb him continually in his pride, "will not allow him to give himself up to his evil cause and to himself and the world. . . . And to this extent he will exist in analogy to Him."[68]

The other aspect of the nature of what determines, stamps and enlightens the believer in Jesus Christ is the restoration of the believer's right and life. It is the Christian attitude on its positive side which is the *analogatum* in a positive sense of Christ's justifying being and activity.

The Christian has forfeited his right and lost his life.

But this right and life have been restored in the act of obedience in which Jesus Christ sacrificed Himself for [the believer], and manifested in His resurrection from the dead. He stands in [the Christian's] place as [his] righteousness and life. If [he] know[s] Him and [himself] in Him—and that is the knowledge of faith —this means that [he] see[s himself] as the one to whom that right and life are given, as the one to whom He has given Himself as righteous and alive for [him].[69]

Barth proceeds again with caution! It would be too much to deduce from the restoration of the Christian, as it has taken place in Jesus Christ, that it has taken place in him, "that before God and man and [himself he] can boast of a right which is under [his] own name, . . . and of a life which [he] can live and enjoy as [his] own life."[70] Only in relation to Jesus Christ can the Christian be sure of his right and his life. On this positive side, too, the history of the Christian does not coincide with that of Jesus Christ, nor is there an exact similarity with Him.

On the other hand, it would be too little if the believer disclaimed all similarity with Jesus Christ; if he thought that, though Jesus Christ ultimately has ordered all things positively in his favour, yet he himself is "so far removed from Him that for the moment [he] do[es] not have anything of it at all, that [he is] still accused of [his] old and recurrent wrong, that [he] can only accuse [himself] in respect of it, that [he] must still fear death as the wages of [his] sin—just as though nothing had happened."[71]

The assertion that there is no assurance of salvation and complete dissimilarity between the believer and Jesus Christ is incompatible with the knowledge of faith.

The true alternative to saying "too much" or "too little" in this respect is *vivificatio*. *Vivificatio* "does not come to a Christian once only but continually . . . [it] does not determine his attitude only occasionally, but is everywhere present—this time as a clear overtone."[72] *Vivificatio* does not mean that for the Christian the new heaven and the new earth have already dawned or come. He is still on this same earth, but because of his *vivificatio* he can and does have confidence. In its light

> little renovations and provisional sanctifications and reassur-ances and elucidations will necessarily penetrate the whole man, who in the knowledge of faith has undoubtedly become a new subject. . . . When a man believes, then, in spite of all the limitations in which he still exists, in the knowledge of the restoration of his right and life as it has taken place in Jesus Christ, he will become a free man, i.e. a man who is no longer a simple servant and victim of his pride, but who is called away from it to the obedience of humility, for which he is also both ready and willing. As he bears that deep wound and accepts that bitter pain of penitence, he will hope for the grace of God and in that hope he will be at bottom a cheerful man . . . he will often enough be assaulted and he will have to fight . . . yet in his relationship with God and man and himself he will be seriously and finally a peaceful man, peaceful because held by the One in whom he is already restored, in whom he is already the righteous and protected covenant-partner of God. . . . He is the response to that which has taken place and been revealed, not in him, but in Jesus Christ for him. And in this attitude he is a copy, a parallel, a likeness of His being and activity for him. In all his imperfection he is a reflection of His perfection, a little light in His great light. He exists, then, in his petty thankfulness for the demonstration of His almighty grace.[73]

Barth's teaching on faith, and its connection with the reality of the Christian's new being has had to be expounded at some length and in much detail because as we have seen Küng states that this reality, though not called "grace" by Barth, corresponds to what Roman theology terms *gratia creata*.

Here, we have a striking example of the progress made by Roman theology in its understanding of Reformation theology. If the Christian's new being (determined by Christ and manifesting itself in analogy to His death and resur-rection) as understood by Barth corresponds to what Roman theology terms *gratia creata*, there is only one possible con-clusion: not only Roman theology but Barth, too, regard the change that takes place in the believer as real. But, if Küng admits that the new being of the Christian is as much a reality for Barth as it is for Roman theology, then he must refute as false and groundless charges such as Bouyer's, who, as we have noted, maintains that Barth holds the grace of God to be His grace only on condition that it gives nothing real, and that the man who believes, by saving faith, is in no way changed from what he was before believing.[74]

We must, however, go a step farther! Although the Council of Trent does not use the expression *gratia creata*, the Tridentine Fathers, according to Küng, describe the same reality with the terms *gratia inhaerens* and *gratia infusa permanens*, i.e. the inner change of man which is true and real.[75] If the reality of the Christian's new being, as understood by Barth, corresponds to what Roman theology calls *gratia creata*, and if *gratia creata* is the same reality as that to which Trent refers as *gratia inhaerens* or *gratia infusa permanens*, then, inevitably, Barth and the Tridentine Fathers must be in basic agreement about the reality of the inner change that takes place in the believer.

Küng claims that there is such a basic agreement between Barth and the Council of Trent; the aim of his work is in fact to produce evidence of such an agreement. But is Küng prepared to draw the conclusion which his own argument inevitably forces upon him? Barth—in whom so many Roman theologians see the true heir of the Reformation—has certainly developed, and at times corrected, the teaching of the Reformers. Yet he is in substantial agreement with them, especially with Calvin, concerning the reality of the inner change wrought by grace in the believer and of his new being in analogy to the death and resurrection of Christ. But if Barth and Trent on the one hand, and Barth and the Reformers on the other are in basic and substantial agreement, what can and must be inferred? If *a* equals *b* and *b* equals *c* in a mathematical equation, then *a* must also equal *c*. If therefore Barth and Trent and Barth and the Reformers are in basic agreement, then Trent and the Reformers must also be in agreement with regard to the reality of the Christian's new being. Yet they are not. The Tridentine anathemas still stand and they are the clearest evidence of the basic disagreement between the Church of Rome and the Church of the Reformation.

Is Küng's concept of grace an advance on the declarations and definitions of the Council of Trent? We are convinced that though he accepts them as authoritative and binding he interprets them—more will have to be said about his methodology later—in the light of the biblical concept of grace which was that of the Reformation but not of the Tridentine Fathers themselves. It is for this reason that he discovers agreements with Barth which would have been alien to the Tridentine Fathers; for their very terminology— *gratia inhaerens* or *gratia infusa permanens*—testifies to an impersonal notion of grace diametrically opposed to what the Reformation rediscovered: grace as God's personal, creative and redemptive act and Word in Jesus Christ.

Küng maintains that what separates Barth and the Roman theologian with regard to the inner change and the new being of the believer is not their reality but the terminology used to define it. While Roman theology calls a created gift "grace", Barth refuses to do so. Küng is of the opinion that as this is a mere question of terminology it is a secondary matter; of primary importance is the fact that both Roman theology and Barth refer to and describe the same reality: the inner change of the Christian and his new being.

But can Küng really claim that what Roman theology means by *gratia creata* is a reality which corresponds to the reality of the Christian's new being referred to by Barth in connection with the event of faith as being creative in character?

Küng, as we have already seen, holds that the grace of God, His favour, is this: "He dwells in us as the Father through the Son in the Holy Spirit, and we may know and love the Father through the Son in the Holy Spirit."[76] This grace—God Himself in His favour—is termed by Roman theology *gratia increata*.[77]

In the light of what he has said about *gratia increata* Küng defines *gratia creata* as follows:

But so that God can show this favour to man, so that the triune God can dwell in this wonderful manner in man, man must be prepared for it; he must have been prepared for it by God Himself. God Himself does this through His indwelling, but in such a way that in the creaturely realm something actually happens and becomes reality. This reality is called in [Roman] Catholic tradition *gratia creata*.[78]

The relationship between *gratia increata* and *gratia creata* is a problem for which Küng accepts Karl Rahner's solution.[79] In his essay on *Some Implications of the Scholastic Concept of Uncreated Grace* Rahner expounds his view as follows:

We need not here go into the familiar controversy . . . as to the meaning of Chapter 7 of the sixth Session of the Council of Trent in the matter of the *unica causa formalis iustificationis*. In this question too we may surely have recourse to the concepts developed in scholastic theology in its treatment of the *visio beatifica*. Just as there the light of glory is seen as the *dispositio ultima quae est necessitas ad formam*, so here an analogous relationship may be assumed to hold between created and uncreated grace. In this regard created grace is seen as *causa materialis* (*dispositio ultima*) for the formal causality which God exercises by graciously communicating His own Being to the creature. In this way the material and formal causes possess a reciprocal priority: as *dispositio ultima* created grace is in such a way the presupposition of the formal cause that it can itself only exist by way of the actual realization of the formal causality. From this objective reciprocal priority there follows further the logical justification for inferring the presence of one reality from that of the other. Because created grace as *dispositio ultima* can only exist along with the actual formal causality of the form for which it is the *dispositio*, it is correct to say: If created grace is given, so too necessarily by that very fact uncreated grace, and hence the whole grace of justification, is communicated to man.

Thus on our view of the relationship between created and uncreated grace there does not exist even the beginning of a possibility of thinking of created grace apart from uncreated grace, and so of thinking of uncreated grace as a fresh gift arising out of a new and independent demonstration of God's grace. We must remember furthermore that created grace alone (as a finite determination of the subject) can be called *forma* in the strict (categorical) sense of the word (as opposed to the divine Being itself, which remains transcendent with respect to the creature in spite of its formal causality); and we must remember that the Council [of Trent] only wished to meet the imputation theory of the Reformers, Seripando and others, but did not wish to determine how created and uncreated (inner!) grace (of which latter it also says precisely "*signans et ungens Spiritu promissionis Sancto*" . . .)[80] are related to each other and together constitute the *single* grace of justification. In view of all this we may say that the Council's teaching on created grace as the *unica causa formalis* of justification does not exclude our conception of the relationship between created and uncreated grace. For in this conception too created grace remains the "unique" formal cause of justification, in so far as it alone is the genuine (categorical) "form" of the justified man, and once it is posited, justification as a whole is really posited with it already. In addition it must be said that chapter 7 of the Tridentine decree on justification only teaches explicitly that the *causa formalis* of justification is wholly *interior* (and thus not an imputed "*causa formalis extrinseca*"), and that conversely therefore the *causa formalis* of justification is interior grace alone. It is true that the Council describes this interior grace in terms which in the theology of the schools hold good primarily of created grace, but it nowhere says that *interior* grace, as the unique formal cause of justification, must be understood *exclusively* of *created* grace.

If on our view created grace is conceived of as the *dispositio* (*causa materialis*) for the *donum increatum*, this is in no way to deprive it of what is attributed to it by theology. In order that it can be a *dispositio* for uncreated grace at all, it does indeed have first of all the character of a *formal* entitative, supernatural determination of the human spirit; as such, however, on our view too all those *effectus formales* can be assigned to it ascribed to it by scholastic theology. Just in so far as and in virtue of the fact that it constitutes man as a subject fit to receive the substantial gift of the divine essence for a future *visio*, it assimilates man to God's nature considered as the principle of His possession of Himself in Trinity; and thus it at once becomes the *causa formalis* of all the properties of man's supernatural elevation.[81]

Rahner adds a revealing and important footnote to the statement we have quoted:

In this sense our view is not in conflict with St. Thomas's

statement (Ia–IIae, 110. 1 ad 2; *De Ver*. q. 27, a, i ad i) that created grace alone and not God Himself is the *"causa formalis"* in respect of supernatural "life". It is through created grace alone that man becomes a subject who is *capable* of knowing and loving God supernaturally, who has the *capacity* for it. But in order that such a supernatural "life" should become actual there is need further of the self-communication of the object of this supernatural life, and this communication is not simply the mere *consequence* of the subjective potency of this life.[82]

Küng, as we have seen, holds that the Tridentine expressions *gratia inhaerens* and *gratia infusa permanens* which indicate the true and real inner change of man correspond to the term *gratia creata* not used by Trent. He also believes that what is achieved by created grace—and this must be in some way the inner change of man or at least its beginning—is the preparation (certainly accomplished by the divine indwelling) for the reception of the favour of God. The implication seems to be that the inner change of man is the *causa materialis*, the *dispositio ultima*, which is the presupposition of the formal causality exercised by God communicating His own being to the creature. If *gratia creata* is the inner change of man or its beginning, then this change being the *causa materialis* of justification is the presupposition of the *causa formalis*, i.e. of the communication of the divine being—of uncreated grace—to man, though it is admitted that both causes are interdependent so that the one cannot be without the other.

Rahner maintains, as we have seen, that his conception of the relationship between created and uncreated grace is not excluded by the Tridentine teaching on *gratia creata* as the *unica formalis causa*. Trent says: *"unica formalis causa est 'iustitia Dei, non qua ipse iustus est, sed qua nos iustos facit'* " —"the sole formal cause [of justification] is the justice of God, not that whereby He Himself is just, but that whereby He maketh us just."[83] For Rahner too, created grace remains the "unique" formal cause of justification in so far as it alone is the genuine "form" of the justified man. But when the Tridentine Fathers speak of interior grace as the *causa formalis iustificationis* it need not be understood exclusively of created grace. Their main concern was not to define the relationship between created and uncreated grace but to make it clear that grace is interior and not imputed.

It would seem that here Küng and Rahner are arguing on the basis of an unwarranted interchange between "result" and "presupposition". As a consequence of this illogical argument they can make *gratia creata*—the inner change of the Christian—become the presupposition of *gratia increata*. Created grace thus becomes in the justification-process more important than uncreated grace, which is God Himself. Their real mistake, however, is to establish a *necessary* reciprocity between *gratia creata* and *gratia increata*, which signifies that the latter is implied and controlled by the former.

Both Küng and Rahner are at fault in not realizing or in ignoring the all-important fact that, where the grace of God is concerned, there is no such *necessary* reciprocity. Grace—God in Christ—acts freely and creatively and unconditionally. When God is gracious He acts in sovereign freedom which excludes *necessary* reciprocity. How could the creativeness of the grace of God possibly depend on being necessarily reciprocated by its creation, i.e. the new being of the Christian? Küng contends that man must be prepared by God for the reception of His favour. But why? When God created *ex nihilo* the heaven and the earth and all that is therein, was what He created prepared by Him for its creation? When He created *ex virgine*, i.e. when He created freely out of the old creation, was man, his action and initiative and even his co-operation, not expressly excluded, since man in the person of Joseph had no part in the birth of Jesus Christ? Nor did God's new creation in Christ depend on the action, initiative and co-operation of the Virgin Mary. Her *fiat*, "be it unto me according to thy Word" (Luke 1 : 38), was not the intimation of her co-operation with God who, since she had assented to His will, could now recreate, but it was the humble acceptance of what He had already willed to be: "Behold, thou shalt conceive in the womb, and bring forth a son, and shalt call His name Jesus" (Luke 1: 31). God's second creation *ex virgine* through the Holy Spirit is prototypical of His recreation of man in Christ through the Holy Spirit: God recreates freely out of the old creation yet without its co-operation. Just as the first creation was not prepared for its being created but came into being by the power of God's Word so there is no preparation when God recreates man in Christ. Or is His Word less powerful when He recreates than when He created at first?

Both Barth and Küng believe that an inner change takes place in man; both hold that this change distinguishes the Christian from other men in whom it has not yet taken place; both view this change as true, real and permanent. It may therefore be said that the reality itself—referred to by Roman theology as *gratia creata* and described by Barth in connection with the event of faith as being creative in character—is for Barth as well as Küng one and the same.

Küng assures us that the Tridentine expressions *gratia inhaerens* and *gratia infusa permanens* testify to, and emphasize, this true and real inner change wrought and brought about in man by grace. Expressed in Christological terms this means that grace, God in His favour, Jesus Christ Himself effects the inner change of man. Barth, we believe, would agree with this statement. He would further agree—because he insists on the unity of the one grace of the one Jesus Christ—that this inner change, this recreation and rebirth, this new being in analogy to the death and resurrection of Christ is the sanctification of the Christian which is his through incorporation into Christ.

Finally (in opposition to an older Protestant scholasticism), Barth would agree that sanctification is not to be thought of in terms of an *ordo salutis* in which it is consequent on and second to justification. We recall here what we quoted from Barth in our debate with Bouyer:

> In the *simul* of the one divine will and action justification is first as basis and second as presupposition, sanctification first as aim and second as consequence; and therefore both are superior and both subordinate. Embracing the distinctness and

unity of the two moments and aspects, the one grace of the one Jesus Christ is at work, and it is both justifying and sanctifying grace, and both to the glory of God and the salvation of man.[84]

While Barth discusses the possibility of a *prius* and a *posterius* in the relationship between justification and sanctification, it is of the utmost importance to note that they are first or second, superior or subordinate only in the *simul* of the one divine will and action. Nowhere does Barth, however, speak of the necessity of a preparation of man, of the recipient of the favour of God in Christ so that the *simul* of the divine will and action can take place; nowhere does he refer to a reality which enables man to know and love God prior to the self-communication of God and actualized by it.

The point at issue here thus indicates a sphere where there is basic disagreement between Barth and Roman Catholic teaching. Grace in this context—Roman Catholic theology would call it *gratia increata*—is for both Barth and Küng the favour of God, it is God in His favour, Jesus Christ Himself. Barth would say that this favour, the self-communication of God in Christ, justifies and sanctifies the vessel, i.e. man, by His will and action of filling it. In our opinion, Küng can hold part but not all of this, and therefore cannot claim that in this instance there is basic agreement between Barth and Roman theology. It seems to us that the notion of *gratia creata* compels the Roman theologian to hold that only a specially prepared vessel can be filled with, and contain, the grace of God: the man who is already prepared for the reception of grace. Being prepared for the reception of grace, he will be filled with it, and so be justified and sanctified because the self-communication of the divine being—*gratia increata*—will actualize the inner change—*gratia creata*—which is the preparation for receiving the favour of God.

Barth certainly speaks of the reality of the Christian's new being, but he regards it as the manifestation and confirmation of the justification and sanctification of man wrought by the grace of God in Christ. The reality described by Roman theology as *gratia creata* is the inner change of man which has taken place in him, or at least has begun to do so prior to the self-communication of God in Christ which is needed to actualize the new being of the Christian.

In summing up we submit the following criticisms of the Roman notion of *gratia creata* and *gratia increata* and their relationship one with another:

1. The doctrine of *gratia creata*—Küng defines created grace as man's preparation by God for the reception of His favour, i.e. of *gratia increata*—does not take seriously enough the creative character of God's mighty act in Jesus Christ which is His grace.

2. The doctrine of *gratia creata* ignores the fact that, when God creates, He does so out of the free grace of His own unconditional love, i.e. He creates by the power of His Word and Spirit without any preparation of, or co-operation with, what He creates. Even though Roman theology admits that the preparation of man for the reception of God's grace is also the work of God, a limitation is imposed on the creative power of His Word and Spirit: God has to achieve His purpose in two stages; He has to act twice before His work—the new being of the Christian—is complete. First, He has to prepare the vessel for the reception of grace and then He has to fill it with grace. In creation "God said" and what He said came to be and "God saw . . . that it was good". Could His grace be any different or less effective in the recreation of man?

3. The implication of the doctrine of *gratia creata* is that the relationship which subsists between Creator and creature, Redeemer and redeemed, is one of *necessary* reciprocity. There is indeed a correlativity or correspondence set up by grace between God and man, but it rests on the free grace of God's own sovereign and creative act. Grace, by its very nature, involves a relation of irresistibility, just because it is God's grace. The necessary reciprocity which is involved in the Roman notion of *gratia creata* and *gratia increata* and their relationship the one with the other, makes God and His work depend on human co-operation. This is quite unacceptable to Reformed theology. Since God is utterly free and sovereign, His grace recreates man in Christ, thus

establishing a correspondence between God and man. Yet there is no *necessary* reciprocity on the part of the new creature—prior to God's mighty act of grace in Christ the new creature is not yet—on which recreation would depend. God creates out of the free grace of His love what He purposes to do in Christ: the new relation of the creature to Himself which is the new being of the Christian.

4. The doctrine of *gratia creata* is based on a psychological understanding of grace—grace is *inhaerens* or *infusa*—instead of being grounded in a dynamic notion of grace. The grace of God in Christ—*gratia increata*—and its relation to the Christian's new being in grace—Roman (though not Reformed) theology would call it *gratia creata*—must be understood in terms of the substitutionary act of God in Christ. Christ took our place that we might be given His place. What is His grace? His grace is that He, though rich, for our sakes became poor, that we in Him might become rich with His riches. But this substitution is irreversible. The Word became flesh, but the flesh did not become the Word; God can become man and make man take His place, but man cannot become God. In terms of grace this means that grace—Jesus Christ—became man that man might be given His place through incorporation into Him, through participation in the grace which is Jesus Christ. But man cannot become grace which is Jesus Christ nor can grace be "applied" to or "infused" into him, for grace, Jesus Christ, is indivisibly one.

It seems that, though he dislikes the term *gratia creata*, Küng must yet adhere to the doctrine described by it because otherwise he would have to reject important aspects of Roman Mariology and even ecclesiology.

We believe that it is true to say that the doctrine of *gratia creata* finds its fullest and final expression in the Roman teaching about the Virgin Mary, especially when she is seen as the archetype of the Church. If Christ is the personification of *gratia increata*, Mary is the personification of *gratia creata*, of that co-operation with grace which, since redemption is impossible without it, is in fact co-redemption.

Everything that is said by Roman theology of *gratia creata* can be predicated in an absolute sense of the Virgin Mary. The fact that she—free from original and actual sin—was the perfect vessel for the reception of grace was certainly the work of God's grace. Owing to God's gracious deed Mary was the most glorious fruit of redemption, the first redeemed of her divine Son, the restored creation, the rose among thorns, the bush that burned and that was not consumed, the mirror of the holiness and righteousness of God. But note that she was all this not only before the incarnation and the death and resurrection of her Son but even before she conceived Him.[85]

Mary was redeemed in view and in anticipation of Christ's incarnation and redemption and on the grounds of His merits. But—does not this make co-operation as important as redemption itself, created grace as important as uncreated grace, the vessel as important as its content, Mary as important as Christ Himself?—only her *fiat* made the incarnation and the redemption of Christ possible.

In his *Mary, Archetype of the Church*, Otto Semmelroth rejects

> any concept of co-redemption in which Mary is interpreted as really co-meriting grace within Christ's work. . . . By it Mary would be the co-worker of her own salvation and she would have to have co-merited to be able to merit at all. A general law would be established saying in effect that Christ's work of redemption cannot take place without Mary's co-operation. We must remember that Mary herself has been redeemed; and whatever she contributes to salvation is a result of the grace of salvation given her during the process of redemption. Grace is therefore preceded by Christ's completed work.[86]

But the point is that Mary was redeemed before the redemption of Christ, i.e. in anticipation of something which her *fiat* alone in the Roman view made possible. Though her own redemption was the result of Christ's redemption, it was also its presupposition without which the result would not have followed.

In Roman theology a distinction is made between *redemptio objectiva*—"the work of Christ the Redeemer alone"

—and *redemptio subjectiva*—"the giving of the fruits of salvation to men when the 'proper disposition' (under the
influence of grace) makes possible the reception . . .".[87]
Semmelroth, "careful to steer the middle course between
errors of excess and defect",[88] holds that the subjective
aspect of redemption is man's willingness and readiness to
accept the divine redemption. Without them the divine
action could not attain its goal. The *fiat* of man required so
that redemption can be effected is, however, not spoken by
men generally and individually, but by one person on behalf
of all men: Mary, whose unique position is grounded in the
fact that she is the archetype of the Church. She speaks in the
name of the Church and receives on its behalf the work of
Christ.[89]

> Accordingly the Church is co-redemptive in the truest sense. If
> she were not, Christ's work—though certainly capable of
> saving—would not effectively save anyone. The Church co-
> operates with redemption—but not in a productive way, for
> Christ alone does this. The Church's co-operation is receptive
> —which does not imply passivity alone. . . .[90]

We can only conclude—in spite of everything Küng has
said about the agreement between Barth and Trent—that, in
the Roman view, Christ, the grace of God, does not save man
but only makes him capable of being saved. Mary, and the
Church of which she is the archetype, by their *fiat* make
man's capability of being saved effective so that he is saved.
Is this not very near to saying that Mary (or the Church) is in
her way a redeemer like Christ Himself?

A further question remains: whether or not justification
and sanctification, redemption and salvation must be
ascribed—owing to the Roman notion of *gratia creata*—partly
to man and partly to Christ. For what *gratia creata* achieved in
an absolute sense in the Virgin Mary and in the Church seems
to be repeated to a limited degree in every Christian. Through
his *fiat* he becomes a co-redeemer with Christ so that his
willingness to be saved—*gratia creata*—transforms his capability
of salvation—achieved by *gratia increata*—into salvation.

We have no intention of imputing to the Roman Church

beliefs which it does not hold. We would, however, claim that the danger of holding such beliefs is implied in the very notion of created grace. We shall refer to this same question again.

> How does it come about that God is gracious to man? . . . to the sinner? And how does the sinner get a gracious God? . . . How does man's justification take place?[91]

These questions are being asked by Küng. Will his answers show that he and Barth, the Church of Rome and the Church of the Reformation are in basic agreement? Can they be when they differ on *gratia creata* and its implications?

3

The Declaring Righteous of the Sinner

As in the case of *grace* as the graciousness of God, Küng begins his exposition of the Roman Catholic teaching on the declaring righteous of the sinner with an exegetical analysis of the term *justification*.

In his view

> justification is only understood Scripturally if it is understood as salvation-event in the operation (*Funktion*) of the covenant of God with man. This covenant is a "contract" but a contract of pure grace.[92]

According to the original biblical meaning—in the Old and the New Testament—justification is a declaration of righteousness in a verdict pronounced by a judge. When in the New Testament the words δικαιοῦν, δικαίωσις, δικαίωμα are used, though the forensic act is not every time stressed, the juridical concept is yet always present. Küng then states the reasons why in his opinion the forensic aspect is so much to the fore when the term δικαιοῦν is used, especially by St. Paul: 1. Paul's dependence on Old Testament terminology which is forensic. 2. The forensic aspect of the synagogical doctrine of justification which was not affected by the Pauline-pharisaic controversy. While Paul's doctrine cannot be construed *a priori* as the antithesis of the pharisaic

teaching, his position was nevertheless reached in the debate
with the Pharisees. His terminology was largely borrowed
from the language of the Pharisees which was that of the Law.
3. The forensic character of the Septuagint cited by Paul.
4. The equation of "to justify" and "to account for righteousness" (Rom. 4; Gal. 3: 6). 5. The obvious forensic note
in the use of δικαιοῦν in the eschatological passages (Rom.
2: 13; 8: 33; 1 Cor. 4: 4). 6. The contrast between δικαιοῦν
and κατακρίνειν (Rom. 8: 33–34; 1 Cor. 4: 3–6) and the use
of the characteristically juridical formula ἐνώπιον αὐτοῦ
(Rom. 3: 20) and παρὰ τῷ θεῷ (Rom. 2: 13: Gal. 3: 11).
7. The use of δικαίωσις (Rom. 4: 25), (where there is a
connection between justification—judgement—death and
resurrection) and of δικαίωμα (which has different connota-
tions but is definitely employed in a forensic sense in Rom.
5: 16, where it is contrasted with κατάκριμα). Finally, there
is an implied judicial basis and note in all the passages
where δικαιοῦν occurs.[93]

In Küng's view the reason why some Roman Catholic
exegetes and theologians do not sufficiently appreciate the
biblical evidence in this respect is that the

> forensic concept of justification could force [them] to accept
> the (allegedly) Lutheran concept of a *purely* forensic declaring
> just. So as to avoid this merely verbal declaration of righteous-
> ness, the verdict of God in justification is often conceived [by
> Roman theologians] as a verdict *after* justification, i.e. as a
> confirmation (*Konstatierung*) by God of the state of grace of
> justified man; but this verdict of God confirming the righteous-
> ness of man must . . . be *secundum veritatem* and so already pre-
> supposes the making righteous of man.[94]

Küng, however, is unable to accept this explanation of the
way in which man is declared righteous. To his mind the idea
of God confirming afterwards "with satisfaction"[95] the
making righteous of man, which has already taken place, is
too anthropomorphic. Küng correctly points out that "the
distinctive feature of the divine declaring just as opposed to
every human judgement is after all that it justifies not the
just but the sinner" (Rom. 4: 5).[96]

The question which now arises is—and here Protestants are completely at one with Küng—

> how can justification be defined as a declaration of righteousness and at the same time how can both the anthropomorphic confirmation and a mere verbal declaration of righteousness be got round?[97]

In answering this question Küng passes from his exegetical analysis of the term justification to its theological explanation as it follows in his view from the Roman Catholic teaching.

Justification is a non-reckoning, a non-imputation. Yet neither what man has done nor what he is can be ignored: man has sinned—he is a sinner. The one and only possibility of justification is that God does not impute sin and guilt (2 Cor. 5: 19). God treats us as if we had not sinned. In spite of his sin the sinner is declared righteous by God.

Küng has no hesitation in saying that the word "justification" as such does mean a declaration of righteousness and not an inner renewal. But is it permissible to conclude that consequently the declaring just of man does not signify his inner renewal? By no means: the exact opposite is true! The Word that declares man righteous is not the word of man but the *vox Domini* and it is *potens in virtute*. The Word of God does what it says. God said: "Let there be light and there was light".

> It is the same in the justification of the sinner: God pronounces the verdict: thou art righteous. And the sinner *is* righteous, really and truly, externally and internally, completely and totally righteous; his sins *are* forgiven and man is righteous in his heart. The voice of God is never lost in a vacuum (cf. Ps. 29: 4–9).[98]

Whether Cardinal Newman's *Lectures on Justification* (1838; revised edition 1874), cited by Küng,[99] really support his own appreciation of the Roman Catholic doctrine of justification is not our concern in this context. The fact remains, however, that Reformation theology, especially as represented by Calvin and above all by Barth, is in full agreement when Küng states:

God's declaration is thus not the mere confirmation of a past or the testimony to an existing fact or the intimation of something merely future; still less is it the declaration of something that never existed nor ever will. The declaration of righteousness is the cause of something that did *not* exist before but now *does.* What man effects by works, God effects by His Word—His Word which is filled with the Spirit and power. . . . It is *verbum Dei efficacissimum.* His verdict is the creative *fiat* of the Almighty. In short, God's *declaration* of righteousness is as *God's* declaration of righteousness at the same time and in the one act the *making* righteous.[100]

Does Küng not strike a truly "Reformed" note when he says:

Certainly the one and the same central event in Jesus Christ is at one and the same time "justification" and "sanctification". . . . But one can only do justice to the fullness of the wealth of this one central event by not running together the characteristic coloration of the two sides into one common greyness meaning anything; rather one must allow justification to be justificattion. . . . And according to Holy Scripture justification means . . . a declaring just, a judicial event. To be sure, it is a right peculiar judgement—not simply a judgement of the judge's wrath but also and above all a judgement of saving grace; not human justice but though justice it is divine love; not a judgement which declares the righteous to be righteous but which by its Word *makes the unrighteous* righteous. . . which incorporates into the body of Christ and leads the lost sinner home to the Father.[101]

When Küng's exegetical analysis and his theological explanation of the term "justification" are considered, the difference in outlook between him and, for example, Bouyer is immediately obvious. We have noted that Küng recognizes that the word justification as such does mean a declaration of righteousness and not an inner renewal. Bouyer, on the other hand, claiming the unanimous support of modern scientific exegesis for his view, avers that δικαιοῦν "can only mean 'to declare officially just someone who is so in reality'".[102] In other words, Bouyer is one of those Roman Catholic theologians who does precisely what Küng refuses to do. He seems to regard the divine verdict in justification as the confirmation of what has already taken place: the inner renewal of man which is thus presupposed. The verdict of God merely confirms a state of grace which is already in existence. The reality of man's righteousness is the cause of God's official declaration.

The fact that Küng moves away from this position testifies to the progress of Roman theology towards a more biblical understanding of justification. But, while those who belong to the Church of the Reformation must and do note this progress with satisfaction, they are not so easily convinced by Küng's other claim that there are no essential differences between the Roman Catholic (i.e. the Tridentine) and the Barthian position in respect of justification. In short, they are not convinced that Küng rather than, for instance, Bouyer represents the official Roman Catholic teaching on justification.

Küng contends that both Rome and Barth understand justification as "a declaring just which makes just".[103] In the case of Barth, Küng is undoubtedly correct. Barth's position may be summarized as follows:

> What we have to say here [i.e. regarding justification], is that in the same judgement in which God accuses and condemns us as sinners and gives us up to death, He pardons us and places us in a new life before Him and with Him. And what we have to show is that this is possible, that the two belong together: our real sin and our real freedom from sin; our real death and our real life beyond death; the real wrath of God against us and His real grace and mercy towards us; the fulfilment of our real rejection and also of our real election.[104]

Barth thus underlines the fact that the work of the righteousness and of the grace of God is genuine. Our sin and our freedom from it, our death and our life, the wrath of God and His mercy, our rejection and our election are therefore neither fictitious nor nominal but real:

> On the left hand . . . it is not at all the case that God condemns man only nominally and that only in appearance He destroys him with his wrong. And it is also not the case that He causes him only nearly or half to die and to perish. Again, on the

right hand, it is not at all the case that He will only partly spare and preserve him, that He will allow or promise or grant him as His creature and elect only a partial right—a bare right to exist. On the contrary, on the left hand it is the case that God judges man and his wrong in all seriousness, that He destroys him genuinely and truly and altogether, that this man has actually to die, that the wrong with which he is identified has actually to be purged and consumed—a whole burnt offering in the flame of which both he and his sin are burnt up, disappearing in the smoke and savour, and ceasing to be. And on the right hand it is the case that God accepts His creature and elect genuinely and truly and altogether, that the faithfulness which He displays to him does not flicker like an exhausted lamp but shines out brightly like the sun. The words pardoning and preserving and maintaining which we have so far used to describe the activity of God on this side are far too weak, because here on this positive side we are dealing with the positive replacement of the wrong which has been set aside, with its crowding out by the new right of man, with the fact that to seal the passing of the dead and unrighteous man God introduces a new and righteous man in his place. In the one case, as in the other, therefore, in His "NO" and also in His "YES", God does for man an honest and perfect work. In the one case, as in the other, He does not fashion a mere *quid pro quo*, a mere "as if ", but actualities (*Realitäten*).[105]

The agreement between Küng and Barth is even more clearly expressed by the following statement in the *Church Dogmatics*:

There is no room for any fears that in the justification of man we are dealing only with a verbal action, with a kind of bracketed "as if", as though what is pronounced were not the whole truth about man. Certainly we have to do with a declaring righteous, but it is a declaration about man which is fulfilled and therefore effective in this event, which corresponds to actuality because it creates and therefore reveals the actuality. It is a declaring righteous which without any reserve can be called a making righteous.[106]

This making us righteous is for Barth real and actual for

we are totally evil when we enter His judgement and totally cleansed when we leave it. In one sentence of God we are both *semper peccatores* and *semper iusti.* The forgiveness of sins consists in the fact that these two predicates do not exclude one another, that they stand opposed, not in dialectical equilibrium, but with a preponderance of the second over the first; in the fact that their sequence is irreversible, that God never creates evil out of good, but good out of evil; in the fact that *semper iusti* is the second and final word which is to be heard and considered at this point. This is God's grace in judgement.[107]

But, while Küng and Barth are in basic agreement, can the same really be said of Barth and Rome, or more precisely of Barth and Trent? Barth himself does not seem to think so. His rejection of the Tridentine decree on justification (Session 6)—"theologically a clever and in many respects a not unsympathetic document"[108]—is certainly complete. He is convinced "that not even the remotest impression seems to have been made upon its exponents [i.e. upon the Tridentine Fathers] by what agitated the Reformers, or, for that matter, Paul himself in this whole question of faith and works".[109]

Barth's general objection to the *Tridentinum* is not so much its lack of understanding for the concern of the Reformation but rather the reason why this appreciation was lacking. He believes "that what was not only to the Reformers but to Paul the climax of justification in its character as a divine work for man was to them [i.e. the Tridentine Fathers] a completely unknown quantity".[110] Some of his more particular objections to Trent are as follows:

1. The death of Christ is the mere *causa meritoria* of justification (Chap. 7).[111] Justification itself is thus transferred "into the sphere of the Church which controls sacramental grace on the one hand, and of the believer who makes use of the Church's means of grace on the other".[112]

2. Justification is described as "a process in the man who enjoys the blessings of the Church's redemptive system and fulfils its demands".[113]

3. The unbiblical notion of "the *gratia praeveniens* in virtue of which even before a man believes and is baptized he is set in motion *ad convertendum se ad suam iustificationem*, that is, to the 'disposing' (Chap. 5[114] and canons 4–5)[115] of himself for

grace as his own *liberum arbitrium*, which has only been weakened (Chap. 1),[116] assenting to it and co-operating with it (*assentiendo et cooperando* [Chap. 5])".[117]

4. The denunciation as a *vana et omni pietati remota fiducia* (Chap. 9)[118] that the Christian may "cling in faith and . . . find comfort in the fact that his sins are forgiven."[119]

5. The unscriptural definition of the relationship between sanctification and justification which "forms the substance of the positive teaching of the *Tridentinum*: . . . justification is only completed in sanctification, in the doing of the good and meritorious works provoked and made possible and accomplished by the grace of justification (Chap. 16)[120]—a grace which only begins with the forgiveness of sins (Chap. 7)[121]."[122]

In spite of this devastating criticism, however, Küng holds the view that there is basic agreement between Barth and Trent in respect of the doctrine of justification. He admits that "the Tridentine Fathers cannot complain about too great an appreciation and sympathetic understanding of their . . . document on the part of Barth".[123] But the point is that, in Küng's opinion, Barth's criticism misfires because it is based once again on a misunderstanding. Barth simply fails to see that a change of emphasis in the definition of a truth does not mean its denial nor does the absence *expressis verbis* of an aspect of a truth signify its rejection.

Barth apparently does not realize that the Council of Trent justifiably reacted against "the extrinsical exaggeration"[124] of the Reformation which seems to permit the inference that the Council does not exclude extrinsicism altogether. "The massive offensive of the Reformers [against the Church of Rome] was followed by an equally massive counter-offensive."[125] The Tridentine answer to the theocentricism of the Reformation was "a certain anthropocentricism"[126] from which it may be inferred that the Council did not reject theocentricism. All that happened at Trent was apparently that the Tridentine Fathers "did not stress the theocentric and forensic aspect as strongly [as did the Reformers]".[127]

Küng makes the somewhat surprising statement that since

"it was not altogether easy to discern the true concern [of the Reformation] in Luther's polemics"—could this mean that the Council of Trent condemned Luther's teaching without really understanding it? ". . . if the Council was not to be misunderstood, the stress had to be put clearly on the other aspect [i.e. the anthropocentric aspect]".[128]

Barth also fails to see that ". . . the Council by no means excluded the forensic–theocentric aspect; it is included."[129] Küng maintains that what Trent rejects and condemns is "merely the extrinsical exclusiveness—*iustificari vel sola imputatione . . . vel sola peccatorum remissione* [canon 11]".[130] According to Küng this means—we shall refer to the whole question of his methodology later on—that Trent condemns only those who say that men are justified "either by the *sole* imputation . . . or by the *sole* remission of sins". In other words what Trent anathematizes is merely the *sola* of the Reformers: *sola imputatione iustitiae Christi—sola peccatorum remissione.* But the Tridentine Fathers do not condemn imputation and remission of sins as such. What is condemned is the exclusion from the justification of men "of the grace and the charity which is poured forth in their hearts by the Holy Ghost and is inherent in them"—*exclusa gratia et caritate, quae in cordibus eorum per Spiritum Sanctum diffundatur atque illis inhaereat* [canon 11].[131] In the same way the Council in no way denies that when men are justified they are reputed to be just but *non modo reputamur, sed vere iusti nominamur et sumus*—"we are *not only* reputed, but are truly called and are just (Chap. 7)".[132]

Küng thus holds that in the Tridentine decree "imputation or the act of the forgiveness of sins and therefore the juridical act of justification are also included".[133] For this very reason he believes that "the description of justification in chapter 4 [of the 6th Tridentine Session]—*translatio ab eo statu [in quo homo nascitur filius primi Adae, in statum gratiae, et 'adoptionis filiorum' Dei per secundum Adam Iesum Christum]*[134] must in accordance with the general interpretation be understood in a double sense: not only in the passive sense of man becoming just but first of all in the active sense as the justifying act of God's sovereignty."[135] What is required is "that the relationship between declaring just and making just is accurately determined . . ."[136] Küng does this by saying that "the one act . . . is as a declaration of righteousness at the same time a making righteous."[137]

This is good "Reformed" theology. Not only Barth but Calvin too would at once agree that in the one act, the one salvation-event, man is declared and also made righteous, he is justified and also sanctified. But we must ask whether Küng's viewpoint is also good Tridentine theology. In support of his position (and of the Council of Trent) Küng cites F. Prat who says:

> So that man may be just before God and God may pronounce him to be just, one of two things is necessary: that God has previously made him just or that He makes him just by His declaration itself. According to the latter hypothesis the justification of the impious is declarative in form but effective in reality. The divine sentence then produces its effect in the same way as the sacramental formulae, the words of consecration, the words of Christ performing miracles. The judicial sense of the word "*justificatio*", which many modern exegetes regard as essential, is thus preserved but at the same time the fictitious justification which is due to a divine judgement contrary to the truth, is avoided.[138]

There is certainly no "fictitious" justification in Reformation theology; for the divine judgement is never contrary to the truth: the sinner is declared righteous and in being declared righteous he is made so. The divine judgement is not contrary to the truth: there is a righteousness on which God bases His sentence. This righteousness is not man's—he has none prior to God's declaration—but Christ's, and, because it is His, it is extrinsic to man. But, when God declares man to be righteous, it becomes his, yet it is his only as the righteousness of Christ.

Is this also the teaching of Trent as Küng—excepting the extrinsical exaggerations of the Reformers—wants us to believe? We recall the two possibilities Prat mentions in connection with the question of how God can pronounce man to be just: either "God has previously made him just or . . . He makes him just by His declaration itself." Is the first of these two alternatives not an accurate description of the Tridentine teaching as long as we remember that man himself co-operates with the prevenient grace of God in the preparation of his justification, of his being made just by God?

The translation from the state in which man was born to a state of grace (Session 6, chap. 4) is certainly impossible in the Tridentine view without regeneration in Christ and participation in the merits of His passion.[139] But this regeneration and participation effect, as we have already noted, the process of translating men from one state to another only if they, moved by *gratia praeveniens*, are "disposed . . . to convert themselves to their own justification, by freely assenting to and co-operating with that . . . grace" (chap. 5).

Careful note should be taken of what, according to Trent, is happening in and to man prior to his actual acceptance of the grace of justification, and of how much he can, does and must achieve by way of preparation for his actual justification, i.e. before God declares him to be righteous: he acknowledges the truth of God's revelation and promise; he understands himself as a sinner; he turns to the mercy of God; he begins to love Christ; he hates his own sin; he (if he is an adult) decides to receive Baptism, to begin a new life and to obey the commandments of God (chap. 6).

All this man achieves before he receives the grace of justification itself; all this man accomplishes prior to his actual justification for which it is the preparation. Admittedly, man can achieve so much because of the operation of prevenient grace in him, but only his assent and co-operation can make its operation effective.[140] In other words, while it is true that man cannot prepare himself for the reception of justifying grace without the assistance of *gratia praeveniens*, it is equally true that prevenient grace cannot prepare man for his justification without his assistance, i.e. his free assent and co-operation.

Since the co-operation of man is required in the preparation of his justification, the Tridentine Fathers inevitably include in it his sanctification. God thus declares righteous the man who, assisted by and assisting, *gratia praeveniens*, is already, at least to some extent, righteous. Trent is therefore able to state that the preparation of man is followed by justification itself, which is not merely remission of sins *sed et sanctificatio et renovatio interioris hominis per voluntariam susceptionem gratiae et donorum, unde homo ex iniusto fit iustus* . . . (Chapter 7).[141]

Is Küng really able to claim that for Trent too the declaring righteous of man and the making him so are achieved in the *simul* of the one divine act? The Tridentine Fathers not only distinguish merely in thought between a *prius* and a *posterius* in the *simul* of the one divine act which is correct; they also reject the *simul* and make God's declaration—the justification of man—the *posterius* which depends for its realization on the *prius* of his sanctification, at least partially achieved by his own co-operation.

Küng counters Barth's anti-Tridentine arguments by asking whether "the time has not come when [Protestants and Roman Catholics] should stop polemizing past each other".[142] He seems to think that, apart from overstressing one or the other aspect of justification—of which both parties were guilty—Protestants and Roman Catholics are really saying the same thing in different ways.

> Protestants speak of a declaring just which includes the making just while [Roman] Catholics speak of a making just which presupposes the declaring just.[143]

But does the division between Rome and the Reformation, between Trent and Barth, really amount to no more than a mere difference in emphasis? Were the Reformers and their followers excommunicated simply because they said the same thing as Trent, but said it differently? We believe—and the historical evidence seems to be with us—that after much preliminary work, long debates and careful deliberations, the Tridentine Fathers condemned the Reformation by defining justification in such a way that the basic difference between them and the Reformers became clear and indisputable.

However much the Reformers and Barth may dislike the Tridentine idea of man's co-operation with the grace of God in the preparation of his justification and of his inner renewal preceding God's declaration of righteousness, they would admit the logic of these assertions, given the premise from which the Tridentine Fathers started and on which they based their declarations and definitions with regard to justification. The premise, in the light of which the whole of the 6th Session of Trent must be understood, is to be found in chapter 1, where in spite of original sin it is said of man: *tametsi in eis liberum arbitrium minime exstinctum esset, viribus licet attenuatum et inclinatum.*[144] In contradistinction to the Reformation, Trent declares that man's free-will, though weakened by sin, is in no way extinguished. As long as he is helped by prevenient grace, man is thus able to co-operate with God, and this he can do before God declares him to be righteous. In other words—and could this be the teaching of the Reformers or of Barth?—he is not dead in his sins, so that God has to raise him to life before he can do anything; he is only weakened by sin, so that a little portion of grace is able to give him the power, the desire and the will to assent to the infusion of the full measure of grace which justifies him.

Given the premise from which the Tridentine Fathers argue, their definitions are perfectly logical, but are they still so once they are understood and interpreted as Küng claims they should be? In his introductory letter to *Rechtfertigung* Barth shrewdly asks Küng "I wonder whether you have discovered all this [forensic—real justification, etc.] yourself there [in the decrees of Trent] *before, during* or *after* you read the *Church Dogmatics* so thoroughly?"[145]

Barth states categorically that because of the Roman teaching as defined by Trent, "the Reformation communions could not reunite with a Church [i.e. the Church of Rome] which held this doctrine, and they cannot accept the call to reunion with it today."[146] Küng on the other hand declares that once misunderstandings are cleared up Trent and Barth are already in basic agreement in respect of the doctrine of justification and that therefore there is now for the Church of the Reformation "no genuine ground for separation from the old [i.e. the Roman] Church".[147]

Küng holds that "the Protestant theologian is never more easily mistaken than when he asserts that this or that is *not* Roman Catholic doctrine."[148] In this connection it is therefore presumably a mistake to say that forensic-real justification, grace, *sola fide*, etc., as understood by Barth, are not Roman Catholic doctrine too. But if we Protestants are mistaken—and how willingly and gladly would we admit our mistake—have we not the right to ask that, in this vital matter of the interpretation of the 6th Tridentine Session, a more official declaration is made, stating clearly that what Küng claims to be the teaching of the Roman Church on justification is in fact its teaching?

4

Justification in the Death and Resurrection of Christ

The chapter on *Justification in the Death and Resurrection of Christ* in Küng's *Rechtfertigung* seems to us crucial for the whole debate with him. Here he attempts to prove conclusively that Barth is the victim of a terminological confusion, which explains his misunderstanding and misinterpretation of the Tridentine decrees with regard to the main issue. Küng defines justification as "the life-giving declaration [of God] that the sinner is righteous".[149] But when is this declaration made? Küng observes correctly that it must not be thought of in too human a fashion "as if God's solemn judgement would have to be pronounced in the case of each single individual (perhaps at the moment of conversion or Baptism)".[150] In his view, Holy Scripture makes it clear that God's gracious judgement is pronounced once for all; for His "proper verdict as a judge is indissolubly connected with

Christ's death on the Cross and His resurrection".[151] It is in them that the sinner is declared to be righteous (Rom. 3: 21–26; 4: 25; 5: 9).

We agree with Küng when he states that, whenever Scripture mentions justification in connection with Christ's death and resurrection, there is always an explicit reference to faith. Only he who believes is justified. It is, therefore, necessary "to see the 'objective' act of justification, which took place on the Cross, together with its 'subjective' realization."[152] Two mistakes must be avoided. The justification which was effected on the Cross must not be separated from its personal realization, its appropriation by the individual. Were this done it would lead to *apokatastasis*. On the other hand, the appropriation of justification by the individual, personal justification, must not be detached from the universal act of justification on the Cross for, were it done, it would lead in one way or another to predestinarianism. Both the universal act of justification, accomplished once and for all on the Cross, and the personal justification of the individual are to be seen as the two aspects of one and the same truth: *All* men are justified in Jesus Christ, only *believers* are justified in Jesus Christ. It is the divine character of the juridical and gracious verdict (*Rechts- und Gnadenspruch*) accomplished once and for all and for all men on the Cross that makes it possible to see "objective" and "subjective" justification together.[153]

Küng holds—and again we agree with him—that God's gracious judgement of sinful man, of all men, unto salvation in the death and resurrection of Christ constitutes the objective aspect of justification. In that death and resurrection God passed His sentence—gracious and quickening—whereby the righteous One was made sin for the sake of sinners and in Him they are pardoned (2 Cor. 5: 21; Gal. 3: 13; Rom. 8: 3). Since in this sense all men are justified by Christ, justification is the concern never merely of the individual but always of the community. The Apostle Paul therefore always sees justification in the framework of the redemption of all men. Thus Küng can say that in Jesus Christ all men are justified and thereby called into the Church, indeed they are embryonically taken into it. . . . The mystery of God's grace, the salvation of all men—Jews as well as Gentiles—hidden in creation, is now "made known by the Church" (Eph. 3: 9f.). Through the Church the individual becomes in faith a partaker of the universal justification. Justification, as it has already taken place in the death and resurrection of Christ [i.e. objective justification], has therefore an essentially ecclesiological character.[154]

It is quite obvious that, if what Küng develops here is the Roman doctrine of justification, it is indeed in essential and substantial agreement with Barth's teaching. A few quotations from the *Church Dogmatics* will vindicate Küng's claim.

Küng refuses to think in too human a fashion of God's declaration of righteousness as if His "solemn judgement would have to be pronounced in the case of each single individual". For Barth too the judgement of God is "the one and total destruction of wrong and all wrongdoers".[155] "On the one side the justification of man in Jesus Christ is the destruction of his wrong and his own setting aside as the doer of that wrong."[156] Barth refers here to the justification of all men in the death and resurrection of Jesus Christ. Jesus Christ

has . . . suffered for all men what they had to suffer: their end as evil-doers; their overthrow as the enemies of God; their extirpation in virtue of the superiority of the divine right over their wrong. . . . Jesus Christ was ready and gave Himself up to suffer and perish and die in that way—in accordance with the perfect righteousness of God. God judged the world in Him—and judged it in righteousness—by delivering Himself up in Him to be judged . . . in our flesh the eternal Son, the man Jesus of Nazareth, rendered the obedience of humility to the eternal Father, thus fully satisfying the righteousness of God in its negative side, the side of wrath. . . . In Him [Jesus Christ] our sin and we ourselves have perished. . . . Taking our place and suffering for us, He did not do what we as wrongdoers are always doing, and He did what we do not do . . . He has not merely suffered for us, but, suffering for us, He has done the right for us, and therefore suffered effectively and redemptively for us. . . . Between us and our past there stands positively and divisively the act of right which is His death. . . . That, then, is the righteousness of God in its concrete form as the righteousness of Christ, as our justification accomplished in Him, on its first and negative side; the gracious and redemptive work of God on the left hand.

On the other side, the justification of man in Jesus Christ is the establishment of his right, the introduction of the life of a new man who is righteous before God. . . . On this second and positive side of our justification as it has taken place in Jesus Christ, we are dealing with something specific which has happened to Him, the Son of God, in His unity with our fellow-man Jesus of Nazareth. As the true Son of God and Son of Man, as our Lord and our Brother, He is not merely the subject but the object of the righteousness in which God vindicates and establishes His right amongst us . . . God acknowledged the right of the One who gave Himself to judge the world by letting Himself be judged in its place . . . God revealed the meaning and purpose of His wrath, His consuming love, to the One who had exposed Himself to it and borne it to the very end. The righteousness of God did not merely take place by Him, in the obedience of His Son acting in His passion for us, but when it had taken place by Him in the act of His death, it was also revealed in Him as the righteousness of the eternal faithfulness and grace of God, as the righteousness of His positive will, which was present from the very first, although only latent in His non-willing, His will to introduce the new and righteous man, His will that this man should live. This is something which Jesus Christ has not done, which has come to Him as the answer to what He had done, but just as real, just as concrete, just as visible, audible, perceptible, just as historical as the death which He took upon Himself and in which He acted passively. We speak of His resurrection from the dead by the glory of the Father (Rom. 6: 4). . . . As He did what He has done in our place, for us, so the answer which God the Father gave Him in respect of His act of obedience applies to us. The good will of the Father, which was hidden in His dying for us and revealed to Him in His resurrection, was and is the good will of God with us. . . . His resurrection is the beginning from which we all come when we leave the past which He has concluded, going forward in Him to the future which is already present.[157]

Küng distinguishes between an "objective" and a "subjective" aspect of the one justification accomplished once for all in the death and resurrection of Jesus Christ. The same distinction between the (objective) justification of all men and its (subjective) appropriation or apprehension by those who believe is made by Barth.

> When we say justification, sanctification and calling, on the one side we are already expounding the relevance of what was done in Jesus Christ, but, on the other, we are expounding only the objective relevance of it and not its subjective apprehension and acceptance in the world and by us men. . . . In the Christian there is an appropriation of the grace of God ascribed to all men in Jesus Christ, a subjective apprehension of what has been done for the whole world in the happening of atonement. . . .
>
> The appropriation of the grace of Jesus Christ ascribed to us, the subjective apprehension of the reconciliation of the world with God made in Him, the existence of Christians, pre-supposes and includes within itself the presence, the gift and the reception, the work and accomplishment of His Holy Spirit. The Holy Spirit is the one eternal God in His particular power and will so to be present to the creature in His being and activity, so to give Himself to it, that it can recognize and embrace and experience Himself and His work and therefore the actuality and truth of its own situation, that its eyes and ears and senses and reason and heart are open to Him and willing and ready for Him. The particular existence of the Son of God as man, and again the particular existence of this man as the Son of God, the existence of Jesus Christ as the Lord who becomes a servant and the servant who becomes Lord, His existence as the Guarantor of truth is itself ultimately grounded in the being and work of the Holy Spirit. He is *conceptus de Spiritu sancto*. And this is the distinctive mark of the existence of the men who perceive and accept and receive Him as the Reconciler of the world and therefore as their Reconciler, who —vicariously for the whole world reconciled by Him—discover that they are His because He is theirs, who on the basis of this discovery and therefore in this special sense exist "in Him", who can be with Him and for Him as He is with them and for them (with and for the whole world). It is the Holy Spirit, the being and work of the one eternal God in this special form, that is still lacking in the world at large. That God did not owe His Son, and in that Son, Himself, to the world, is revealed by the

fact that He gives His Spirit to whom He will. The hand of God the Reconciler is over all men. Jesus Christ was born and died and rose again for all. The work of atonement, the conversion of man to God, was done for all. The Word of God is spoken to all. God's verdict and direction and promise have been pronounced over all. To that extent, objectively, all are justified, sanctified and called. But the hand of God has not touched all in such a way that they can see and hear, perceive and accept and receive all that God is for all and therefore for them, how therefore they can exist and think and live. To those who have not been touched in this way by the hand of God the axiom that Jesus Christ is the Victor is as such unknown. It is a Christian and not a general axiom; valid generally, but not generally observed and acknowledged . . . they [i.e. those who are not Christians] do not know their justification, sanctification and calling as they have already taken place in Jesus Christ. But the hand of God has touched and seized Christians in this way—which means the presence and activity of the Holy Spirit. In this special sense Christians and only Christians are converted to Him. This is without any merit or co-operation on their part, just as the reconciliation of the whole world in Jesus Christ is without its merit or co-operation. . . . The free grace of the sovereign God has in relation to them the special form that they themselves can reach after it. . . . Therefore the being and work of Jesus Christ, the One and All of His achievement and the relevance of it has also this—shall we call it for the sake of clarity, subjective?—dimension, in which the same One and All is now in the eyes and ears and hearts, in the existence, of these men, Christians, who are specially taken and determined by His Holy Spirit. They have over the rest of the world the one inestimable advantage that God the Reconciler and the event of reconciliation can be to them a matter of recognition and confession, until the day when He and it will be the subject of His revelation to all eyes and ears and hearts, and therefore of the recognition and confession of all men.[158]

Now, as has been said, Küng holds that, since from an objective point of view all men are justified by Christ, they are called into the Church and indeed "embryonically taken into it". Therefore for him justification, as it has already taken place in the death and resurrection of Christ, has "an essentially ecclesiological character". Here again he can rightly claim agreement with Barth.

Barth rejects the notion of an older Protestant theology which "proceeded at once from the objective demonstration of divine grace to its subjective apprehension in the life of man, i.e. the individual Christian."[159] He calls it "an intolerable truncation of the Christian message" with the almost inevitable result "that the great concepts of justification and sanctification came more and more to be understood and filled out psychologically and biographically, and the doctrine of the Church seemed to be of value only as a description of the means of salvation and grace indispensable to [the] individual and personal process of salvation."[160]

Barth holds that

the Holy Spirit is not a private spirit, but the power by which the Son of God (*Heidelberg Catechism, Qu. 54*) "has from the beginning of the world to the end assembled out of the whole race of man, and preserves and maintains, an elect congregation." But He assembles and preserves and maintains it, not as a pile of grains of sand or as an aggregate of cells, but as a community of those of whom each one can individually recognize and confess by His power "that I am a living member of the same, and will be so for ever." Within this particular group of problems it is clearly a matter of a correspondence, a reflection and repetition of the relationship between the objective ascription and the subjective appropriation of salvation. Salvation is ascribed to the individual in the existence of the community, and it is appropriated by the community in the existence of the individuals of which it is composed. . . .

The "pillar and ground of truth" (1 Tim. 3: 15), the salt of the earth, the light of the world, the city set on a hill, is the community of God and not the individual Christian as such, although the latter has within it his assured place, his indispensable function, and his unshakeable personal promise. It is not he but the *ecclesia una sancta catholica et apostolica* that stands (in close connection with the Holy Spirit) in the third article of the Creed. It is the Church which with its perception and experience of the grace of God stands vicariously for the rest of the world which has not yet partaken of the witness of the Holy Spirit. It is the Church which in this particularity is ordained to the ministry of reconciliation and the witness of the grace of God in relation to the rest of the world. It is in its existence, therefore— and only in the sphere of its existence [also] in that of individual

Christians—that the salvation ascribed to the world is appropriated by man. It is primarily in it that there is fulfilled in the sphere of sinful man and his world, as the work of the Holy Spirit of Jesus Christ, the subjective apprehension of the atonement objectively made by Him.[161]

When Küng speaks of "the essentially ecclesiological character" of justification and says that "... the mystery of God's grace, the salvation of all men ... is now 'made known by the Church' (Eph. 3: 10)" he is not thinking in terms of a merely epistemological relationship between justification and the Church. For him, as for Barth, the act of God in justification is basically corporative, i.e. God's election of and covenant with Israel, and is individual only within this corporate election and covenant.

Küng's citations from Roman authorities show how strongly he emphasizes the corporate aspect of justification. He quotes for instance E. Tobac:

> There cannot be any doubt ... that justification viewed as the effect directly obtained from the death of Christ has in the eyes of St. Paul a collective meaning. ... The divine decree of justification directly affects the community and only indirectly individuals. These latter are not incorporated into the messianic community because they are justified but participate in the collective justification because they are introduced into the community.[162]

Th. Soiron, also cited by Küng, holds that

> Christ as the everlasting Word summing up the words of the Father about the whole creation and all mankind and Christ as the everlasting Word having assumed the nature of the whole human race as it presents itself (*sich darstellt*) since Adam's fall is embryonically we men in our collective capacity (*das Wir der Menschheit*); in it Christ and mankind, head and body, are embryonically united as the one divine person. Hence follows the important consequence: all that as God-man He does, says, suffers, sacrifices and prays is all done for mankind—and even more—mankind has done all that embryonically in Him in His Spirit. Therefore mankind is fundamentally redeemed in Him ...[163]

Finally a quotation from Michael Schmaus:

His [Christ's] obedience and His love are therefore our obedience and our love, His death and resurrection are our death and resurrection. He did it in our stead. *He sacrificed (offerte) as the representative of all.* In Him mankind stood on Golgotha before the face of God and submitted to the judgement of the Father. In Him mankind has satisfied the justice of God.[164]

Küng's viewpoint, however, with regard to the ecclesiological character of justification, can be seen even better and more clearly in his exposition of and agreement with Barth's teaching on the election and rejection of Israel and on the atonement in relation to the covenant.[165]

For Barth, Jesus Christ is both "the electing God"[166] and "elected man".[167] All men are elected in this one man.

Those whom God elects He elects "in Him", not merely "like Him", but in His person, by His will, and by His election. . . . What can this election be, then, but more grace, a participation in the grace of the One who elects, a participation in His creatureliness (which is already grace), and a participation in His sonship (which is eminently grace)?[168]

Jesus Christ is both the electing God and elected man. He is also both the elected and the rejected man.

. . . in the election of Jesus Christ . . . God has ascribed to man the former, election, salvation and life; and to Himself He has ascribed the latter, reprobation, perdition and death.[169]

Thus Jesus Christ is rejected by God that all men may be elected in Him.

The ecclesiological character of justification, its corporate nature and the fact that it is an incorporating act is stressed by Barth—and Küng is in obvious agreement with him—when he says:

The election of grace, as the election of Jesus Christ, is simultaneously the eternal election of the one community of God by the existence of which Jesus Christ is to be attested to the whole world and the whole world summoned to faith in Jesus Christ. This one community of God in its form as Israel has to serve the representation of the divine judgement, in its form as the Church the representation of the divine mercy. In its form as Israel it is determined for hearing, and in its form as the Church for believing the promise sent forth to man. To the one elected community of God is given in the one case its passing, and in the other its coming form.[170]

God's election of grace in Jesus Christ is the eternal ground of justification. The divine election is God's eternal covenant with man—in Jesus Christ God elects Himself as the God of the covenant and thus man as His covenant-partner.

Jesus Christ is the atonement. But that means that He is the maintaining and accomplishing and fulfilling of the divine covenant as executed by God Himself. He is the eschatological realization of the will of God for Israel and therefore for the whole race. And as such He is also the revelation of this divine will and therefore of the covenant. He is the One for whose sake and towards whom all men from the very beginning are preserved from their youth up by the longsuffering of God, notwithstanding their evil heart. And in this capacity He reveals that the particular covenant with Israel was concluded for their sake too, that in that wider circle it also encloses them. He is the servant of God who stands before God as the representative of all nations and stands amongst the nations as the representative of God, bearing the judgements of God, living and testifying by the grace of God—Himself the Israel elected and called to the covenant and to be the mediator of the covenant. And in that capacity He reveals that this covenant with Israel is made and avails for the whole race.[171]

Reconciliation and, more particularly, justification, for which the covenant is the presupposition, are the fulfilment of the covenant. Its fulfilment

consists in the fact that God realizes His eternal will with man, that He makes the covenant true and actual within human history. It consists in the historical proclamation attested in the Old Testament, and the historical existence attested in the New, of the Mediator, that is, of the eternal Word of God and therefore of God Himself in His historical identity with the man Jesus of Nazareth: in the coming of His kingdom on earth . . .[172]

Both Barth and Küng agree, therefore, that justification is

essentially "ecclesiological" in character not only because the salvation of all men in Jesus Christ is now "made known by the Church" but because the act of God in justification is basically corporate and incorporating, since election in Christ is the election of the community and only within it of the individual.

In the light of what has already been said Protestant theology could not possibly object to Küng stressing three points in connection with the events of justification:

1. The *personal* character of justification: What is involved is not an organic natural process accomplished by "graces" but

a personal standing with Christ before the Father.[173]

2. The *seriousness* of justification:

Faith does not simply dissolve into love; what is involved is not the trivial (*harmlose*) reconciliation of two lovers who have quarrelled but the righteous (and gracious) judgement of the Lord of heaven and earth.[174]

3. The *theocentricity* of justification:

What is involved is not primarily an inner human process of salvation; not a not-having and a being-infused with, a *habitus* and graces, not the *iustificatio passive considerata* but *God's* wrath and grace, *His* divine act of gracious judicial decision, the *iustificatio active considerata*; what is involved is not in the first place "on earth peace, goodwill toward men" but "glory to God in the highest", not in the first place the justification of man where man gets his right but the *self-justification of God* where God gets His right in His eternal will as Saviour and Creator (*in seinem ewigen Heils- und Schöpferwillen*).[175]

Küng concludes that in justification the emphasis must be put not on its subjective but on its objective aspect. While it is true that justification must be apprehended by the individual—only he who believes is subjectively justified —the decisive act of justification took place in the death and the resurrection of Christ. Not man and his faith change the situation as it originally subsisted between God and the sinner, nor do man and his faith complete salvation—the salvation-event took place once and for all in the death and the resurrection of Christ. All man can do is actively to acknowledge in faith that the real change in his human situation took place in those saving-events.

There can be no doubt that what Küng expounds as the doctrine of justification is in agreement with the teaching of Barth. But once again the question arises of whether what Küng expounds is the *Roman Catholic* doctrine of justification? Can the Tridentine decree really be understood in terms of a forensic-real justification which has taken place once and for all in the death and resurrection of Christ and is grounded in them? In other words, is the Tridentine doctrine of justification in basic agreement with the teaching of Barth in spite of his criticism and rejection of it?

In Küng's view Barth completely misunderstands Trent because he "overlooked the fact that the Tridentine concept of justification is . . . not closed but open, i.e. it is complementary."[176] While justification is for Barth primarily the judgement of God in the death and the resurrection of Christ, "Trent understands 'justification' primarily . . . as the process of justification (*Rechtfertigungsvorgang*) in man . . . these two [concepts] do not exclude but include each other."[177]

Küng believes that Barth "played off his concept of justification against the Tridentine one instead of appraising active and passive justification as the two necessary aspects of one and the same justification. He thus falls a victim to the difference in terminology."[178]

But what is the difference in Barthian and Tridentine terminology? According to Küng it is this:

> . . . the "objective" salvation-occurrence (*Heilsgeschehen*) on the Cross which Barth calls in accordance with Scriptural usage "justification", is denoted for the most part by [Roman] Catholics with the equally Scriptural term "redemption" (*Erlösung*) and is thus distinguished from "justification" as the "subjective" salvation-occurrence.[179]

Somewhat reproachfully Küng therefore asks:

How could Barth overlook the fact that in the Tridentine decree the *capitula* on justification in the "subjective" sense (chapters 3ff.; Denz. 1523ff. [795ff.] are preceded (preceded!) by a short (no one called this aspect in question) but very important (*gehaltvoll*) chapter on "redemption" (*Erlösung*), i.e. precisely on "justification" in the "objective" sense?[180]

Küng is quite sure that the nucleus of everything Barth is trying to say about objective justification, i.e. the redemption or justification of all men in the death of Christ, is in fact said by Trent in the chapter *De dispensatione et mysterio adventus Christi*:

> When it came to pass, that the heavenly Father, "the Father of mercies, and the God of all comfort" [2 Cor. 1: 3], when that blessed "fulness of the time was come" [Gal. 4: 4], "sent unto men, Jesus Christ, His own Son"—who had been, both before the Law, and during the time of the Law, to many of the holy fathers announced and promised—"that He might both redeem the Jews who were under the Law" [Gal. 5: 4], and that "the Gentiles, who followed not after justice," might attain to justice [Rom. 9: 30], and that all men "might receive the adoption of sons" [Gal. 4: 5]. Him "God hath set forth as the propitiator, through faith in His blood for our sins [Rom. 3: 25], and "not for our sins only, but also for those of the whole world" [1 Jn. 2: 2]—*hunc*, "*proposuit Deus propitiatorem per fidem in sanguine ipsius, pro peccatis nostris*", "*non solum autem pro nostris, sed etiam pro totius mundi*".[181]

Now if this view is right, Küng has unearthed an appalling truth which has been buried for centuries: Protestant theologians—Barth amongst them—have been the victims of their own carelessness. They have overlooked on the one hand the difference in Protestant and Roman Catholic terminology and on the other the fact that, even when the same term is used both by Protestants and Roman Catholics, it may not have the same meaning and signification for them. When, therefore, Protestant theologians like Barth criticize a Roman concept in the light of their own terminology or on the basis of their own signification of terms, the inevitable result is: confusion and misunderstanding!

What better example is there than the doctrine of justification? In the Reformation view justification is by grace alone, i.e. by Christ alone. The Roman Catholic teaching, formulated and defined by Trent, is unacceptable to the Church of the Reformation because, though justification for the Tridentine Fathers is also by grace, it depends on the assent and co-operation of man initiated by grace as well.[182] The Church of the Reformation has been calling Rome in question for 400 years because that Church assigns an active part to man in his justification. How can man possibly co-operate with the free and sovereign declaration of God that the sinner is righteous in Christ? But now Küng tells us that Reformation theology frames the right question wrongly. When the question is correctly framed it is obvious that Rome also denies human co-operation in justification.

Protestant theologians—somewhat bewildered—point to the relevant chapter in the Tridentine decree where the assent and the co-operation of man are expressly mentioned in connection with his justification. Küng reassures them: this is merely a terminological misunderstanding. The human co-operation asserted by Trent is not co-operation in justification, or rather not in justification as that is understood and defined by Protestant theology. For example, what Barth means by justification is not so called by Roman theology. As a rule the Roman theologian does not term the objective salvation-occurrence, accomplished once for all in the death and the resurrection of Christ, justification; he calls it redemption, in which there is naturally no human co-operation. Here, then, we have agreement *in nuce* between Trent and Barth. On the other hand, when the Tridentine Fathers speak of human assent and co-operation in justification, they do not refer to the objective declaration of God made once for all in Christ, but to the subjective process in man, i.e. his personal justification, by which objective justification is apprehended and appropriated by him in faith.

How much brighter the hope of Christian unity would appear to be if what separates the Church of Rome and the Church of the Reformation was merely a question of terminology needing some re-adjustment. But is Küng not over-

simplifying the issues that have divided Christendom since
the sixteenth century? What he is saying, in effect, is that for
400 years Protestants and Roman Catholics have never
really talked to each other. They have always talked past
each other. Note: since the sixteenth century the Church of
the Reformation has opposed the Church of Rome by upholding the doctrine of justification by grace alone. In doing
this none of its theologians—not even Barth—has ever
realized that, had any of them only looked properly at
chapter 2 in the 6th Tridentine Session, they would have
found essentially the same teaching on justification (or at
least on what they themselves call justification) as they have
in their own Church. Nor has any of them ever discovered
that in Trent's definition of justification the human co-
operation referred to does not apply to the objective salvation-
event accomplished by Christ but to its appropriation by
man. But note further: For 400 years the Church of Rome
has upheld its anathemas against the Church of the Reformation without being aware of the fact that, at least with regard
to the doctrine of justification, its objections to, and final
rejection of, the Reformation were the result of a regrettable
misunderstanding. For, had the Tridentine Fathers only
known that apart from the theocentric "over-emphasis"
needing correction, justification in the Protestant sense is
basically the same as redemption in the Roman Catholic
sense, and that what Roman Catholics term justification, i.e.
the appropriation of objective justification, is not denied by
Protestants, they would surely not have outlawed a movement whose main concern was to acknowledge and re-affirm
the Scriptural truth that man is saved by Christ alone without his own co-operation.

But is Küng's argument that Barth is the victim of a
terminological confusion really convincing? It should be
noted at this point that the distinction between the objective
redemption of Christ and the subjective justification of the
individual believer is not known to post-Reformation
Protestantism. In Baptist theology, for instance, we find a
distinction which closely corresponds to that which according

to Küng was made by the Council of Trent. Baptism administered only to adult believers is regarded by Baptist theology, not as the sign and seal of the Gospel of redemption, but as the sacramental or symbolic expression of the believer's own state as being saved and converted. This unbiblical view of Baptism is based on the equally unbiblical distinction between an objective redemption which has already taken place once and for all in the finished work of Christ and a subjective salvation as the saving appropriation of objective redemption by the individual.

Thus, the distinction between objective and subjective justification, between redemption and salvation, between the work of Christ done once for all and its appropriation by man, is not unknown in Protestant theology. Nor is the idea of human co-operation in salvation foreign to Protestant theology: while redemption is recognized as the work of Christ alone, human co-operation is required for salvation; for it is only when man appropriates redemption by personal decision manifesting itself in his "conversion" that he is actually "saved". Man thus co-operates with God in his salvation by fulfilling certain conditions: faith, regeneration, conversion.

But the unbiblical distinction between redemption and salvation within Protestantism is not confined to Baptist theology. It is also found in the federal theology of Calvinist scholasticism where a distinction is made between the covenant of redemption—the covenant between the Father and the Son—and the covenant of grace—the covenant between God and man with Christ as Mediator. While salvation is the promise of the covenant of grace it is conditional upon personal faith.

Both Baptists and the federal theologians of Calvinism ignore the fact that, even if a distinction between objective redemption and subjective salvation or justification is maintained, they must be seen as two aspects of one and the same event; for not only objective redemption but also its appropriation are already accomplished and completed in Christ. Christ's work is accomplished not only from the side of God towards man—objective redemption—but also from the side of man towards God—the appropriation of redemption.[183]

Not only redemption but also salvation, not only objective but also subjective justification, has already taken place in Christ, the Elect One in whom all men are elected. It is for this reason that true Reformed theology has always stressed the distinction between the active and the passive obedience of Christ. Justification (or redemption) has taken place objectively in Christ; He submitted to the judgement of the Father upon our sins which He took upon Himself in our human nature and bore on our behalf. This is His passive obedience.

But justification (or salvation) has also taken place subjectively in Christ. Christ our representative, standing before God in our humanity, has already fulfilled all the "conditions" on which the subjective appropriation of redemption or justification depends. It is He who believes, trusts and loves God, and He does so in our humanity, in our name and on our behalf. This is His active obedience.

In his commentary on *The Epistle to the Philippians* (1927) Barth writes that the positive thing in faith, i.e. "the *collapse* of *every* effort of his [man's] own capacity and will, and the recognition of the absolute *necessity* of that collapse",[184]—"is not . . . the act of human but the originally *divine* faith. For it is not in virtue of the human but in virtue of the *divine* faithfulness that what man in faith knows to be true and real *is* in fact so—that God with *His* righteousness takes the lost creature's part, that the latter *as* lost is righteous."[185]

Is it really possible to hold as Küng does that Barth misunderstands the Tridentine teaching on justification because he is unaware of the difference in the terminology used by Trent and by him? Since the distinction between objective redemption and subjective salvation, which is very similar to the supposed Tridentine distinction between objective redemption and subjective justification, is not unknown within Protestantism, Küng's view of a mere terminological confusion on Barth's part does not seem to be very likely.

We now return to the question we have already raised: is what Küng expounds really the *Roman Catholic* doctrine of justification? His Church has not (at least not yet) condemned his exposition of it and thus has raised great hopes in Protestant circles. But will there ever be more than hope —we are speaking here as fallible men who "see through a glass, darkly"—as long as the Mariology of the Roman Church, to which we have already referred, testifies to its beliefs in human co-operation with redemption? Küng's methodology, of which we will have to speak later, may enable him to interpret or re-interpret the semi-pelagianism of Trent in an orthodox, i.e. Scriptural, fashion, but does Roman Mariology not remind us continually that his Church upholds in the person of Mary the doctrine of man's co-operation in some way with his redemption?

It is beyond the scope of this enquiry to discuss controversies concerning the exact place of Mary in redemption that go on within the Roman Communion. Theological opinions ranging from extreme Marian maximalism to Marian minimalism differ as to the nature and extent of her co-operation with Christ.

A. Deneffe understands Mary's co-redemption "in the light of direct co-operation with objective redemption",[186] i.e. with Christ's own work of redemption. Mary is thus placed beside Christ as a co-principle of salvation.

W. Goossens, on the other hand, states that "unless the Church should judge otherwise, one may and should deny the thesis of a direct co-operation with objective redemption."[187] In his opinion Mary's co-operation extends only to subjective redemption, i.e. to the imparting of the fruits of objective redemption to individuals.

H. M. Köster holds that

the covenant between God and man requires the assent of man to be legitimate and effective . . . Mary as the head of mankind gave this assent. . . . The sole cause of redemption is the work of Christ but mankind must say "Yes" to it. Only through this "Yes" was the covenant really achieved. A representative of the whole of mankind must say "Yes". Christ cannot be this representative because according to Scripture He belongs to the divine side of reality and is not a human person. According to the will of God Mary has this representative significance. The action of Christ and that of Mary are a unity.[188]

Semmelroth, steering a middle course between Marian maximalism and minimalism, believes that "a complete denial of Mary's co-operation (except for the imparting of fruits) would not do justice to ... papal texts".[189] These "deal clearly with direct co-operation with the redemption, not just the imparting of its fruits to individuals".[190] In support of his own view Semmelroth quotes M. J. Scheeben:

> There is an ancient ecclesiastical concept, attested to a thousand times, or rather, an explicitly documented dogma resulting from the way the Protogospel was taught in the Vulgate (*ipsa conteret caput tuum*), that states that the effects of Christ's redemption should be attributed in a very real sense to His mother, as a principle.[191]

It seems thus to be a fair conclusion to say that the majority of Roman theologians, backed by papal documents, extend Mary's co-operation as the representative of mankind not only to subjective redemption but to objective redemption, to the redemptive work of Christ itself, the effectiveness of which must in a very real sense be attributed to her.

When we remember that, according to Küng, redemption and justification in the objective sense are interchangeable terms, human co-operation does not seem to be restricted to the appropriation of objective justification but to that objective justification itself.

We readily and gladly admit that the teaching of Barth and the teaching of Trent, as understood and interpreted by Küng, indicate a measure of agreement. But can Trent be interpreted (as is done by Küng) against the background of official Roman teaching, especially of Roman Mariology? The terms *assentire* and *cooperari*, though somewhat suspect, point to an important truth which Protestants have no intention of neglecting. But all depends on how human assent and co-operation are related to (objective) justification. Are they the condition or the consequence of its effectiveness?

Am I effectively justified on condition that I co-operate, or do I co-operate because I am effectively justified?

We believe—unless the Church of Rome declares officially otherwise—that, even if the Tridentine decree refers not to objective but to subjective justification, human co-operation in the appropriation of objective justification is understood, not as the consequence of objective justification being effective through the Holy Spirit, but as the condition of its becoming effective.

If the appropriation of objective justification is the condition of man's salvation then his salvation is partly God's work and partly his own. If on the other hand man's salvation is through the Holy Spirit the consequence of an already accomplished salvation, it is then wholly and exclusively the work of God. We believe that this vital issue still divides the Church of Rome and the Church of the Reformation.

Is Küng really in agreement with Barth in seeing objective and subjective justification as two aspects of one and the same salvation-event, i.e. does he interpret both aspects christologically? We believe that in the Tridentine decree itself subjective justification is not merely the anthropological "correction" of the Reformers' theocentric over-emphasis. In subjective justification, as Trent sees it, man tries to share in the work of Christ. The Tridentine interpretation is, in our view, anthropologically instead of being strictly christologically orientated and determined. We must now raise the question of whether Küng himself really interprets both aspects of the one justification strictly christologically.

5

The Appropriation of Justification "Sola Fide"

Neither Roman Catholics nor Protestants dispute the fact that subjective justification, i.e. the appropriation of objective justification, is achieved by faith. It is therefore agreed that there is an indissoluble link between the apprehension of the objective salvation-event and faith.

Faith and its nature have already been referred to in connection with Bouyer's defence of *fides caritate formata* and with Barth's teaching on the reality of the Christian's new being. We must now deal with the part faith plays in justification, when man appropriates individually and personally what Christ has already done for all men.

Küng is at one with Barth (and with the Reformers) in saying that man is justified not by works, nor by faith and works, but *sola fide*. He is convinced that "the formula *sola fide* can be understood in an orthodox [i.e. Roman Catholic] sense" and that for this reason "the Lutheran *sola*" can be understood "as the meaningful clarification of Rom. 3 : 28"[192] (which Luther translates "by faith *alone*"). In support of his view he calls attention to the fact that the *particula exclusiva* was used in pre-Reformation translations of the Bible as well as by Augustine, Thomas Aquinas and Bellarmine. Küng claims that the Council of Trent did not object to the formula *sola fide* as such.

He cites L. Villette who in dealing with the *Tridentinum* observes that in an earlier version of the famous canon 9 (Session 6) the following words were to be found: "faith alone . . . in the sense in which this is understood by the heretics of our time."[193] Since in Villette's view it is obvious that faith must be so understood no further reference was made to it by Trent and it was omitted from the final version of canon 9.[194] Villette also holds that in the Tridentine condemnations the word "faith" even when used absolutely is always to be understood in the sense in which the heretics understand it. Thus the rule which was valid in the condemnations of Baius and Jansen also applies to the Council of Trent: . . . *quamquam nonnullae aliquo pacto sustineri possent, in rigore et proprio verborum sensu ab assertoribus intento . . . damnamus* —"although some of their theses can in a certain sense be sustained, in the strict and proper sense of the words which they themselves maintain . . . we condemn them."[195]

In the light of all this, Küng concludes that "what matters . . . is not the formula but its meaning."[196] And how right he is! In his *Grundlagen der Dogmatik II*, Otto Weber reminds us that Pelagius, of all people, was apparently one of the first to use the formula *sola fide*, the same Pelagius who believes that Rom. 3: 28 excludes not "the works of the law" but only the *lex ceremonialis*. Weber observes rightly that "this cloud of witnesses [i.e. those who use the term *sola fide*] may suggest the question of what the *particula exclusiva* really wants to say".[197]

What then is the true meaning of *sola fide*? In Küng's view the formula is correctly used when it is meant to express the utter inability of man to justify himself. *Sola fide* signifies the rejection of any kind of self-justification on the part of man.

> . . . the man . . . who expects nothing of himself but everything of God; who is wholly open to Him who is his only refuge is the man who does not do works (*werkt*) but *believes* and who for this reason radically excludes any kind of "self-glorying".[198]

Thus Küng can say:

> Man is therefore justified by the grace of God alone; man achieves nothing . . . but he simply submits himself to God's justification; he does not do works, he believes: *"ex eo enim, quod credit in Deum iustificatem, iustificationi eius subiicit se, et sic recipit eius effectum"* (Thomas Aq. *In Rom.* 4: 5).[199]

Paul as well as John and the Synoptics always connect justification, not with love, but with faith for—as Thomas Aquinas says—"by virtue of the fact that [man] believes in the God who justifies him and submits himself to His justification he receives its effect". In other words, Küng believes that

> justification happens by faith *alone* in so far as no work, not even a work of love, justifies man but only faith, the trust, the yielding of oneself to God, the surrender to God's grace, the *sese subiicere iustificationi et ita recipere eius effectum.*[200]

Küng holds that this linking of faith with trust or confidence, of *fides* and *fiducia* is Scriptural. While in the New Testament the primary meaning of πίστις is the acceptance of the Christian *kerygma*, i.e. its acceptance as true, the close relationship between *fides* and *fiducia* cannot be disputed.

Faith as the Bible understands it includes confidence, which is particularly true when πίστις is mentioned in connection with justification.

Küng's description of faith "sounds" very "Reformed", especially when he adds:

> This believing (*gläubige*) confidence is not first of all assent to abstract truths but is the acceptance (*Bejahung*) of a person. It is the trusting faith in God and in Him whom He has sent. Faith in God is decided in the faith in Jesus Christ; He is the "Truth". "This is the work of God, that ye believe on Him whom He hath sent" (Jn. 6: 29). Jesus Christ always requires faith in Himself, and the centre of the apostolic *kerygma* is faith in Christ as the Lord, faith in the death and resurrection of Jesus Christ.[201]

We are completely at one with Küng when he observes that "it is clear which *fides sola* (Denz. 1559 [819])[202] and which *fiducia sola* (Denz. 1562 [822])[203] are condemned by Trent . . ."[204] He is convinced that, with regard to faith, the Tridentine definitions only exclude a *fiducia* which boasts and does not exert itself:[205]

> . . . yet it is not to be said that sins are forgiven or have been forgiven to any one who boasts (*iactanti*) of his confidence (*fiduciam*) and certainty (*certitudinem*) of the remission of his sins, resting (*quiescenti*) on that alone.[206]

He then invites his readers to compare this passage which condemns *iactare* and *quiescere* with Canon 12 (Session 6):

> If any one says that justifying faith is nothing else but confidence (*fiduciam*) in the divine mercy which remits sins for Christ's sake; or, that this confidence alone (*fiduciam solam*) is that whereby we are justified: let him be anathema.[207]

It would be foolish to deny that, from the earliest beginnings of the Reformation down to the present day, Protestants have constantly been tempted to misinterpret the *sola fide* of the Reformers. Some of them, regarding their *sola fiducia* as a good and meritorious work, may even have believed that it justifies them and so have struck at the very foundation of the Evangelical Church. But Küng would admit that the

Tridentine Fathers were not concerned with Protestant failures to understand aright the true teaching of the Reformation. What Trent condemned was that teaching itself and with it the *sola fide* and the *sola fiducia* of the Reformers.

But—and this is the vital point—what did Trent reject? Was it merely the *particula exclusiva*, i.e. another "over-emphasis" of the Reformers which was anathematized? We maintain that this was not the case. As a matter of fact the *sola* has blurred the real issue that divides Rome and the Reformation in connection with "faith". What Trent objected to, and therefore rejected, was the *fides* and the *fiducia* themselves as the Reformers understood them. The Tridentine Fathers would have anathematized these Reformation concepts even if they had been used without the *particula exclusiva* by the Reformers.

When the Tridentine Fathers, referring to Rom. 3: 22 and 24, say "man is justified by faith and freely", they immediately add this qualification: "those words are to be understood in that sense which the [Roman] Catholic Church has always unanimously held and expressed".[208] And in what sense has the Roman Church always understood "faith"? Küng holds that "faith" includes "confidence", especially in connection with justification; it is the believing confidence which "is not first of all assent to abstract truths but is the acceptance of a person".[209]

But is this really the Tridentine view of faith? *In Lexikon für Theologie und Kirche* (*Lexicon for Theology and the Church*), a Roman Catholic standard work of the highest scholarly repute, J. Trütsch says regarding the Tridentine notion of faith:

> As against the Protestant doctrine of "*fiduciary faith*" the Council of Trent has clearly defined what it would properly call faith: the act of the assent of the understanding (*Verstandeszustimmung*) which submits itself to God and accepts the truth of revealed doctrine.[210]

As against the Reformers' concept of fiduciary faith, the Tridentine Fathers define it as *credere vera esse quae divinitus revelata et promissa sunt.*[211] Faith is thus knowledge and assent —the Christian holds for truth those things which are divinely revealed and promised. This definition is of course correct *so far as it goes*, and to that extent Protestants agree with it: faith is also *notitia* and *assensus*. It is, however, not only knowledge and assent but also *fiducia*. "What is true faith"? asks the *Heidelberg Catechism* and then gives the classic Protestant answer based on Scripture and so combining all aspects of faith:

> It is *not only* a certain knowledge whereby I hold for truth all that God has revealed to us in His Word, *but also* a hearty trust which the Holy Ghost works in me through the Gospel, that not only to others, but to me also, forgiveness of sins, everlasting righteousness and blessedness, are given by God, out of pure grace, for the sake of Christ's merits alone.[212]

The Tridentine definition not only omits this last aspect of faith—trust—but actually rejects it. The "hearty trust . . . that . . . to me also forgiveness of sins, everlasting righteousness and blessedness are given by God" is, in the Tridentine view, *iactare*, boasting, and is therefore condemned.

Is our contention that the Tridentine concept of faith excludes *fiducia* unfair? We do not think so, especially when we consider how this concept of faith as mere assent was further developed in two important Roman documents. These are the *Catechismus Romanus* which might be regarded as a commentary on the Tridentine definitions and the (infallible) decrees and declarations of Vatican I.

While mentioning that the word "faith" (*fides*) has various meanings in Scripture, the *Roman Catechism* defines the faith which is required to obtain salvation as assent. Faith is that "by virtue of which we give our entire assent to the things which are divinely handed down (*cuius vi omnino assentimur iis quae tradita sunt divinitus*)."[213] The end proposed to man as his ultimate happiness is, however, beyond his understanding. He must receive the knowledge of it from God.

> This knowledge (*cognitio*) is actually nothing but the faith by virtue of which we can hold as valid that which the authority of

our most holy mother Church approves as being handed down by God (*cuius virtus efficit ut id ratum habeamus, quod a Deo traditum esse sanctissimae matris ecclesiae auctoritas comprobarit*).[214]

Faith is thus knowledge of, and assent to, the truth as far as it is confirmed by the Church to be divinely revealed and handed down.

While it could be argued, and actually has been, that the *Catechismus Romanus* is not a binding presentation of, and commentary on, Roman doctrine, there can be no doubt of the correctness of its concept of faith from a Roman Catholic point of view. This is corroborated by the binding and infallible decrees and declarations of Vatican I. In its chapter *de Fide*[215] the assent of faith necessary for salvation is not related in any way to *fiducia*.

> Faith itself, even when it does not work by charity, is in itself a gift of God, and the act of faith is a work appertaining to salvation, by which man yields voluntary obedience to God Himself, in assenting to and co-operating with His grace, which he is able to resist (*fides ipsa in se, etiamsi per caritatem non operetur, donum Dei est, et actus eius est opus ad salutem pertinens, quo homo liberam praestat ipsi Deo obedientiam, gratiae eius, cui resistere posset, consentiendo et cooperando.*)[216]

Even more clearly than the *Catechism Romanus* Vatican I makes the meaning of the Tridentine decrees explicit, and so stresses the authority of the Church in setting forth that to which the assent of faith is to be given.

> All those things are to be believed with divine and Catholic faith which are contained in the Word of God, written or handed down, and which the Church, either by a solemn judgement, or by her ordinary and universal magisterium, sets forth to be believed as having been divinely revealed (*ab Ecclesia . . . divinitus revelata credenda proponuntur*).[217]

It seems to us certain that in defining faith as "the act of the assent of the understanding", as a *credere vera esse*, Trent's intention was—in deliberate opposition to the Reformation— to exclude *fiducia* from its concept of faith. This, of course, does not mean that in the Tridentine view faith is excluded

from justification. We are quoting again from Trütsch's
article in *Lexikon für Theologie und Kirche*:

> Although this faith [i.e. the act of the assent of the understanding] without works (i.e. hope and love) is "dead" (Denz. 1530 [800])[218] it has its significance within the justification-process (*fides est humanae salutis initium, fundamentum et radix iustificationis*) ... Denz. 1532 [801].[219, 220]

Faith is the beginning of human salvation, the root and ground
of justification.

Even if Küng is correct in saying that Trent was not
opposed to the formula *sola fide* as such, but only to the wrong
kind of the "by faith alone", it is now quite clear which kind
of *sola fide* is condemned: fiduciary faith, a faith which is
confident of justification here and now. Faith, as the
Tridentine Fathers understand it, cannot be sure and
certain of justification—if it were it would be "boasting".
"Justified by faith" understood "in that sense which the
[Roman] Catholic Church has always unanimously held and
expressed" means that faith is only the beginning of salvation
—man appropriates by faith, not salvation itself, but only its
initium; his faith is the foundation and the root of all justification—he thus appropriates, not justification itself, but
only the *fundamentum* on which it stands and the *radix* from
which it grows.

Küng would no doubt raise objections to our interpretation
of Trent. He maintains that it is not the right but only the
wrong *fiducia* that is condemned by the Tridentine Fathers.
The right kind of *fiducia* is a confidence which, in view of its
own sinful weakness, in fear and trembling expects everything humbly and hopefully from the revelation of God. It is
a confidence that believes in the divine promises, especially
in the forgiveness of sins obtained by Christ.[221]

We can assure Küng that Protestants are fully aware of
St. Paul's unequivocal instruction that if there is any
καύχησις, any glorying or boasting to be done it must be
ἐν κυρίῳ, in the Lord. (2 Cor. 10: 17). Those who stand in
the true tradition of the Reformation, from Luther and

Calvin to Barth, though sorely beset by the sin of pride, do not boast of or glory in their confidence, but, looking away from themselves to Jesus Christ, who is the only ground of their *fiducia*, they glory in the Lord. But in doing so—and here they basically differ from Trent—they are sure and certain that from every point of view, objectively and subjectively, they are justified here and now; for what God has promised—redemption as well as justification, objective as well as subjective, is now fulfilled in Christ.

This is the heart of the matter, the real point at issue between Rome and the Reformation, between Barth and Trent. Is then the object of the Christian's confidence, his justification, i.e. its appropriation, realized? Does my *fiducia*, whose only ground is Jesus Christ, enable me to say: here and now I am justified, here and now my sins are remitted, here and now God's declaration of righteousness puts me in the right and so makes me righteous in Christ; or must I be content with contemplating a future justification: now I can hope that I will be justified, now I can be confident that my sins will be forgiven?

Although *fiducia* is not omitted by Trent, its reference is not to the present but to the future. This is shown by the Tridentine definition of confidence. While Faith is *credere vera esse*,[222] confidence is *spes fidentes Deum . . . propitium fore*[223]— the hope which trusts that God will be propitious. The object of *fiducia* in the Tridentine view is therefore not yet realized, its realization, however confidently expected, is not yet assured. In other words, *fiducia* is to be thought of in terms of a hope still to be fulfilled.

This is confirmed by Villette whom Küng cites in support of his position. Villette holds that the chapter on justification (Session 6, chapter 6)

> obviously aims only at one aspect of the Reformed teaching on faith . . . the subjective certainty and assurance of being justified. It is this assurance which the Council [of Trent] declares to be vain and impious, not the faith itself which accompanies it . . . Canon 12 (Session 6) . . . surely shows the insufficiency of faith-confidence to effect justification but it does

not say as much as that this faith-confidence is bad in itself or harmful.[224]

And what is "faith-confidence"? Villette states that the

description of hope [in Session 6, chapter 6][225] corresponds almost literally to that of the faith-confidence of the innovators; it allows, however, for two precise definitions of importance: on the one hand, the reason (*motif*) for this confidence is not the subjective feeling of believing and of being justified but the objective promise of God; on the other hand, this confidence is not set on a present and realized object (justification already granted) but on a future object (*Deum sibi propitium fore*).[226] This double nuance allows a distinction to be made between simple "faith-confidence", the legitimacy of which the Council recognizes, because it assimilates it into the necessary movement of theological (*théologale*) hope, and what is usually called "fiduciary faith" or "special faith", which is a purely subjective conviction condemned by the Council. Thus, in so far as the innovators affirm the necessity of simple "faith-confidence" for justification or the sacraments, their thought conforms to that of [Roman] Catholics. . . . On the other hand, in so far as Protestants cling to "fiduciary faith" alone they are condemned by the Council which declares it to be "vain, useless and dangerous": it is without a valid foundation and risks making the subject forget the reality of his weakness and of his precarious dispositions.[227]

Protestants would readily agree that the ground of the Christian's confidence could never be his own pious feeling of believing or of being justified, but Jesus Christ and He alone. But, because Christ alone is the ground of *fiducia*, there is assurance that in Him God's promises of redemption and justification are now fulfilled. The object of *fiducia* is, therefore, not to be realized in the future, but is realized objectively and subjectively in Christ here and now.

The Reformers and Barth do not assert that the Christian requires nothing but faith (thus excluding love and hope), nor do they deny that *fiducia* is only one of several aspects and dimensions of faith. Both the Reformers and Barth affirm, however, that justification is *sola fide* to the exclusion of love and hope and that man apprehends it *sola fiducia*.

Because Trent anathematizes this position[228] Barth calls Romanism "another gospel".[229] He admits that faith has for Paul "other dimensions than that in which in relation to man's justification it is *fiducia divinae misericordiae peccata remittentis propter Christum*". But

> there can also be no doubt that in the contexts in which he connects δικαιοσύνη and πίστις faith is just this and nothing but this: the confidence of sinful man in the demonstration of the undeserved faithfulness of God as given in Jesus Christ, a demonstration in which he finds that his sins are forgiven. If there is any corresponding faithfulness of sinful man to the faithful God, it consists only in this confidence. As he gives God this confidence, he finds himself justified, but not otherwise. That was what the Reformers maintained. They did not have the unequivocal backing of Paul for all their statements. But they undoubtedly had it for this statement.[230]

Barth's statement should be carefully noted: "As he [i.e. man] gives God this confidence, he finds himself justified." If Barth is not referring here to subjective justification, to the apprehension and appropriation by the individual of what Christ has done objectively for all men, what else could subjective justification possibly be? And because he is speaking here of subjective justification *sola fiducia*, which is expressly rejected by Trent, he calls Roman Catholicism "another gospel". Yet Küng says that Barth's criticism of Rome misfires because owing to a terminological confusion he criticizes what Trent intends as a statement on subjective justification in terms of his own teaching on objective justification. But is it really possible to find basic agreement between Barth's view that, as man gives God this confidence, he finds himself justified *but not otherwise*—i.e. the appropriation or apprehension of justification *sola fiducia* and the Tridentine anathema against anyone who says that *vel eam fiduciam solam esse, qua justificamur?*[231] We do not think so. Our contention can easily be tested by asking quite simply what part is assigned to love in justification by Barth and Trent respectively. We asked a similar question in our debate with Bouyer.

Küng observes that

> faith is strongly stressed in Barth's doctrine of justification. But
> he [i.e. Barth] does not for this reason depreciate love. The
> relationship between faith and love is to be regarded as
> corresponding to the relationship between justification and
> sanctification. Here too there are two moments in the one
> action.[232]

In order to prove that his interpretation of Barth is correct,
Küng cites some key-passages from the *Church Dogmatics*.
Although Barth distinguishes between faith and love, he
does not separate them:

> Love as self-giving stands contrasted with faith as reception. Yet
> on the divine side we do not have in the humiliation and
> exaltation of Jesus Christ, and therefore in justification and
> sanctification and the work of the Holy Spirit which reveals
> them two separate divine actions, but two undivided and
> simultaneous, although distinguishable, moments or forms of
> the one divine action. Similarly, on the human side faith and
> love, reception and surrender are two indivisible but disting-
> uishable moments of the one vital movement and act which
> constitutes Christian existence. The contrast then is only
> relative, and we can hardly speak of love without (in other
> terms) making use of the views and concepts with which faith
> has also to be described, or of faith without attributing to it
> certain features which in the strict sense are those of love.[233]

Although justification and sanctification, faith and love
can never be separated, they must yet be distinguished from
each other. In doing so Barth gives no part to love in justification, which is for him exclusively connected with faith:

> ... there can be no question of a justification of man by his love
> to God—perhaps as a continuation or actualization of his
> justification by faith. Certainly the divine direction, the direc-
> tion into love to God, can never be lacking in the man who has
> subjected himself to the divine sentence in the knowledge of it.
> But it is the pardoning sentence of God alone which is the basis
> of fellowship between God and man, and which therefore justi-
> fies man. And the fact that he is justified is something which he
> finds to be true and actual only in faith. That he can love, i.e.
> seek God, is his freedom to live in that fellowship on the basis

which has been laid down by God and God alone. But because we are here dealing with human activity, with the sum of the Christian *ethos* and its always doubtful fulfilment, it can as little contribute to the setting up of that fellowship and therefore to justification as can faith itself as the human recognition that it has been set up.

It amounts to this, that in love man is occupied with something else and he ought always to be so. It would completely destroy the essential character of Christian love as the freedom given to man and to be kept by man if we tried to burden it with the, in itself, impossible and superfluous task of accomplishing or actualizing or even completing the justification of man. No one can and will love God who does not believe. No one can and will love God except in the grounding of his being in the fellowship with God realized in that divine judgement. If we are to be justified by faith, in faith we will not look either at our works or our sins. Similarly in love—in the works of our love to God—we will not consider the possibility of trying subsequently to fulfil or to complete of ourselves that grounding of our being.[234]

If Küng is able to accept Barth's statements, then he is really in agreement not only with Barth himself but also with Calvin. But we believe that, were he to accept this position, Küng would be rejecting Tridentine doctrine.

Our opinion here is shared by some of Küng's Roman Catholic critics. One of them (who is by no means unsympathetic) Heinrich Stirnimann, O.P., reviewed Küng's *Rechtfertigung* in the *Freiburger Zeitschrift für Philosophie und Theologie* and then answered in the *Schweizerische Kirchenzeitung* some of the objections to his review raised by Küng in that same journal. For Stirnimann the real *"nervus quaestionis"* lies mainly in the question of whether or not love participates in the act of justification. Barth, in his opinion, excludes love in this respect. According to Roman Catholic doctrine, on the other hand, what is involved is more than a simple recognition of the work of God. Stirnimann holds that the decisive factor from the point of view of man is his "return" (*Rückkehr*), his "contrition" (*Reue*) which must derive from supernatural love to God. For this reason faith as well as love are constitutive elements in the justification-occurrence.

Neither faith nor love are the work of man but are effected by divine grace, the only active principle of the justification of the sinner. Stirnimann believes that both in his presentation of Roman doctrine and in his assessment of the controversy with Barth, Küng completely loses sight of the inner connection of these fundamental points.[235]

Stirnimann also holds that

on the basis of the decisive passages [in Thomas Aquinas] (I/II, q. 113 and *De ver.*, q. 28) it cannot be doubted that love belongs not in some "hidden way" but formally and explicitly as an act to the substance of the justification-process. *"Simul in iustificatione impii cum motu fidei est etiam motus caritatis"* [in the justification of the impious there is simultaneously with the movement of faith also the movement of love] (I/II, q. 113, a. 4, ad 1. cf. *De ver.*, q. 28, a. 4, ad 3). Nor does the *Tridentinum* speak of a justification by faith to which love would be added merely as "fruit and result". Faith and love belong according to it [Trent] constitutively to the justification-occurrence: *Nam fides, nisi ad eam spes accedat et caritas, neque unit perfecte cum Christo, neque corporis eius vivum membrum efficit.* [For faith, unless hope and charity be added thereto, neither unites man perfectly with Christ, nor makes him a living member of His body.][236] The proper end (*Abschluss*) of justification which belongs to its nature is the sinner becoming a "living member" of the Body of Christ again, the "friendship" with God shining again in the full sense.[237]

What divides Trent and Barth according to Stirnimann is thus the place of love in the justification-occurrence. What Trent affirms positively: i.e. that love belongs formally, explicitly and constitutively to the process of justification— is denied by Barth who connects faith only with justification and love with sanctification. Reformation theology teaches that, though faith and love cannot be separated, they, as already said, must be distinguished, just as justification and sanctification, though inseparable, are yet distinguishable. From a Roman Catholic point of view, however, justification and its appropriation are apparently not by faith alone but also by love, for otherwise how could love belong formally, explicitly and constitutively to the justification-occurrence?

Küng is thus criticized by a scholar of his own Communion because he discovers a basic agreement between Barth and Trent, which, in Stirnimann's opinion, is impossible once the Tridentine decree is correctly understood. We too find this same divergence between Barth and Trent. But how wide the gulf between Barth and the Tridentine Fathers really is becomes even more evident when we look more closely at Küng's own concept of faith, of "justifying faith".

For Küng, faith, *fides viva*, which alone justifies "does not exclude but includes contrition (*Reue*) for sins; it produces no works (not even works of faith) to justify itself—justification by living faith does not at all mean justification by faith *and* works. But it [faith] wants to be active in works: *fides quae per caritatem operatur* (Gal. 5: 6)."[238] But faith does not only work through love, it actually contains an embryonic love (*eine keimende Liebe*); even "dead" faith has this indwelling embryonic love. "Otherwise how could it grasp (*erfassen*) the mercy of God if it had not at least an embryonic love? How could it [faith] trust (*ein Vertrauen haben*) in the Redeemer without a secret longing (*Verlangen*) for Him?"[239] Thus "love is not absent in justification nor can it be".[240]

This is far from the Reformation concept of faith as the vacuum, the empty vessel, which is to be filled with Christ, as *fides a Christo formata*. But is Küng's concept of a faith which contains an embryonic love and a secret longing for Christ not equally far removed from Barth's notion of faith?

"Faith"—says Barth—"is the simple discovery of the child which finds itself in the father's house and on the mother's lap."[241] Faith is the choice of that "for which [man] is already chosen by the divine decision and beside which he has no other choice".[242] Faith is thus a simple acknowledgement of what God has already done objectively, really and ontologically in Christ. [243] "I may close my eyes, I may shut them as tight as I can or I may turn away from the sun, but this does not alter the fact that the sun shines on me too, and that I have eyes to see it." [244] Faith therefore is simply that we open and use our eyes and do not "persist in the darkness which has been penetrated and dispersed in Him".[245] Faith is the acceptance of the fact that "all this [i.e. both our justification and sanctification, both our regeneration and conversion in Christ] has been done and is in force . . . so that it is just as true and actual in our lives as it is in itself."[246] And when Barth speaks of the creative (*kreatorischen*) character of faith, to which we have previously referred, this is meant to describe the faith of the Christian, which, as a witness to Christ, simply confirms "the alteration of the human situation, which has taken place in Jesus Christ".[247] We have already heard what Barth has to say about the relationship between faith and love in connection, not with justification (!), but with the Holy Spirit: faith and love are two indivisible but distinguishable moments of the one movement which constitutes the Christian life. In our debate with Bouyer we learned that in principle Calvin said the same 400 years ago. But neither Calvin nor Barth ever confuse faith and love. There is no question of discovering even an embryonic love or a secret longing in faith which would make it "justifying faith". How could they do so? If faith has in it an embryonic love, it would no longer be the empty vessel that is to be filled with Christ, who alone justifies. Faith would be active itself in justification. In Christ man is justified and sanctified, he believes and loves at one and the same time.

It is impossible to separate justification and sanctification: they are two aspects of the one divine action. It is equally impossible to separate faith and love: on the human side they are two aspects of one and the same act. It is, however, necessary, as was said, to distinguish them in thought. Faith is the reception of Christ, who justifies; love is the surrender of the believer to the Christ, who sanctifies. Man loves the moment he is justified, or appropriates justification, but he is not justified because he already loves God, or is already longing for Him.

We hold that Küng's concept of faith is basically different from that of Barth. He understands faith as *fides formata caritate* however embryonic the indwelling love may be. He says so himself. He mentions for instance San Felice and J. Contarini, who in defence of the *sola fides* at the Council of

Trent found it sufficient to say that the reference was to the *fides formata caritate.*[248]

But, though Küng clearly states that faith includes contrition and contains both an embryonic love and a secret longing for Christ, so that love is not and cannot be absent in justification, Stirnimann is not satisfied. What is too "Roman" for us is not "Roman" enough for him. We reject Küng's notion of faith because, though it appears in the guise of the *sola fide,* it is still essentially the typically Roman *fides caritate formata* and not the Reformation *fides a Christo formata.* Stirnimann criticizes Küng's notion of faith on the ground that he does not state definitely, clearly and strongly enough what is so obviously taught by Thomas Aquinas and the Tridentinum: love—a mere embryonic love will not do— belongs formally, explicitly and constitutively to the justification-process and does so as an act.

If Stirnimann is correct in his understanding of Trent— and we believe that he is—the gulf that separates Rome and the Reformation, Trent and Barth, is now apparent in all its breadth. The proper and essential end of justification is the sinner's becoming a living member of the body of Christ again and the shining again of his friendship with God. But in this case who then is subjectively justified, who appropriates justification? Is it really the sinner? The Tridentine Fathers certainly say that we are justified freely (*gratis autem iustificari ideo dicamur*);[249] but how and why are we justified freely, i.e. without faith and works, without merits on our part? Their answer is: "*quia nihil eorum, quae iustificationem praecedunt, sive fides, sive opera, ipsam iustificationis gratiam promeretur*—because none of those things which precede justification—whether faith or works—merit the grace itself of justification."[250, 251] What the sinner receives freely is *not* justification but only the grace of justification. And what happens when the sinner has freely received this grace? Is it not true that, once this grace has been received, man— co-operating and assenting—does not hear and appropriate a verdict of acquittal but, as we have said before, he is taken into a process set in motion. This process is sanctification, of

which justification is a part. At the end of the process sanctified man is justified. If, as Stirnimann says, the end of
justification is accomplished when the sinner again becomes
a living member of the Body of Christ and his friendship with
God shines once more, it cannot be the sinner, but it must be
the just, who is justified, at least man who is in a state of
grace.

But this is the teaching neither of the Reformers nor of Barth:

> The justification of man as determined and accomplished and
> pronounced in the divine sentence is both at once in this order
> and sequence: it is *creatio ex contrario*, but *creatio*; *iustificatio impii*,
> but *iustificatio*. . . . The justification of man begins in his past
> and it is completed in his future. But as his past as a sinner is
> still his present, so his future as a righteous man is already his
> present. The fact that although he is still a sinner he is already
> righteous, that in the same present in which he comes out of his
> past as a sinner he goes forward to the future as a righteous
> man—this fact is the promise addressed to him in the judge-
> ment and sentence of God. There is no doubt that it speaks of
> his future. This other man, the righteous, the one he was not
> and still is not, is the man he will be. This future is promised to
> him as the past is repudiated. But the promise that he will be
> this man is addressed to him here and now, today, in the midst
> of the present. It is not an uncertain promise like the hopes
> which he might create for himself or which might be created
> for him by circumstances and relationships and even other men.
> It is the promise the power of which is the irrevocable decision
> of God in which he is already this other man, the righteous.[252]

The irrevocable decision of God is that in Christ the sinner
is already this other man, the righteous. In Christ man is
what he is to be. Barth leaves no doubt at all that this change
in the human situation comes about without the co-operation
of man but solely by His verdict of acquittal whereby the
sinner is justified. We do not believe that this is the doctrine
of Trent, as we observed when we dealt with the same question, but looked at it from a different angle, in Chapter 3 of
this section: the appropriation of justification is in the
Tridentine view only the beginning of a process of sanctification at the end of which God pronounces His verdict, not

on the sinner, but on the just, at least on him who, having received freely the grace of justification, assented to and co-operated with it, and so is sanctified. From the point of view of the Reformation (and in this Barth is its true heir), the foundation and source of Christian assurance is what Christ, the grace of God has done *for* us. This is why justification is central! Central for Trent is what the grace of God is doing *in* us. Sanctification incorporating justification is for this reason the centre, and it is a sanctification to which man must assent and with which he must co-operate before he is saved.

Now, when we examine Küng's teaching from every angle, does he not say after all fundamentally the same?

> In so far as justification occurs by faith alone and not by the works of man, it is not . . . sanctification (in the strict "subjective"-ethical sense); the divine justification would otherwise become the self-justification of man (this is clearly expressed by Trent, cf. Denz. 1532 [801]). In this sense sanctification follows on justification. . . . But in so far as justification as the effective judicial verdict of God makes man ontologically (*seinsmässig*) righteous or holy, it is . . . sanctification (in the sense of the "objective"-ontic-making holy (*Heiligmachung*) effected by God); the divine justification would otherwise be an empty, merely verbal declaration (this aspect is expressed by Trent in Denz. 1528 [799] and 1561 [821]).[253]

Küng describes the relationship between the "objective"-ontic making holy (*Heiligmachung*) and the "subjective"-ethical sanctification (*Heiligung*) thus:

> The righteousness or holiness given to man by the justification of God is the necessary foundation for every moral sanctification, and, conversely, sanctification is the effectuation (*Wirksamwerden*) and the fulfilment of the holiness founded by justification (*durch die Rechtfertigung grundgelegte Heiligkeit*). . . . As faith must be active in love so justification must be effectual (*wirksam*) in sanctification. In all human sanctification it is obvious that what is involved can never be a human completion but only an effect (*Auswirkung*) of the divine work.[254]

All this seems to be very near to the position of both the

Reformation and Barth—until we look again at Küng's notion of faith. He says that "in justification the sinner can give nothing but what he receives from the grace of God".[255] But what he receives—this is surely a fair deduction—he can give, for instance faith which is a gift of God's grace.

We have already seen that faith for Küng though under a slightly different aspect is basically *fides caritate formata*, it is thus as for Trent a *virtus theologica*. As such it is effected by grace but it is as a *virtus* infused into man and so his. Man cannot give anything but what he has received—that, however, he can give. And so he can and does give in justification what he has received from God, his faith with its embryonic love, a faith which already loves. Faith, as a *virtus* infused into man, presupposes the co-operation between man's will and God's grace. Trent speaks of the co-operation and the assent of man quite clearly, openly and definitely. Küng qualifies these as much as possible. The *cooperari* and *assentire* are not active co-operation but passive collaboration; it is "*Mitwirken nicht im Sinne eines Mitwerkens, sondern eines Mitmachens.*"[256] *Assentire* is "in its passivity a highly active saying 'Yes and Amen' of the contrite sinner who is raised up by God's gracious verdict as a judge"; *cooperari* is "passive collaboration (*Mitmachen*) with what God alone has put into effect (*ins Werk gesetzt*)".[257]

But does not Küng overlook something vital? Otto Weber puts his finger on it: Man collaborates only passively— "[er] macht . . . mit" but what does he contribute to this collaboration—"*was bringt er dazu mit*"? "Does he remain who he is, and so come under the influence of . . . *gratia*? Or does he become another by the favour of God?"[258] In other words, is faith the root and foundation of a justification still to be subjectively appropriated but as yet not realized? Or is it the trust, the *fiducia* that "to me also, forgiveness of sins, everlasting righteousness and blessedness are given by God", i.e. the trust that I am justified, both objectively and subjectively? We believe that Küng's notion of faith is too Tridentine to allow him to say really that the sinner is subjectively justified here and now. Fundamentally he says what Trent does: he who collaborates is not acquitted right away but comes under the influence of sanctifying grace; this is the process of sanctification at the end of which, if he is in a state of grace, he is justified.

At the end of the last paragraph we asked whether Küng's own interpretation of both aspects of the one justification, and thus also of its appropriation, is strictly christological. Although he goes farther than any other Roman theologian we know, we believe that fundamentally he remains Tridentine in his teaching on subjective justification, which is determined not christologically but anthropologically. What then is subjective justification; what is meant by justified *sola fide*?

In *Justification, its Radical Nature and Place in Reformed Doctrine and Life*, T. F. Torrance gives an excellent summary of what we believe to be the position of both the Reformers and of Barth.

Jesus Christ was not only the fulfilment and embodiment of God's righteous and holy act of *dikaioma*, but also the embodiment of our act of faith and trust and obedience toward God. He stood in our place, taking our cause upon Him, also as Believer, as the Obedient One who was Himself justified before God as His beloved Son in whom He was well pleased. He offered to God a perfect confidence and trust, a perfect faith and response which we are unable to offer, and He appropriated all God's blessings which we are unable to appropriate. Through union with Him we share in His faith, in His obedience, in His trust and His appropriation of the Father's blessings; we share in His justification before God. Therefore when we are justified by faith, this does not mean that it is *our* faith that justifies us, far from it—it is the faith of Christ alone that justifies us, but we in faith flee from our own acts even of repentance, confession, trust and response, and take refuge in the obedience and faithfulness of Christ—"Lord I believe, help thou mine unbelief". . . . [Thus] justification has been fulfilled subjectively as well as objectively in Jesus Christ, but that objective and subjective justification is objective to us. It is freely imputed to us by grace objectively and we through the Spirit share in it subjectively as we are united to Christ. His subjective justification becomes ours, and it is subjective in us as well as in Him, but only subjective in us because it has been made subjectively real in our own human nature, in our own human flesh in Jesus, our Brother, and our Mediator.[259]

Here subjective as well as objective justification, the two aspects of one and the same salvation-event, are christologically determined. The strict christological orientation is missing in Küng when it comes to the subjective aspect of the one justification. He goes farther than Trent but does not go far enough. We rejoice that His Church allows him to go as far as he does but Rome will have to progress much farther before Christian unity can become a visible reality.

One more question must be asked in connection with Küng's teaching on justification. How can he interpret Trent as evangelically as he does? This brings us at last to his methodology.

6

Küng's Methodological Principles

While Küng's own teaching on justification meets some of the criticisms and objections of the Reformation, and so constitutes a *rapprochement* between Roman Catholic and Protestant theology, the Reformed theologian is rather taken aback by the boldness of Küng's assertion concerning the true meaning of the Tridentine definitions of justification.

This may be exemplified by referring once again to Canon 11 of the 6th Tridentine Session: *Si quis dixerit, homines iustificari vel sola imputatione iustitiae Christi, vel sola peccatorum remissione, exclusa gratia et caritate, quae in cordibus eorum per Spiritum Sanctum diffundatur atque illis inhaereat, aut etiam gratiam, qua iustificamur, esse tantum favorem Dei: an. s.*[260] From an historical point of view it is quite clear that, whatever the exact nature of their teaching may have been, the Tridentine Fathers rejected the Reformation doctrine of justification. In their preliminary discussions, as in their final declarations and definitions, they refused to approach in any way the position of the Reformers, and at least intended to assert that God justifies by the infusion of grace, thus excluding the

Reformation view of justification by the imputation of righteousness. We came to the conclusion that they regarded grace as a "physical entity in the human subject" and not as "a being and attitude of the living God Himself". Consequently, what is involved in justification according to Trent is in our opinion not so much "His-being-gracious" but "my-having-grace".[261]

Küng on the other hand gives the primacy very definitely to forgiveness and imputation in justification, which is a declaring righteous and only as such also a making so. What has been denied by most Roman theologians up to the present day, and was in the opinion of a majority of Roman as well as Protestant scholars rejected and condemned by Trent (Session 6, chapter 7), is now positively affirmed by Küng as the true teaching of Trent and therefore of the Church of Rome.

This contradiction between the traditional understanding of the Tridentine teaching and Küng's new interpretation of it becomes even more obvious in relation to the last part of Canon 11: *gratiam, qua iustificamur, esse tantum favorem Dei.*

Küng maintains that in this statement the nature of grace as the favour of God is *clearly* affirmed.[262] Whatever else the Tridentine Fathers may have done, they certainly did not affirm *clearly* that grace is the favour or the kindness or the graciousness of God. Here again, what has never been very much to the fore in Roman theology since the Middle Ages (to say the least of it)—namely grace as the favour of God in Jesus Christ—is according to Küng *clearly* affirmed in the binding definitions of Trent, and is therefore claimed to be the official and authoritative teaching of the Church of Rome.

Küng is far too good a scholar not to be aware of the difficulties with which his interpretation of the Tridentine teaching confronts, not only Protestant, but even Roman Catholic theologians. How does he succeed in substantiating his claim that the decrees of Trent are capable of his interpretation? Küng is able to do so by applying more strictly and radically than other Roman theologians several methodological principles which may be summarized as follows:

1. His first methodological principle, at least by implication, is that in determining the authoritative meaning of a dogma, the private theological opinions of those who formulated it are neither binding nor of consequence.[263] In his article *The Evangelical Possibilities of Roman Catholic Theology*, George A. Lindbeck makes an assertion regarding the methodology of Roman theologians which is probably unacceptable to them. Lindbeck holds that

> in practice if not in theory, dogma [from a Roman point of view] is related to theology somewhat as the constitution of a state is related to its laws, or as a law is related to its interpretations. Just as a skilful lawyer may discover possibilities of interpretation which were previously undreamt of and which, in fact, contradict what was thought to be the clear intent of the formulators of the law or constitution, so also Roman Catholic theologians often discover loop-holes in the dogmatic system.[264]

While this lawyer-like technique with regard to dogmatic interpretation may appear to Protestants to be somewhat dishonest, Lindbeck hastens to the defence of Roman theologians. He reminds Protestants that from a Roman Catholic point of view

> it is also [Roman] dogma that only a part of theological truth has been explicitly defined, and that the Scripture liturgy, the Fathers and Doctors, are also norms for theology. So when a Roman Catholic theologian does violence to what seems the clear historical meaning of a dogma in order to make it harmonize with other authorities, he may actually be performing his dogmatically imposed task.[265]

In interpreting the Tridentine decrees Küng uses this lawyer-like technique. He is not concerned, as it were, with the mind of the lawgiver or with what the lawgiver intended the laws to mean, but only with their actual text. In other words, not the private theological opinions of the Tridentine Fathers, which determined at least to some extent their definitions, but the actual text of the definitions themselves are interpreted by him and made to harmonize with other authorities, i.e. Scripture.

Canon 11 of the 6th Tridentine Session condemns anyone who says that "the grace, whereby we are justified, is only the favour of God". Everything depends on the meaning of *esse tantum favorem Dei*. It is beyond dispute that for the Reformers grace was only, i.e. nothing else than, the favour of God in Jesus Christ; grace was Jesus Christ Himself. It is also clearly established that the Council of Trent condemned the Reformation position. Küng acknowledges that from a biblical point of view grace is not a *habitus* within man but primarily the favour and kindness of God. The Council of Trent would have rejected this statement. When Küng's methodological principle is applied to Canon 11 it does not matter to him whether or not the Tridentine Fathers as private theologians and individuals intended to say that grace is not the favour of God but rather a physical entity infused into man. What really matters is that what they did say can be interpreted as meaning: grace is also the favour of God but not exclusively so. Since the Tridentine canon does not declare that grace is in absolutely no sense the favour of God, Küng is able to hold that grace is in fact primarily the favour of God.

No one should rashly accuse Küng of lacking in candour nor should his methodology be dismissed as dishonest. He bases his interpretation of dogma on an eminently sound principle. Just as the exegete is not concerned, or at least should not be concerned, primarily or exclusively with the mind of Mark or Luke but with their witness to Jesus Christ, so the theologian, in interpreting the dogmas of the Church, cannot base his conclusions on the intentions of those who formulated the dogmas but only on the formulations themselves. Not what the Tridentine Fathers intended to say but what they actually did say became authoritative for the Roman Church.

There is, however, one noticeable flaw in Küng's argument. If, in determining the authoritative meaning of a dogma, the private theological opinions of those who formulated it are irrevelant, does the same irrelevancy not extend to the private opinions of its interpreters? Protestants would hold that Küng has the authority of Scripture for his teaching on grace as the favour of God, but has he the authority of his Church? Does he not rather express a private theological opinion which will remain personal until the Roman magisterium declares authoritatively that his interpretation of the Tridentine decrees is indeed that of the Roman Church?

As we have already seen, Küng himself admits that post-Tridentine Roman theology has often not taken seriously enough what he believes to be clearly affirmed by the Council of Trent, i.e. grace is the favour of God. Is not the most likely reason for this omission on the part of Roman theology that grace as the favour of God was either not affirmed or at least not clearly affirmed by Trent? Protestants are inclined to ask whether Küng is not rather more faithful to the Apostolic witness and rather less so to the Tridentine Fathers, while Roman theology has hitherto been rather more faithful to Trent and less so to the witness of the Apostles.

2. Küng's second methodological principle is that a dogma must be understood against the background of the historical period in which it was formulated. A dogma is intended to define, not the whole truth of the divine Revelation, but only that part and aspect of it which have been misinterpreted or corrupted. Consequently, the interpretation of a dogma must be related to the particular heresy it condemns. Küng is of the opinion that

> most dogmatic definitions are polemical formulae directed against heresies; they are walls of defence against error. . . . The uniform basic structure and the continuity of the dogma remain intact. But the Church, concentrating all its power on that part of divine Revelation which is endangered, illuminates, as it were, the dark spot with a searchlight and brings everything unmistakably and distinctly to light through the agency of an exact, precise and universally understandable formula.[266]

Küng believes that this applies to almost every dogma:

> Not only the Council of Trent but every Council from Nicaea

to Vatican [I] has had concrete opponents in view and has spoken polemically into a definite direction. It is not for nothing that everywhere in *Denzinger* the [names of the] opponents who are addressed appear in brackets: *contra Arianos, Macedonianos . . . contra Novatores saec. 16 . . . contra materialistas, pantheistas!*[267]

The function of a dogma is thus primarily negative and defensive—it is *norma negativa*. When this methodological principle is applied to the decrees of the Council of Trent, it seems that the primary and principal task of the Tridentine Fathers was, not to declare and to define what justification is, but what it is not.

It is, of course, perfectly correct that in many instances the function of a dogma is indeed defensive and negative: defensive—it secures the Church against the invasion of error; negative—it defines what the deep mysteries of God, which cannot be defined, are *not*.

A rather unconvincing part of Küng's methodological approach is his idea that, for instance, from the defensive and negative Tridentine declaration *Si quis dixerit . . . gratiam, qua iustificamur, esse tantum favorem Dei: anathema sit* a positive assertion regarding grace can, and almost must, be deduced. Although anyone who says that grace is "only the favour of God" is anathematized by the Tridentine Fathers, their declaration affirms *clearly* all the same that grace *is* the favour of God.

Protestants are, of course, in full agreement with Küng's biblical theology: grace is the favour of God, it is Jesus Christ. They are, however, not at all sure that his interpretation of the Tridentine decrees and definitions is accurate, though they would like to think that it is. They rejoice that his teaching has not been officially repudiated by the Roman Church. But they would prefer his "private" theological opinion to obtain a more official recognition in his Church. Then, and only then, could there be real peace between the Evangelical and Roman understanding of grace.

3. The third methodological principle employed by Küng is that, since dogmatic definitions are never final pronounce-

ments, they can be re-formulated and re-stated not only terminologically but also conceptually and so be clarified and improved. Protestant theologians will have no difficulty in recognizing here a principle which the Reformation applied to all traditional theological statements. The Church often uses for its dogmatic formulations the terminology and the thought-forms of philosophical systems prevailing at particular times in history without, however, being bound to them. When new philosophical systems produce a new terminology and new concepts, they may serve the Church in clarifying and improving its dogmatic definitions. But, since these are always merely finite statements, often with a historically conditioned emphasis, they never exhaust the fullness of the truth.[268]

> The implicit truth-content so far as it is divine truth always surpasses its explicit formulation. . . . A truth of faith can therefore always be articulated by a . . . still more complete, adequate and perfect formula.[269]

Now this is good and sound "Reformed" theology. At the Reformation the Church, its doctrine and structure, was "re-formed" in accordance with, and in submission to, the Word of God. The finite character of dogmatic definitions having been acknowledged, the traditional formulations of the faith were cited to appear at the bar of the Word of God to be reconsidered and judged. As a result of this judgement doctrinal statements were often re-formulated, and so clarified and corrected. Genuine Reformation theology has, however, always recognized that even after clarification and correction the improved dogmatic declarations are still finite statements, which are capable of further correction and improvement in the light of the Word of God. No modern theologian has reminded the Church—the Church of the Reformation and perhaps even the Church of Rome— more often and more forcibly than Barth that to be *ecclesia reformata* the Church must always be *ecclesia semper reformanda*.

The question arises in connection with Küng's methodology whether the application of the principle adopted by him goes far enough. He holds that dogmatic definitions can be amplified and improved. They can even be replaced by formulae, which are not merely terminologically, but also conceptually different according to new historical circumstances and perspectives. But though he agrees that there may be amplification, completion, perfection, in short a development of dogmatic definitions, there could never be any replacement of content. The content of a formula is immutable.

> The dogmatic definitions [of the Roman Church] go unerringly and directly (not merely approximately) to the heart of the truth—thus they are irrevocable. . . . This embodying of the revelation-truth in a new form of thought and speech by the Church is accomplished, however, not primarily by human-theological thinking but, as the effect of the incarnation, brought about in the Church by the operation of the Holy Spirit of Jesus Christ.[270]

As long as the Holy Spirit is not identified with the mind or "soul" of the Roman Church, and His operation involves the confrontation of the Church with the objective Word of God, and not the approbation of the subjective ideas of the Church itself, no exception can be taken to Küng's point of view. Protestants must, however, insist that dogmatic formulae are correct only if, even after development, they are still explicitly or implicitly based on, and warranted by, the written Word of God. Even after Küng's clarification Protestants will find it difficult enough to recognize in the Tridentine decrees the biblical doctrine of justification. If the magisterium of the Roman Church endorsed Küng's clarification and interpretation of the Council of Trent with regard to the doctrine of grace, Protestants would not be able to deny the similarity between the Roman and the Barthian understanding of grace. They feel, however, that the division between the Church of the Reformation and the Church of Rome will finally be overcome only if more radical use of Küng's third methodological principle is made in respect of Roman dogmas which have no Scriptural warrant. When it comes to dogmas like the Immaculate Conception and the Bodily

Assumption of the Virgin Mary, neither clarification nor improvement, neither change of terminology nor even of concept would satisfy the Church of the Reformation. These dogmas do not stand the test of the truth of the Word of God and must therefore be replaced by a Mariology which is Scriptural.

4. Küng's fourth methodological principle is that, though a truth of faith may at times be forgotten by the Church, yet it is never lost but always believed by the Church:

> If whole eras of theological thought are not to be misjudged, regard must be had to the fact that all the truths of faith need not at all times be equally important in the Church's conscious-ness.[271]

Does this mean that at the time of the Council of Trent the Roman Church reacting against the Reformation was less conscious of the doctrine of grace and more so of other pressing problems? Küng's explanation on the basis of his methodological principle is this:

> "While the dark spot"—presumably the most grievous heresy at a particular time—"is bathed in the clearest light, other areas are no longer directly illuminated; they are not, however, simply in total darkness. Yet to the human eye they fade into the half-light or even obscurity. These truths are not lost to the Church, they are always there to be believed. But they do not shine so clearly as before until the human eye becomes accustomed to the new light and can once more see and appreciate what lies round about and beneath this truth."[272]

Protestants are once again at one with Küng. Since the role of a dogma is often defensive, a particular aspect of the faith which is under attack is stressed and sometimes even overstressed at the expense of other aspects. But, while we are in agreement with Küng's methodological principle, the results he obtains confront us with various difficulties.

What was the dark spot which had to be illuminated in the 16th century? Was it the doctrine of grace which Roman theology had obscured, or was it the Reformation which restored the biblical meaning of grace? If the dark spot was the unbiblical doctrine of grace, that prevailed in scholastic theology, why did Rome reject and outlaw the Reformation? If it was the Reformation, how can there be basic agreement between the Tridentine and Barthian teaching on grace? Since Barth and the Reformers are in basic agreement, the same should be true of Trent and the Reformation. Yet Trent condemns the Reformation and its teaching on grace. Is Küng's interpretation of Barth wrong or of Trent? Since Barth himself testifies that Küng rendered his teaching accurately and interpreted it correctly, we come reluctantly to the conclusion that what Küng develops as the Roman teaching is not, or at least is not yet, officially the teaching of his Church. But his methodological principle is, of course, correct. It is proved correct, however, not by the Council of Trent but by the Reformation. It was the Reformation which illuminated the dark spot—the then current unscriptural doctrine of grace—and it is still doing so through, for example the theology of Barth, while the half-light still prevails in the official and authoritative declarations of the Roman Church.

But in spite of all our reservations the positive value of Küng's methodology can hardly be exaggerated. The application and use of his methodological principles enable him to reinstate the written Word of God as the primary and positive source of theology. Although in the Roman (and therefore in Küng's) view official dogmatic definitions are infallible and their content is immutable, their function according to Küng is, as it were, preventive: by laying down what Scripture does not say or mean, these definitions prevent the theologian from misinterpreting the Word of God. It may perhaps be possible to call them a secondary and negative source of theology. Küng accepts the absolutely binding authority of the doctrinal documents of his Church. They are for him not signposts which merely indicate a direction, but they show the path which must be followed.[273]

Küng claims that the Roman theologian is in a positive way conscious of being absolutely bound to the teaching of his Church. What Küng means is that the Roman theologian in searching the Scriptures does not reach his conclusions as an independent Christian to conform afterwards also to the doctrines of his Church as *norma negativa*. He searches the Scriptures, and in doing so he is already conscious of being absolutely subject to the teaching of his Church. In spite of the positive way in which the Roman theologian is supposed to be free we would still maintain that Küng's use of dogmatic definitions is negative. They are signposts that indicate not the way to be followed but the way not to be followed. In other words, their function is to prevent the Roman interpreter of the Bible from falling into error. As long as he does not choose the way which the dogmatic definitions show to be wrong, he is free to search the Scriptures, which are the directly tangible Word of God, and so the primary and positive source of theology.[274]

It would be futile to suggest that Küng has removed the obstacles that stand in the way of Christian unity. He has, however, shown the way in which it can and must be done, i.e. by the reinterpretation of dogmatic definitions in the light of, and subject to, a norm outside themselves. Only the Roman Church can, of course, decide whether this reappraisal of its definitions is correct from its own point of view. In other words, Küng's greatest achievement is that his methodology, though sometimes not radical enough, has enabled him to reinstate Holy Scripture as "the directly tangible Word of God" and "the centre of . . . theology",[275] i.e. as the norm to which all definitions must be submitted. He thus points to the fact—and this is the important service he has rendered especially to Roman theology—that not dogmatic formulations but the Word of God itself is, and must be, the basis of the interconfessional debate, because it alone will enable Protestants and Roman Catholics to join in re-thinking and re-stating what they believe and ought to believe as disciples of their common Lord, who speaks to them in the Holy Scriptures.

But are other Roman theologians, and, above all, the Roman magisterium, willing to accept the primacy of the written Word of God as the basis of the Protestant–Roman Catholic dialogue? Does Küng himself not say that the definitions of the magisterium of the Roman Church prevent him from falling into error, when he is searching the Scriptures? In the Protestant view some of these definitions are glaring examples of the errors into which the Church of Rome has already fallen, because it has not given the primacy to Scripture. Cardinal Bea lays it down as a fundamental rule for the relationship with the "separated brethren"—and one may assume that as the President of the Roman Secretariat for the Promotion of Christian Unity he has the authority to do so—that "sound work for unity must first of all safeguard the integrity of [Roman] Catholic dogma...".[276]

But if this is so, is a dialogue between the Church of the Reformation and the Church of Rome possible? If the pronouncements and definitions of the magisterium of the Roman Church prevent its theologians from falling into error, does it not mean that, whenever they debate a controversial issue with their Protestant partners, they are bound to give the right answer ultimately, while their non-Roman counterparts unless willing to bow to the superior knowledge of Rome, are fated always to give the wrong answer? Do not the claims of the Roman Church erect an insurmountable barrier to Christian unity, and make the interconfessional debate futile? It is to this problem we must now apply ourselves.

NOTES ON PART II

1. At the time of writing an English translation of H. Küng's *Rechtfertigung* was not available.

2. R., pp. 11–12.

3. Cf. R., p. 12.

4. R., p. 13.

5. R., p. 274.

6. R., p. 105.

7. R., p. 15.

8. C.D., I/1–IV/2 (10 volumes) were published between 1932 and 1955; IV/3 (first and second half) was published in 1959.

9. R., p. 11.

10. Cf. R., p. 12.

11. Cf. R., pp. 97–101.

12. Cf. R., pp. 41–45.

13. C.D., IV/1, p. 79.

14. R., p. 41.

15. C.D., IV/1, pp. 79–80; cf. R., pp. 41–42.

16. C.D., IV/1, p. 82; cf., R., p. 42.

17. Cf. C.D., IV/1, pp. 88–89; R., p. 42.

18. C.D., IV/1, p. 84; cf. R., pp. 42–43.

19. Cf. C.D., IV/1, pp. 84-87; R., p. 43.
20. C.D., IV/1, p. 87; cf. R., p. 43.
21. C.D., IV/1, p. 87.
22. C.D., IV/1, pp. 87-88.
23. C.D., IV/1, p. 88.
24. C.D., IV/1, p. 88.
25. C.D., IV/1, p. 88.
26. Cf. R., p. 44.
27. R., p. 44.
28. C.D., IV/1, pp. 89-92; cf. R., pp. 44-45.
29. R., p. 45.
30. R., p. 45.
31. R., p. 44.
32. R., pp. 44-45.
33. R., pp. 195-6.
34. R., p. 196.
35. R., p. 196.
36. R., p. 196.
37. R., p. 197.
38. R., p. 197.
39. R., p. 198.
40. R., p. 198.
41. Trent, Session 6, *Prooemium*, Denz. 1520 (792).
42. R., p. 198.
43. Cf. R., p. 199.
44. R., p. 199.
45. R., p. 200.
46. R., p. 201.
47. R., p. 201.
48. R., p. 201.
49. Trent, Session 6, Canon 11; Denz. 1561 (821); Schaff II, p. 113.
50. Cf. R., pp. 202-3.
51. C.D., IV/1, p. 749; cf. R., p. 91.
52. C.D., IV/1, p. 751; cf. R., p. 91.
53. C.D., IV/1, p. 752; cf. R., pp. 91-92.
54. Cf. R., p. 92.
55. C.D., IV/1, pp. 749-50; cf. R., p. 92.
56. C.D., IV/1, pp. 752-3; cf. R., p. 93.
57. Cf. R., p. 93.
58. C.D., IV/1, p. 770.
59. Cf. R., p. 94.

60. C.D., IV/1, p. 770.
61. C.D., IV/1, p. 770.
62. C.D., IV/1, p. 771.
63. C.D., IV/1, p. 771.
64. C.D., IV/1, p. 771.
65. C.D., IV/1, p. 771.
66. C.D., IV/1, p. 771.
67. C.D., IV/1, p. 772.
68. C.D., IV/1, p. 772.
69. C.D., IV/1, pp. 772-3.
70. C.D., IV/1, p. 773.
71. C.D., IV/1, p. 773.
72. C.D., IV/1, p. 774.
73. C.D., IV/1, p. 775.
74. Cf. S.F.P., p. 185.
75. Cf. R., p. 204.
76. R., p. 200.
77. Cf. R., p. 200.
78. R., p. 200.
79. Cf. R., p. 200.
80. Trent, Session 6, Chapter 7; Denz. 1529 (799); Schaff II, pp. 94-95.
81. Karl Rahner, S.J., *Some Implications of the Scholastic Concept of Uncreated Grace* in *Theological Investigations*, Vol. I, *God, Christ, Mary and Grace*, trans. by Cornelius Ernst, Baltimore and London, 1961, pp. 341-2.
82. *Ibid.*, pp. 342-3.
83. Trent, Session 6, Chapter 7; Denz. 1529 (799); Schaff II, p. 95.
84. C.D., IV/2, pp. 508-9.
85. Cf. Michael Schmaus, *Katholische Dogmatik*, Vol. 5, *Mariologie*, München, 1955, p. 193 (hereafter referred to as M. Schmaus, *Mariologie*).
86. Otto Semmelroth, S.J., *Mary, Archetype of the Church*, trans. by Maria von Eroes and John Devlin, Dublin, 1963, pp. 73-74 (hereafter referred to as O. Semmelroth, *Mary*).
87. *Ibid.*, p. 72.
88. *Ibid.*, p. 62.
89. Cf. *ibid.*, pp. 61-91.
90. *Ibid.*, p. 83.
91. R., p. 205.
92. R., p. 206.

93. Cf. R., p. 208.
94. R., pp. 208-9.
95. R., p. 209.
96. R., p. 209.
97. R., p. 209.
98. R., pp. 210-11.
99. Cf. R., pp. 209-10.
100. R., p. 211.
101. R., pp. 212-13.
102. S.F.P., p. 181.
103. R., p. 213.
104. C.D., IV/1, p. 516.
105. C.D., IV/1, pp. 542-3.
106. C.D., IV/1, p. 95; cf. R., pp. 77-78.
107. C.D., II/2, p. 757.
108. C.D., IV/1, p. 624.
109. C.D., IV/1, pp. 624-5.
110. C.D., IV/1, p. 625.
111. Denz. 1529 (799); Schaff II, p. 95.
112. C.D., IV/1, p. 625.
113. C.D., IV/1, p. 625.
114. Denz. 1525 (797); Schaff II, p. 92.
115. Denz. 1554-5 (814-15); Schaff II, p. 111.
116. Denz. 1521 (793); Schaff II, p. 89.
117. C.D., IV/1, p. 625.
118. Denz. 1533 (802); Schaff II, p. 98.
119. C.D., IV/1, p. 625.
120. Denz. 1545-50 (809—10); Schaff II, pp. 107-10.
121. Denz. 1528-31 (799-800); Schaff II, pp. 94-97.
122. C.D., IV/1, p. 625.
123. R., p. 213.
124. R., p. 215.
125. R., p. 215.
126. R., p. 215.
127. R., p. 215.
128. R., p. 215.
129. R., p. 215.
130. R., p. 215; cf. Denz. 1561 (821); Schaff II, p. 112.
131. Denz. 1561 (821); Schaff II, pp. 112-13.
132. R., pp. 215-16; Denz. 1529 (799); Schaff II, p. 95.
133. R., p. 216.

134. Denz. 1524 (796); Schaff II, p. 91.
135. R., p. 216.
136. R., p. 217.
137. R., p. 217.
138. F. Prat, La Théologie de Saint Paul, Vol. 2, Paris, 1949, p. 229; quoted from R., p. 217.
139. Denz. 1524 (796); Schaff II, p. 91.
140. Cf. C.D., IV/2, p. 497.
141. Denz. 1528 (799); Schaff II, p. 94.
142. R., p. 218.
143. R., p. 218.
144. Denz. 1521 (793); Schaff II, p. 89; cf. also Session 6, Canon 5, Denz. 1555 (815); Schaff II, p. 111.
145. R., p. 13.
146. C.D., IV/2, p. 498.
147. R., p. 274.
148. R., p. 124.
149. R., p. 218.
150. R., p. 218.
151. R., p. 218.
152. R., p. 219.
153. Cf. R., pp. 219-20.
154. R., p. 221.
155. C.D., IV/1, p. 553.
156. C.D., IV/1, p. 552.
157. C.D., IV/1, pp. 552-6.
158. C.D., IV/1, pp. 147-9.
159. C.D., IV/1, p. 149.
160. C.D., IV/1, p. 150.
161. C.D., IV/1, pp. 149-50.
162. E. Tobac, Le Problème de la justification dans S. Paul, Louvain, 1908, p. 224s; cf. R., p. 221.
163. Th. Soiron, Die Kirche als Leib Christi, Nach der Lehre des hl. Paulus, Düsseldorf, 1951, p. 219f.; cf. R., p. 222.
164. Michael Schmaus, Katholische Dogmatik, Vol. II/2, Gott der Erlöser, München, 1955, p. 350; cf. R., p. 225.
165. Cf. R., Chapters 4-6.
166. C.D., II/2, p. 103.
167. C.D., II/2, p. 116.
168. C.D., II/2, p. 121.
169. C.D., II/2, p. 163.

170. C.D., II/2, p. 195.
171. C.D., IV/1, pp. 34–35.
172. C.D., IV/1, p. 67.
173. R., p. 227.
174. R., p. 227.
175. R., p. 227.
176. R., p. 228.
177. R., p. 228.
178. R., p. 228.
179. R., pp. 228–9.
180. R., p. 229.
181. Session 6, Chapter 2; Denz. 1522 (794); Schaff II, pp. 89–90.
182. Cf. Session 6, Chapter 5; Denz. 1525 (797); Schaff II, p. 92.
183. *Church of Scotland Report on Baptism*, 1959, pp. 30–31.
184. Karl Barth, *The Epistle to the Philippians*, trans. by James W. Leitch, London, 1962, pp. 101–2.
185. *Ibid.*, p. 102.
186. Quoted from O. Semmelroth, *Mary*, pp. 72–73.
187. Quoted from O. Semmelroth, *Mary*, p. 77.
188. Quoted from M. Schmaus, *Mariologie*, p. 329.
189. O. Semmelroth, *Mary*, p. 79.
190. *Ibid.*, pp. 78–79.
191. *Ibid.*, p. 79.
192. R., p. 243.
193. Cf. L. Villette, *Foi et sacrement*, Diss., Paris, 1954, IV, 111s; R., p. 243.
194. Denz. 1559 (819); Schaff II, p. 112.
195. Denz., 1980 (1080); cf. L. Villette, *Foi et sacrement*, IV, 111s and R., p. 243.
196. R., p. 244.
197. Otto Weber, *Grundlagen der Dogmatik*, Vol. II, Neukirchen–Moers, 1962, p. 350 (hereafter referred to as O. Weber, *Grundlagen II*).
198. R., p. 245.
199. R., p. 246.
200. R., p. 246.
201. R., p. 249.
202. Session 6, Canon 9.
203. Session 6, Canon 12.

204. R., p. 248.
205. R., p. 248.
206. Session 6, Chapter 9; Denz. 1533 (802); Schaff II, p. 98.
207. Denz. 1562 (822); Schaff II, p. 113.
208. Session 6, Chapter 8; Denz. 1532 (801); Schaff II, p. 97.
209. R., p. 249.
210. *Lexikon für Theologie and Kirche*, 2nd Edition, edited by Ed. Joseph Höfer and Karl Rahner, Vol. 4, Freiburg, 1960, p. 919.
211. Session 6, Chapter 6; Denz. 1526 (798); Schaff II, p. 93.
212. *Heidelberg Catechism*, Q. 21 in T. F. Torrance, *The School of Faith, The Catechisms of the Reformed Church*, London, 1959, p. 72.
213. Part I, Chapter 1. 1.
214. *Ibid.*
215. Session 3, Chapter 3.
216. Denz. 3010 (1791); Schaff II, p. 244.
217. Denz. 3010 (1791); Schaff II, pp. 244–5.
218. Trent, Session 6, Chapter 7; Schaff II, pp. 95–96.
219. Trent, Session 6, Chapter 8; Schaff II, p. 97.
220. *Lexikon für Theologie und Kirche*, op. cit., p. 919.
221. Cf. R., 248.
222. Denz. 1526 (798); Schaff II, p. 93.
223. *Ibid.*
224. L. Villette, *op. cit.*, IV, 114; quoted from R., p. 248.
225. Denz. 1526 (798); Schaff II, p. 93.
226. *Ibid.*
227. L. Villette, *op. cit.*, IV, 115; quoted from R., pp. 248–9.
228. Session 6, Canon 12; Denz. 1562 (822); Schaff II, p. 113.
229. C.D., IV/1, p. 626.
230. C.D., IV/1, p. 626.
231. Session 6, Canon 12; Denz. 1562 (822); Schaff II, p. 113.
232. R., p. 86.
233. C.D., IV/2, pp. 730–1.

234. C.D., IV/1, pp. 104–5; cf. R., pp. 86–87.

235. Heinrich Stirnimann, O. P., *Rechtfertigung in dialektischer Besinnung* in *Freiburger Zeitschrift für Philosophie und Theologie*, Vol. 4, 1957, Nr. 3, p. 321.

236. Trent, Session 6, Chapter 7; Denz. 1531 (800); Schaff II, p. 96.

237. Heinrich Stirnimann, O. P., *Zur Rechtfertigung in dialektisch—katholischer Besinnung* in *Schweizerische Kirchenzeitung*, Luzern, Nr. 52, 1957, p. 652.

238. R., p. 250.

239. R., p. 250.

240. R., p. 250.

241. C.D., IV/1, p. 748.

242. C.D., IV/1, p. 748.

243. Cf. C.D., IV/1, p. 747.

244. C.D., IV/2, p. 410.

245. C.D., IV/2, p. 410.

246. C.D., IV/2, pp. 369–70.

247. C.D., IV/1, p. 752.

248. Cf. R., p. 250.

249. Trent, Session 6, Chapter 8; Denz. 1532 (801); Schaff II, p. 97.

250. *Ibid.*

251. In a recent article, *Das tridentinische Rechtfertigungsdekret im Lichte spätmittelalterlicher Theologie*, (*Zeitschrift für Theologie und Kirche*, Tübingen, Nr. 3, 1964, pp. 251-282) Heiko A. Obermann tries to show that the meaning of the above-quoted text of the Tridentine decree is not as clear and unambiguous as it might appear to be at first sight. The usual translation of the text is: "none of the things which precede justification—whether faith or works—*merit* the grace itself of justification." But the Latin verb translated "merit" is *promereri* and not *mereri*. The late mediaeval sources and the debates of Trent themselves lead Obermann to believe that *promereri* is not a synonym or a poetic form of *mereri*. At the time of the Council

of Trent *promereri* had acquired the meaning of *vere* or *proprie mereri* and was used by the Tridentine Fathers in the sense of "to merit truly or properly" or "in the full sense". Obermann therefore holds that the correct translation of the relevant passage in the Tridentine decree is: "none of those things which precede justification— whether faith or works—merit *in the full sense* the grace itself of justification" (p. 263). Obermann comes to the following interesting conclusion:

1. The intention of Trent was to exclude—prior to the reception of justifying grace—only the *merita de condigno* but not the *merita de congruo*.

2. *Promereri* is deliberately distinguished from *mereri*. *Promereri* refers to the *merita de condigno*, *mereri* to the *merita de congruo*.

3. At the beginning of the Tridentine debate on justification the Franciscan party was on the defensive, but it gained sufficient power and influence for its views on the question of the *meritum de congruo* to gain acceptance.

4. The attempt of the Thomist party to introduce *meretur* instead of *promeretur* in the final text of the Tridentine decree failed. The *meritum de congruo* was successfully defended; this is expressed in the final formulation where not *meretur* but *promeretur* is found (p. 278).

Obermann himself admits that a great deal of research is still to be done in this connection, but if his view is found to be correct, it would be impossible to maintain, as Küng does, that there is a basic agreement between the Barthian and the Tridentine teachings on justification.

252. C.D., IV/1, pp. 592–5.

253. R., pp. 260–1.

254. R., p. 261.

255. R., p. 244.
256. R., p. 257.
257. R., p. 257.
258. O. Weber, *Grundlagen II*, p. 351.
259. T. F. Torrance, *Justification: Its Radical Nature and Place in Reformed Doctrine and Life*, in *Christianity Divided, Protestant and Roman Catholic Theological Issues*, ed. by David J. Callahan, Heiko A. Obermann, Daniel J. O'Hanlon, S.J., London and New York, 1961, pp. 293–4.
260. Denz. 1561 (821); Schaff II, pp. 112–13.
261. R., pp. 196–7.
262. Cf. R., p. 202.
263. Cf. George A. Lindbeck, *The Evangelical Possibilities of Roman Catholic Theology*, in *Lutheran World*, Publication of the Lutheran World Federation, Vol. VII, Nr. 2, September 1960, p. 145.
264. *Ibid.*, p. 143.
265. *Ibid.*, p. 145.
266. R., p. 109.
267. R., p. 113.
268. Cf. R., p. 108.
269. R., p. 108.
270. R., p. 108.
271. R., p. 213.
272. R., p. 109.
273. Cf. R., p. 123.
274. R., p. 123.
275. R., p. 123.
276. Augustin Cardinal Bea, *The Unity of Christians*, ed. by Bernard Leeming, S.J., London, 1963, p. 81.

PART III

BARRIERS TO CHRISTIAN UNITY

I

The Difficulties and Limitations of the Protestant–Roman Catholic Dialogue

IT MUST BE clearly understood that though Protestants and Roman Catholics are once again engaged in a doctrinal debate, any kind of ecumenical romanticism confusing a dream with reality would misjudge the true situation and so lead to disappointment. If the results of the recent Protestant –Roman Catholic encounter are to be assessed properly a realistic view of them must be resolutely adopted.

While it is true that the dialogue is making progress it should not be forgotten that the partners in it, though they speak to each other, do not stand side by side but face each other across a gulf—the rift which runs through the Church of Jesus Christ.

Any false ideas that might be held about the results and achievements of the Protestant–Roman Catholic debate are dispelled by one of its most important participants: von Balthasar. This theologian regrets Barth's refusal to regard the Church of Rome as a sister Church and his repudiation of it as a false Church in whose confession the one true Church of Jesus Christ cannot be recognized.[1] On the other hand, von Balthasar admits that he cannot take Barth's anathema amiss since he himself as a Roman Catholic must repeat the anathema of the Council of Trent against the Church of the Reformation.[2]

The partners in the dialogue thus face each other not as isolated individuals but as members of their respective Churches. It is for this reason that in the name of the Truth they seek, they "deny the presence of the true Church on the other side".[3] Thus the question arises whether a dialogue in which each partner presupposes that the other belongs to the false Church can be serious.

From the Protestant point of view conversation with Roman Catholicism is possible because in looking across to the other side the partners do not see a *different reality;* what they see according to Barth is the same reality, i.e. the One Holy, Catholic and Apostolic Church, but they *see it differently.*[4] While Barth therefore has no hesitation about repudiating the Church of Rome as a false Church, he yet admits that "here [i.e. in the Roman Catholic Church] is churchly substance. Here is embedded the knowledge that the Church is the house of God. The substance may perhaps be distorted and perverted, but is not lost."[5] He goes on to say that "the Reformers never contended, and we also cannot contend that this insight [i.e. the insight 'that God, in the house which is His house, is and remains the Lord of the house'][6] is hidden from the [Roman] Catholic Church. . . . Because the Church [of the Reformation] was resolved to let this insight shine purer and clearer and prevail more consistently (only comparatives exist when we are speaking of the will of men) the Church was established in contrast to Roman Catholicism as the *Protestant* Church".[7] Barth concludes that "because it would not and could not be anything but a Protestant *Church*, a restoration of the substance of the Church; the Roman Church became and is now in our eyes an heretical Church."[8]

The Roman Catholic partner enters into the dialogue with the same presuppositions. The Tridentine anathema against the Reformation holds good. Yet von Balthasar can have a dialogical relationship with Protestants because they are "our baptized brethren in Christ and thus members of His Body which is a visible body; they are therefore members who should by right belong to the *Una Sancta Catholica*."[9]

If it is granted that the dialogue between the Church of Rome and the Church of the Reformation is not an amicable exchange of platitudes but a theological debate designed to enable both partners to inquire together into the truth, then the truth itself—and not Roman Catholic or Protestant presuppositions about it—must be acknowledged to be the norm to which the partners should submit both themselves and their presuppositions in an act of common obedience. Whenever this common subjection to the Truth is wanting, and one partner imposes his own presuppositions upon the other as the ultimate norm that he must adopt, the dialogue becomes pointless. For then the dialogical relationship is superseded by a camouflaged forensic relationship in which one partner—or each partner in turn—assumes the role of the judge pronouncing sentence on the accused.

With admirable objectivity von Balthasar investigates the possibility of the inter-confessional dialogue and concludes that such a debate is definitely "a Christian possibility within the faith and its analogy".[10] But he is very careful to explain how he conceives of this "Christian possibility":

> For ultimate reasons I can affirm in faith the infallibility of the Pope and the Immaculate Conception of Mary and at the same time I can understand why someone else rejects them for penultimate reasons. . . . What I reject is not totally alien to me, it is a possibility which I know but which I have left behind because it was neither the ultimate nor the decisive one.[11]

No one could deny or even doubt the sincerity von Balthasar brings to his debate with Protestantism. But what must be questioned is whether in this particular connection he speaks as the partner and not as the judge who, while understanding the reasons for the accused's error and sympathizing with him, dismisses his appeal. Is it to the Truth that von Balthasar subjects the dialogue, or is it to the Roman Catholic understanding of the Truth?

The Protestant partner, however, must needs raise yet another question. Can his Roman Catholic vis-à-vis, given his particular point of view, speak as anything else than the judge? In his book From Limbo to Heaven. An Essay on the Economy of the Redemption, Vincent Wilkin, S.J., lays down the fundamental principles governing the solution of a theological problem and the necessary conditions which according to Roman Catholicism must be fulfilled:

It [the solution of the problem] must, of course, be acceptable to the authority of the Church [of Rome]. At once I state that I automatically withdraw anything and everything in these pages which does not meet with the Church's approval.[12]

No matter how determined the Roman Catholic partner may be to renounce the role of the judge, he must in stating his view always make this same proviso and ultimately has to refer "anything and everything" to the final court of appeal—the Church of Rome with its infallible and irrevocable judgement. What Wilkin says cannot be regarded as a personal opinion. It is a mere reflection of the attitude taken up in this matter by the Church of Rome whose doctrines he accepts without question.

It is precisely for this reason that Joseph Klein whose important collection of essays *Skandalon um das Wesen des Katholizismus* ("Skandalon" about the Nature of Catholicism) which has not attracted the attention it deserves, believes that debates with Roman theologians are virtually pointless. He holds that

the reasons why debates with [Roman] Catholicism are so extraordinarily difficult is that even a tendency to adopt a critical or negative attitude towards it is regarded as an insult and affront to the divinely appointed bastion of the infallible truth. Such an attitude is therefore rejected as a basis for entering into genuine controversies. From a [Roman] Catholic point of view true concern for the Gospel—i.e. concern that is not misguided—can only exist under the supervision of the infallible magisterium [of the Roman Church]. . . . Any kind of concern for religion that is not directed towards the ends of [Roman] Catholicism leads to error and has no objective right to exist. . . . The [Roman] Catholic partner in the controversy embodies the irrefragable personified *reservatio mentalis* on the ground of the "as-if" standpoint he is obliged to take. While the non-Catholic makes no personal reservations and acts autonomously under the guidance of truthfulness in the quest for the truth, this attitude is impossible for the [Roman] Catholic; he is necessarily heteronomous. To try—even in good conscience—to withdraw from his duty must necessarily mean going beyond the methodological doubt which alone is permissible for him and to transgress thus is most sinful.[13]

Klein asserts that, if the regulations of the Roman Church are rightly understood, it is open to no Roman Catholic, on grounds of faith and conscience, to reject his Church's claim to possess the truth and its right to exercise authority over him. In other words, he must regard the magisterium of his Church as the final court of appeal.[14]

Klein traces this totalitarianism to the fact that the developing Church of Rome transformed the true "skandalon", the "skandalon" of the Cross of Christ:

> After the reign of God had appeared on earth in Jesus Christ the representation of the ever living Christ in the visible Church substituted the "skandalon" of the absolute intolerance of its truth for the offence and foolishness of the Cross. This "skandalon" is grounded in the Church's judicial thinking and is at its disposal; the Church achieved this by converting the *existentiell* personal truth into juridical truth and by creating for itself an absolute authority in an infallible theoretical doctrine. This doctrine is controlled by men, and is given out by the Church as the *depositum fidei* with which it has been entrusted.[15]

In Klein's view debates with members of the Church of Rome lead nowhere since "ecclesiastical authority [i.e. the Roman Church] knows only obedience in face of its own theory of faith and imposes silence even when it becomes a lie."[16]

Klein holds that the gulf between the Church of Rome and the Church of the Reformation is unbridgeable:

> Luther started from the belief in the possibility of a fundamental change in the historical Church. No one denies this and all theologians and historians at least know today that this goal was not impossible to attain then but has become so. The offence Luther took was dogmatized and in the same way the guilt of his "skandalon" remains a matter of dogma. Thus his offence became even greater and became evident for all times. Joan of Arc was vindicated and there are those who desire the canonization of Savonarola, but with regard to Luther the [Roman] Church cannot retreat. Luther's scandal will only be purged for the Church [of Rome] when the last Protestant returns into its bosom. Should the Church [of Rome] canonize

Luther he would have lived in vain. He must remain a scandal
for the Church [of Rome] because he pointed to the "skandalon" of God.[17]

Klein's objections and arguments against Roman Catholicism must be neither ignored nor minimized. They go in a
very real sense to the root of the difficulty confronting the
Protestant partner everywhere in the dialogue with Roman
Catholicism. The difficulty arises not from any dishonesty
on the part of the Roman Catholic partner but from the
very nature and structure of his Church. The Church of
Rome claims infallibility for its dogmatic definitions—
these definitions are therefore incapable of modification in
substance though not necessarily, as we were told by Küng,
in form and terminology. The dialogical relationship
between those who represent the two Churches is thus
continually in danger of being used to conceal a forensic
intention on the part of the Roman Catholic partner; the
Protestant partner is ultimately summoned to the bar of the
Church of Rome, itself the judge of its own case, itself
the court of appeal in its suit with another Church.

The Protestant partner, however, is not always innocent
or free from blame. Klein, for instance, holds that "[Roman]
Catholic thought is determined by the objectivism of
theoretical truth and not by the imperative of *existentiell*
truthfulness".[18] This is, to be sure, a legitimate criticism of
the Roman Catholic position. As the subjective self-
understanding of the Roman Church unfolds, its magisterium
infallibly and irreformably defines doctrinal innovations,
amplifications and multiplications as dogmas whose acceptance is necessary for salvation; in other words, the Church's
subjectivism is objectified and becomes the truth.

But does Klein—and we may take it that he represents a
whole school of Protestant thought—not proceed on similar
lines in asserting that religious thought must be determined
by "the imperative of *existentiell* truthfulness"? In his opinion
"the personal truth (*die personale Wahrheit*) of the Gospel
requires . . . the personal *existentiell* decision (*die persönliche
existentielle Entscheidung*) of an 'I' who, being in fellowship

with the 'Thou' of his God, must vindicate itself before Him."[19] It would appear that Klein is simply changing over from obedience to the subjective decisions and definitions of the Roman Church to the equally subjective decisions and definitions of the individual believer. Truth is truth only in so far as it is truth *pro nobis*, truth for us. For Klein the term *pro nobis* has a subjective meaning: it is the individual conscience or decision elevated to the status of the final court of appeal.

Klein asserts that "the humanization and naturalization of the Gospel in the objectivizations of the Roman Church can only be maintained by rational and juridical means with the result that faith loses its depth by becoming obedience towards human authority!"[20] The Protestant partner who argues in the inter-confessional dialogue as Klein does immediately lays himself open to the Roman Catholic objection that the Protestant personalism and existentialism that equate individual subjective understanding of truth with truth itself or with its norm, must inevitably lead to an "objectivization" of subjective personal concepts which excludes objectivity and introduces the arbitrary.

The Protestant partner who insists on being guided in the dialogue with the Church of Rome by "*existentiell* truthfulness" and not by the objective Word of God (whose objectivity is self-determined) is equally guilty with his Roman Catholic counterpart of replacing the dialogical relationship by the forensic; for the magisterium of the Roman Church he simply substitutes his own conscience and his own personal understanding of truth.

In actual fact neither the "infallible" magisterium claimed by Rome nor the "inalienable right of private judgement" dear to so many Protestant hearts can possibly be the ultimate criterion of the truth of the Truth of God.

But now a question arises which beyond doubt is the most difficult and complicated of all. This is *the* crucial question which continually threatens the progress and even the very existence of the Protestant–Roman Catholic dialogue. It is therefore a question that *a fortiori* has to be faced so that the dialogue may not be based on a *false hope*. This question concerns what may be called the "ecclesiastical" attitude of the Roman Communion towards the Churches of the Reformation.

As has already been seen, both parties are constantly tempted to transform the dialogical relationship into a purely forensic one and even tend to do so. Protestants and Roman Catholics alike assume that they are in a position to pass judgement on each other, acting as a judge towards the prisoner at the bar. Now we have to consider the further and seemingly insuperable difficulty that arises from Rome's assertion that no possible case can be made out for the "Churches" of the Reformation *as Churches*.

It is precisely this attitude that can be detected in the first Encyclical of Pope Paul VI *Ecclesiam Suam* (1964). Its themes are the self-understanding, the renewal and the dialogue of the (Roman) Church. The partners in the dialogue of the Church with the world are: 1. All men, 2. Those who believe in God (monotheists, i.e. Jews, Moslems, etc.) and 3. The separated Christian brethren. Finally, there is the dialogue within the Church of Rome itself.

Since there is to be a dialogue of the Roman Church with the "separated brethren" several points in *Ecclesiam Suam* ought to be noted. Here it is stated quite unequivocally that the Church of Rome cannot be accused of unfaithfulness. The living heritage of the original apostolic tradition received by the Roman Church has been kept intact. If reform (*renovatio*) is therefore spoken of in this connection this cannot be understood in the sense of change but only in the sense of confirming and strengthening the obligation to preserve the aspect Christ has given to the Church.[21]

Paul VI makes it clear that, though the Roman Church possesses the treasure of truth and grace (*veritatis et gratiae thesaurus*), it is not enough simply to preserve and defend it.[22] The inheritance received from Christ must be spread, offered and proclaimed. Matt. 28: 19—"Go ye therefore and make all peoples disciples"—is quoted. This is the last commission of Christ to His Apostles. The very name of "Apostle" indicates to them their ineluctable mission.[23] Then follows the Pope's definition of what he expects Roman Catholics to understand by the *colloquium*—the dialogue—: *Ad Nos quod attinet, intimam huiusmodi caritatis impulsionem, quae eo tendit, ut in externum ipsa transeat donum caritatis, usitato iam nomine colloquium appellabimus*—"to the inner impulse of this sort of love which endeavours to make itself the external gift of love we would give the now familiar name of dialogue".[24]

In other words, the dialogue from a Roman Catholic point of view is to be a giving and a receiving, a communication and an acceptance which, to be sure, is perfectly correct. Paul VI is, however, very careful to assign the task of giving and communicating to the Roman Church alone and that of receiving and accepting to any other party that may be involved in this rather strange dialogue. The non-Roman partner may be permitted to raise questions concerning forms of piety, canon law, worship, etc. These may be examined to satisfy his justified demands.[25] But the dialogue as such is nothing else than the communication by the Roman Church of its treasure of truth and grace to other communities. But how can a dialogue so defined conform to the rule laid down in the *Decretum de Oecumenismo* (1964)? This decree, referring to the desirability of knowing the separated brethren better, states that much can be gained through theological encounters "where each can deal with the other as an equal"—*ubi unusquisque par cum pari agat.*[26]

But can there be "equality" in theological encounters when the communities to which the separated brethren belong are not the equals of the Church of Rome? And equals they cannot be, for the Roman Church claims to be *the Church*.

When he opened the third session of Vatican II (September 1964) Paul VI stressed this point very strongly in his allocution:

In the sign of the Holy Cross in whose honour we have concelebrated Holy Mass,[27] we open today the third session of the Second Ecumenical Vatican Council. The Church is actually here. Here we [i.e. Pope and bishops] make the Church (*Ecclesiam efficimus*) because we are members of the Mystical Body of Christ; for God has granted us the inestimable favour of His grace so that we should believe in Him and being washed by the waters of Baptism be constituted through charity the sacred and visible People of God. We make the Church because we are its ministers (*administri*), its priests stamped with a special character; by our sacramental ordination we have received marvellous and weighty powers making of us a sacred hierarchy entrusted with functions meant to perpetuate in time and to extend on earth the saving mission of Christ. Finally, we make the Church because as teachers of the faith, pastors of souls, stewards of the mysteries of God (1 Cor. 4: 1), we represent here the entire Church, not as delegates or deputies of the faithful towards whom our ministry is directed, but as fathers and brothers who personify the communities entrusted to the care of each one of us, and as a plenary assembly legitimately convoked by us. We [i.e. the Pope] have called the Council in virtue of our office which unites us with all of you as your brother, as the bishop of Rome . . ., as the humble but true successor of the Apostle Peter—at whose tomb we are devoutly gathered and therefore as the unworthy but true head of the Catholic Church (*indignus sed verus Moderator Ecclesiae catholicae*) and Vicar of Christ, Servant of the Servants of God.

Since we represent in our persons and in our sacred functions the universal Church we proclaim this Council ecumenical: here is the celebration of unity, the celebration of that catholicity by which the Church gives evidence of its wonderful strength, its marvellous faculty to make men brothers and to welcome within its embrace the most diverse civilizations and languages, the most individualized liturgies and types of spirituality, the most varied expressions of national, social and cultural genius, harmonizing all in felicitous union, yet always respecting legitimate variety and complexity.[28]

On this view the dialogue must become purely instructional. It cannot be denied, of course, that the dialogue between the Churches must be carried on at a "pedagogic" level amongst others. But, for it to be valid as dialogue, a willingness to learn as well as an intention to teach must be shown by both sides. Does Rome show that willingness? It seems to us that by "unchurching" its Protestant inter-

locutor—and what else is the implication of the papal allocution—the Roman Church endangers the very possibility of
true dialogical relationship based on *mutual* instruction and
education. By arrogating to itself the role of the teacher who
instructs his Protestant pupil in the true faith, Rome makes
the unwarranted assumption that here is a backward (or
recalcitrant) scholar who must ultimately reach the stage of
deferring to superior knowledge and wisdom and of returning
to the bosom of the one and only Church—the Church of
Rome. Given such premisses, however, can there in fact be a
genuine debate at all?

It is an easily verifiable fact of history that, even when the
struggle with Rome was at its height, and consequently
controversy at its bitterest, the Reformers never unchurched
Roman Catholics so completely and uncompromisingly as the
Church of Rome unchurches Protestants. It is, of course,
perfectly true (or there would have been no Reformation)
that the Reformers condemned and rejected the Roman
Church as an unreformed, heretical or false Church, and
sometimes even referred to it as apostate. Yet neither Luther
nor Calvin ever denied the fact that, since the Word of God
creates the Church, the Church exists wherever that Word is
preached and received and the Sacraments are correctly
administered. This rather was one of their main tenets. The
Reformers were therefore able to discern *vestigia ecclesiae*—
traces of the Church, the *true* Church—even in the unreformed Church of Rome. In spite of that Church's refusal to
be corrected according to the Word of God, and of the corruption and perversion that inevitably followed, Rome still
continued to be in some way and measure a Church. This was
precisely the reason why Luther and Calvin not only recognized the validity of Baptism administered in and by the
Church of Rome but at no time required re-ordination of
those Roman Catholic priests who had adhered to the
Reformation, and who entered upon the ministry of the
Evangelical Church.

In his letter *Concerning Rebaptism* written in January 1528
to two pastors apparently living in a Roman Catholic diocese

who had sought his advice on how to deal with Anabaptist teaching, Luther defined his attitude towards the Papal Church:

> In the first place I hear and see that such Rebaptism is undertaken by some in order to spite the Pope and to be free of any taint of the Antichrist. In the same way the foes of the Sacrament want to believe only in bread and wine, in opposition to the Pope, thinking thereby really to overthrow the Papacy. It is indeed a shaky foundation on which they can build nothing good. On that basis we would have to disown the whole of Scripture and the office of the ministry, which of course we have received from the Papacy. We would also have to make a new Bible. . . . We on our part confess that there is much that is Christian and good under the Papacy; indeed everything that is Christian and good is to be found there and has come to us from this source. For instance we confess that in the Papal Church there are the true Holy Scriptures, true Baptism, the true Sacrament of the altar, the true keys to the forgiveness of sins, the true office of the ministry, the true catechism in the form of the Lord's Prayer, the Ten Commandments, and the articles of the Creed . . . I contend that in the Papacy there is true Christianity, even the right kind of Christianity and many great and devoted saints. . . . But when we oppose and reject the Pope it is because he does not keep to these treasures of Christendom [i.e. Scripture, Baptism, Creed, etc.], which he has inherited from the apostles. Instead he makes additions of the devil and does not use these treasures for the improvement of the temple [i.e. Christendom].[29]

It is significant that in the *Augsburg Confession* the German Reformers—John Calvin signed the *Augustana* at a later date—expressly claimed that they taught nothing "discrepant with the Scriptures, or with the Church Catholic, or even with the Roman Church, so far as that Church is known from writers [the writings of the Fathers]".[30] The Reformers thus in no way denied the name and the nature of a Church to their Roman opponents but rather maintained that "the dissension [was] concerning certain (traditions and) abuses, which without any certain authority [had] crept into the churches. . . ."[31] In other words the "churchly substance" of the Roman Church was not denied but the Reformers denounced and condemned the distortion and corruption of this substance and called for its reformation.

The *Augsburg Confession* was immediately attacked and refuted by Roman theologians and its *Apology* written by Philip Melanchthon in 1530 was equally unsuccessful in bringing about a reconcilation with Rome. Yet the Reformers did not change their basic attitude towards the Roman Communion; they continued to recognize in it a Church, or at least acknowledged that there were churches within that Communion.

In his *Lectures on Galatians*—delivered after the publication of the *Augsburg Confession* and its rejection by Rome—Luther commenting on the words "to the churches of Galatia" (Gal. 1: 2) wrote:

Jerome raises an important question here: Why does Paul call "churches" those that were no churches? For Paul, he says, is writing to the Galatians, who had been led astray and turned away from Christ and from grace to Moses and the Law. I reply: When Paul calls them the "churches of Galatia", he is employing synecdoche, a very common practice in Scripture. Writing in a similar vein to the Corinthians, he congratulates them that the grace of God was given them in Christ, that is, that they were enriched in Him with all speech and all knowledge (1 Cor. 1: 4–5). And yet many of them had been perverted by false apostles and did not believe in the resurrection of the dead, etc. So today we still call the Church of Rome holy and all its sees holy, even though they have been undermined and their ministers ungodly. For God "rules in the midst of His foes" (Ps. 110: 2), Antichrist "takes his seat in the temple of God" (2 Thess. 2: 4), and Satan is present among the sons of God (Job 1: 6). Even if the Church is "in the midst of a crooked and perverse generation", as Paul says to the Philippians (2: 15), and even if it is surrounded by wolves and robbers, that is, spiritual tyrants, it is still the Church. Although the city of Rome is worse than Sodom and Gomorrah, nevertheless there remain in it Baptism, the Sacrament, the voice and text of the Gospel, the Sacred Scriptures, the ministries, the name of Christ, and the name of God. Whoever has these, has them; whoever does not have them, has no excuse, for the treasure is still there. Therefore the Church of Rome is holy, because it has the holy name of God, the Gospel, Baptism, etc.

If these are present among a people, that people is called holy. Thus this Wittenberg of ours is a holy village, and we are truly holy, because we have been baptized, communed, taught, and called by God; we have the works of God among us, that is, the Word and the sacraments, and these make us holy.

. . . Therefore the Church is holy even where the fanatics are dominant, so long as they do not deny the Word and the sacraments; if they deny these, they are no longer the Church. Wherever the substance of the Word and the sacraments abides therefore, there the holy Church is present. . . . Thus our brief answer to this question is this: The Church is universal throughout the world, wherever the Gospel of God and the sacraments are present.[32]

These passages, written at a time when no opportunity was lost of discrediting the opponent, clearly show that for Luther what determines whether a community is or is not a Church is the actual reality of Christ's presence in Word and sacraments. Since it has the holy name of God, the Gospel, Baptism, etc., each and all of which in some sort actualize Christ Himself, the Church of Rome is holy, i.e. it is a Church in spite of all abuse and misuse—corrupt and unreformed to be sure, but nevertheless a Church.

John Calvin reached similar conclusions. In his *Reply to Sadolet* who had tried to woo the Genevans, his "very dear brethren", back to the See of Rome, Calvin vindicated the necessity for reforming the Church. This necessity arose because

the light of divine truth had been extinguished, the Word of God buried, the virtue of Christ left in profound oblivion, and the pastoral office subverted . . . impiety so stalked abroad, that almost no doctrine of religion was pure from admixture, no ceremony free from error, no part, however minute, of divine worship untarnished by superstition.[33]

Calvin claimed that those who fought against such evils did not declare war against the Church but rather helped it in its dire distress. Sadolet may object and say that it was arrogant "to boast that the Church is [with Calvin and his friends] alone and to deny it to all the world besides".[34] But

Calvin did not deny it "to all the world besides" and was therefore able to write:

> We, indeed, Sadolet, deny not that those over which you preside are churches of Christ, but we maintain that the Roman Pontiff, with his whole herd of pseudo-bishops, who have seized upon the pastor's office, are ravening wolves, whose only study has hitherto been to scatter and trample upon the Kingdom of Christ, filling it with ruin and devastation.[35]

However harsh Calvin may have been in his judgement of what he believed to be the corruption and perversion of the Roman Church—and his opponents were certainly no less harsh in their judgement of him—he did not deny that there were churches within the Roman Communion; though these were in desperate need of correction and reformation, they were nevertheless churches.

In the final version of his *Institutes*—published seventeen years after his *Reply to Sadolet*—Calvin's argument is unchanged:

> However, when we categorically deny to the papists the title of *the Church*, we do not for this reason impugn the existence of churches among them. . . . I call them churches to the extent that the Lord wonderfully preserves in them a remnant of His people, however woefully dispersed and scattered, and to the extent that some marks of the Church remain—especially those marks whose effectiveness neither the devil's wiles nor human depravity can destroy.[36]

While the Reformers thus contended for "the true and lawful constitution of the Church"[37] and "the lawful form of the Church",[38] believing as they did that in the Church of Rome "Christ lies half buried", they did not unchurch their Roman Catholic opponents completely but admitted that, since some marks of the true Church remained, the Roman Church was still a Church.

Further evidence of this willingness on the part of the Reformers to recognize the Roman Communion in some sense as a Church, or at least to admit that Christ (however unrecognizably) was present in it, comes from a rather unexpected quarter, as unexpected perhaps for Protestants as for Roman Catholics: John Knox, usually regarded as the most rigidly, uncompromisingly and unreasonably anti-Roman of all Reformers. One might mention in passing the fact—remarkable for the sixteenth century—that during the period of Knox's Reformation in Scotland, which was frankly and undeniably anti-Roman, and is therefore considered by many as a veritable reign of terror, only one Roman Catholic was put to death (1571): Archbishop John Hamilton of St. Andrews, and he was hanged not for being a Roman Catholic but because he was judged to be a traitor to his country.

More important in the context of our inquiry, however, is Knox's theological attitude towards the Church of Rome. A citation from his *Answer to a Letter of a Jesuit named Tyrie* (1572) shows that in common with the other Reformers he did not unchurch Roman Catholics as completely as they unchurched Protestants and that he, too, admitted God had preserved to some extent His truth even in the Church of Rome. To Master Tyrie, Knox has this to say:

> Yea, we are further bold to affirm, that if ever it shall please God to bring the Kirk of Rome to her original purity, that she shall not be ashamed to embrace and reverence the pure Kirk of Scotland as her dearest sister, and next resembling her in all things, before pride and avarice, joined with idleness and riotous living, corrupted her ministers, and the inventions of men were preferred to God's simple truth. We say yet again, that whenever the Kirk of Rome shall be reduced to that state in which the apostles left it, we are assured that she shall vote in our favour, against all such as shall deny us to be a Kirk, if God continue us in that simplicity which this day is mocked by the world. . . .
>
> If Master Tyrie, or any other of that sect, blame us of railing (as commonly they used to do, when we speak the truth) then let him and them consider, that we learned not of Martin Luther what kind of men the papists were, but that which we speak and affirm now, we have received of the papists themselves. For this has been the merciful providence of God towards His little flock ever from the beginning, that when a universal corruption began to spread itself, then some were

raised, as it were one or two amongst the whole multitude, to admonish the present age and posterity to come, how far men had declined from the original purity, that God might at least have some testimony that the verity of God was not altogether buried in the earth.[39]

As far as Luther and Calvin are concerned it is somewhat surprising that both cite the Papacy (which in their view was the principal cause of the corruption and perversion of the Christian faith) as evidence and proof that the Church of Rome is in fact a Church.

In his letter *Concerning Rebaptism* Luther quotes 2 Thess. 2: 4:

The Antichrist takes his seat in the temple of God [and then he adds] If now the Pope is (and I cannot believe otherwise) the veritable Antichrist, he will not sit or reign in the devil's stall, but in the temple of God. No, he will not sit where there are only devils and unbelievers, or where no Christ or Christendom exist. For he is an Antichrist and must thus be among Christians. And since he is to sit and reign there it is necessary that there be Christians under him. God's temple is not the description for a pile of stones, but for the holy Christendom (1 Cor. 3: [17]), in which He is to reign. The Christendom that now is under the Papacy is truly the Body of Christ and a member of it. If it is His Body, then it has the true Spirit, Gospel, Faith, Baptism, Sacrament [of the Lord's Supper], keys, the office of the ministry, prayer, Holy Scripture, and everything that pertains to Christendom. So we are all still under the Papacy and therefrom have received our Christian treasures.[40]

In 1550 Calvin, commenting on the words "In the temple of God" in 2 Thess. 2: 4, reached a similar conclusion:

This one word fully refutes the error or rather stupidity of those who hold the Pope to be the vicar of Christ on the ground that he has a settled residence in the Church, however he may conduct himself. Paul sets Antichrist in the very sanctuary of God. He is not an enemy from the outside but from the household of faith, and opposes Christ under the very name of Christ. The question, however, is asked how the Church may be referred to as the den of so many superstitions, when it was to be the pillar of the truth (1 Tim. 3: 15). My answer is that it is so referred to not because it retains all the qualities of the Church but because it has still some of them left. I admit, therefore, that it is the temple of God in which the Pope holds sway, but the temple has been profaned by sacrileges beyond number.[41]

Whether the Reformers' identification of the Papacy with Antichrist is still acceptable to the majority of Protestants is not the point here. What is important, however, is that neither Roman Catholics nor Protestants should misunderstand the attitude and standpoint of the Reformers with regard to the Pope.

In his *Lectures on Psalm 45* delivered in 1532 Luther commenting on verse 10 defined his views on the Papacy:

. . . in the battle against the Pope and against the diabolical argument he throws at the Church—that although the Pope is a sinner in his own person, he nevertheless has a legitimate office and administration which we must obey—in that matter we can defend ourselves with no other sword than this verse and the command to us: "Hear, look, and incline your ear." We should say, as Paul says to the Jews in Romans 9: "I hear the fathers. I hear the Church. I hear the office, that the Pope sits in the ministry of the Word, that he has Baptism, that he has the fellowship and title of the Church. But I will make a distinction and not let myself be caught by this argument: 'The Pope says this, therefore you must do it.' For here we are enjoined: 'Hear'. Therefore, if the Pope teaches something that is in accordance with the Word, I will listen and do it. But if he speaks contrary to the Word, I will not listen."

But this argument weighs much more heavily on the heart if Satan throws it up to you alone. "Look, you are only a single individual, and you want to destroy this most beautiful government, set up so skilfully. What if there are errors and sins in the Papacy, what are you? Are you really free of errors or sins? Then why do you cause confusion and start a disturbance in the tabernacle of the Lord, since you can object to nothing except errors and sins, which abound in you too?" This really causes distress, as it is apparent that Paul, too, really struggled with this argument, Romans 9. Therefore you must accustom yourself to applying all energy to apprehending the Word, to hearing the Word, seeing the works of God, and believing. For whoever does not do this will be overcome by Satan. So we reply that we do not charge the Pope with his personal errors and sins. Although we must condemn these, we nevertheless excuse and forgive them, just as we want ours to be forgiven us. Therefore our conflict with the Pope is not over private and personal offences and sins but over teaching and the hearing of the Word. For besides their own sins, the Pope with his followers also impugn the glory and grace of God and Christ Himself, of whom the Father says, "Hear Him" (Matt. 17: 5). The Pope would take this hearing away from Christ and draw us to himself, and us who are Christ's disciples he would turn from Christ to himself. This is what we are fighting about. The question is not whether there are errors or sins of life, but about higher things: "Did the Son of God die for our sins and rise again? Have you preached and should you preach about Him? Should He be heard?" Since the Pope seeks to prohibit this by throwing up the authority of the Church, we say: "Get behind me, Satan (Mark 8: 33). We forgive you your sins, but we do not forgive you the blasphemies and denials of Christ, nor do we acquiesce in them. For Christ is greater than the Church that you hold up against us. Indeed, since your Church persecutes the Word of Christ, it is not the Church of Christ, but of Satan".[42]

In the *Schmalkald Articles* Luther states his real objection to the Pope precisely and tersely:

There stand before us all his [the Pope's] bulls and books in which he roars like a lion (as the angel indicates in Rev. 12: 1f.), ever declaring that no Christian can be saved unless he be obedient and subject to him [the Pope] in all the things he wishes, says or does. All this is nothing else but to say: although you may believe in Christ and have everything in Him that is necessary to salvation, yet it profits you nothing unless you revere me [the Pope] as your God and are subject and obedient to me.[43]

John Calvin is equally severe in his condemnation of the Papacy. He calls Leo X (1513–21) "cruel", Clement VII (1523–34) "bloodstained" and Paul III (1534–49) "truculent".[44]

But Calvin's real argument against the Papacy is not concerned with individual popes but with the attitude of the whole Papacy towards the Gospel. He is convinced that

227

there is no other reason why the pontiffs rage with such madness against the reviving doctrine of the Gospel, and stretch every nerve to suppress it; why they incite all kings and princes to persecute it—except that they see that their whole kingdom will fall and crumble as soon as Christ's Gospel gains sway.[45]

These are indeed hard words, but are they basically so very different from what some modern Roman Catholic scholars have to say? Referring to the period following upon the death of Innocent III (1216) Küng holds that

> the Pope became dependent on France, this leading in the fourteenth century to the "exile" of the Popes in Avignon; then came the disastrous building-up of the system of curial taxation, the encroachments of commercialization and nepotism in the Church's affairs, the whole leading to an almost unimaginable degradation of the Papacy.[46]

Küng's opinion of the Renaissance Papacy inaugurated after the final return of the Popes from Avignon (1418) is as follows:

> . . . despite much good in the Church of that time, especially among the people, a rapid and catastrophic increase in worldliness set in, in head and members; there was an unprecedented decline in the morals of the Roman Curia, the bishops, the cathedral chapters and the clergy; an appalling increase in proletariacy among the lower clergy; a decadent, turgid theology, often rating lower in men's minds than Canon Law; a discontent with the Church which was swiftly building up to frustration. The common battle-cry of the best spirits, whether sorrowful or impatient or enraged, was "Reform!" *Gravamina* —lists of grievances—and proposals for reform multiplied without end.[47] . . . It still seemed that Church reform would be possible only through an Ecumenical Council. But the Renaissance Popes wanted neither a Council nor any serious reform.[48]

If the invective freely used by Luther and Calvin (their Roman opponents were not backward when it came to vitriolic abuse) was removed from their attacks on the Papacy it would be discovered that their views on the spiritual state of the Papacy, of the Renaissance Papacy in any case, was not so very different from the conclusions reached by many present-day Roman Catholic scholars. A careful reading of the Reformers would make it clear that, when they refer to the Pope as Antichrist, they are not attacking or condemning the person of the Pope but the institution of which the individual Pope is the representative and embodiment.

Calvin denounces the Pope as "Christ's most hateful enemy, the supreme foe of the Gospel, the greatest waster and scatterer of the Church, the cruellest slaughterer and butcher of all the saints"[49] but then goes on to say: "Here I am not blaming the vices of men, but I am showing that the Papacy itself is directly contrary to Church order."[50]

The real reasons for Luther's and Calvin's objection to and rejection of the Papacy were not moral but theological: not the scandalous lives of individual popes but the claims made by the Papacy as an institution determined the attitude of the Reformers.

Luther stated his reasons in the *Schmalkald Articles*, already quoted; Calvin does so in the *Institutes*:

> We ought consequently to follow this as the chief indication in searching out Antichrist, especially when such pride leads even to the public scattering of the Church. Since, therefore, it is clear that the Roman pontiff has shamelessly transferred to himself what belonged to God alone and especially to Christ, we should have no doubt that he is the leader and standard-bearer of that impious and hateful kingdom.[51]

The Reformers identified the Papacy with Antichrist because to them it was theologically unacceptable that the existence of the Church and membership in it, and so (at least indirectly) the salvation of men, should be claimed by the Papacy to be dependent on the subjection and obedience to the Pope, who as the universal bishop of the Church and the vicar of Christ, was the guarantor of its existence and unity. The fundamental concern of the Reformers was the centrality of Christ: any institution—in this case the Papacy —that in the name of Christ substituted obedience to the Church for obedience to the Lord of the Church was Antichrist.

Roman Catholics may understandably be offended by the

teaching of the Reformers and many Protestants may feel that this aspect of Reformation theology is now best forgotten. Yet neither Roman Catholics nor Protestants should overlook the positive side of the Reformers' arguments against the Papacy. The Reformers made it abundantly clear that Antichrist can arise only in the Church and not outside. Luther and Calvin asserted that the Pope was Antichrist. Since Antichrist, however, is predestined to sit in the temple of God they postulated at the same time—and this is the positive aspect of their theology which is so important for the Protestant–Roman Catholic dialogue—that the Church of Rome is in fact a Church.

In former controversies and in the present dialogue the Protestant position has always been that such debates are actually made possible by the fact that both Communions are Churches and have in common all that is "Christian and good". The separating factor is not the treasure of Christian good they possess—possession of which makes both of them Churches—but the different apprehensions and applications of what they possess.[52]

Therefore in the dialogue the Protestant is not concerned with unchurching the Roman Catholic partner, his aim is rather that, in common subjection to the Word of God, he and his interlocutor should learn and continue to learn to understand and use "everything Christian and good" so that through reformation and amendment both Churches may become visibly what they already are—the One Holy, Catholic (Universal) Church.

Edmund Schlink gives an excellent summary of the Protestant position:

> The oneness of the Church is not in the first place the oneness of its members: it is rather the oneness of Christ who in all places and at all times acts upon them. By Word and Sacrament the one and the same Christ has called and ingrafted them all into Himself; in the multiplicity of the gifts of the Spirit the one and the same Christ is working now. Every member of the Church is elected by the one God, called by the one Christ, and is renewed and receives the gifts of the one Holy Spirit. There-

fore, notwithstanding all their apparent tensions, differences, factions and local divisions we must believe that those who have faith in Christ, are baptized into Him and receive His Body in the Lord's Supper, are really one—and in fact are *the reality* created in Christ by God through the Holy Spirit. Because those, who believe in Christ, are baptized into Him, and receive His Body, are one, they should strive after unity; because they *are* one they *should be* one. [53]

The Reformers and their heirs do not unchurch Roman Catholics; they consider that, in some way or other, the Roman Communion forms part of the Holy Catholic Church which they recognize as being at least present in the Church of Rome. The Roman attitude towards the Church of the Reformation, however, is quite different and much more radical.

Until recently no papal pronouncements, conciliar findings, or official statements by the Holy Office ever referred to Protestant communities as *Churches*. If the term "Church" was employed at all by Roman Catholics with regard to Protestant communities it was used in a non-theological sense. It is gratifying to learn that the decree *de Oecumenismo* testifies to some progress in the ecumenical thinking of the Roman Church. Chapter 3, part 2 of the decree bears the title: *De Ecclesiis et Communitatibus ecclesialibus in Occidente seiunctis*—The separated Churches and ecclesial Communities in the West. It should, however, be noted right away that there are very definite omissions in the decree *de Oecumenismo*; for instance, no attempt is made to specify the Communions in the West which are "Churches" and those which are merely "ecclesial Communities"; no definition is given of what is required of a Christian community to be called a "Church".

But, on the other hand, the decree contains, implicitly at least, the recognition that the "separated Christians" in the West are not merely groups of individuals but that they are in fact "ecclesial Communities". Their "ecclesial" character is acknowledged by reference being made in the decree to their sacramental life. Not only Baptism but also the Lord's

Supper is mentioned. Since the Sacrament of Orders is wanting in the separated communities, these have, in the Roman view, been unable to preserve the eucharistic mystery in its fullness. But the Church of Rome now recognizes that "nevertheless in commemorating the Lord's death and resurrection in the Holy Supper [these communities] are professing that it signifies life in communion with Christ and are looking for his coming in glory"—*tamen, dum in Sancta Coena mortis et resurrectionis Domini memoriam faciunt, vitam in Christi communione significari profitentur atque gloriosum Eius adventum exspectant.*[54]

But, while there is definite progress in the ecumenical thinking of the Roman Church, its claims have in no way been abandoned: it and it alone is the one and only true Church. On the contrary, Rome reaffirms its claims in the decree *de Oecumenismo*: ". . . the Catholic Church has been enriched with the whole truth revealed by God and with all the means of grace"—*Ecclesia catholica omni a Deo revelata veritate et omnibus mediis gratiae ditata sit.*[55]

This surely signifies that the Christian communities in the West separated from Rome, whether they are called "Churches" or "ecclesial Communities", have not been enriched with the whole truth revealed by God nor with all the means of grace and that therefore they are not and cannot be recognized as the *Ecclesia* or as *Ecclesiae* in the full theological sense.

2

Christology

The Protestant–Roman Catholic dialogue demonstrates that by a removing of emotional and psychological barriers and by a discussing of the real theological differences it is possible to discover that the two Communions hold much in common. Now there is at least an indication of the direction in which the Churches will have to go if they are ever to be visibly one in Christ.

It would, of course, be foolish to deny that theological obstacles continue to strew the road to unity. They do it so effectively that the disciples of Jesus Christ, the one Lord of the Church, must still qualify their membership in His Body by prefixing the words "Protestant" or "Roman Catholic" to their name of Christian.

In 1927 Barth, in his lecture on *The Concept of the Church* to which we have already referred, voiced the opinion that Protestants and Roman Catholics could discuss all other things, and significantly he added: "I do mean *all* other things—Papacy and sacraments, dogma and ritual",[56] if agreement could be reached on the question of the nature of the Church.

Since 1927 the growing concern for Christian unity has resulted in a continual increase in the number of subjects examined by Protestant and Roman Catholic scholars in their dialogue. Writing thirty-five years after Barth's lecture, the daring venture of 1927, Küng in *The Living Church*, dealing with the ecumenical perspectives, asks where the chief theological and practical difficulties of unity lie and then gives the following answer: "Not in the understanding of Christology, not in the understanding of the justification of the sinner, not in the understanding of the sacraments, but in the understanding of *the Church*."[57]

The implication of Küng's statement seems to be that the understanding of justification, Christology, etc., is *per se* the same in the Church of the Reformation and the Church of Rome so that it can no longer be regarded as a divisive factor.

We believe that Küng's assessment of the situation is over-optimistic. He seems to confuse the agreement between individual theologians which may exist—Barth's doctrine of justification and his own is an example—with agreements between Churches which in the case of the subjects he cites do not yet exist.

Leaving aside justification, is it really correct to say that neither theological nor practical difficulties arise between Protestants and Roman Catholics, for instance, in their understanding of Christology?

Would Küng agree that in the incarnation the Son of God took upon Himself man's *fallen* humanity? Is this issue, which was not altogether settled at the Reformation,—the Reformers did not speak unambiguously on this subject—not a very live one in connection with the Roman and Protestant understanding of Christology?

For Barth, this whole question is of vital importance from a Christological point of view. When we remember once again that many Roman theologians regard him as the true heir of the Reformation some weight must be given to his Christological understanding in this respect.

From Barth's point of view it is essential to realize that the Son of God did not just become man in a general sense but that He became specifically and concretely *the man* who is under the judgement of God whose wrath he has incurred. Thus in Jn. 1:14 "the Word was made flesh" the term σάρξ "includes not only the concept of man in general but also . . . the narrower concept of the man . . . whose existence has become one exposed to death because he has sinned against God. Flesh is the concrete form of human nature marked by Adam's fall . . . the form of the destroyed nature and existence of man as they have to be reconciled with God."[58]

Would Roman theology really be at one with us in saying that He whose name was Wonderful Counsellor, the Mighty God, the Everlasting Father, the Prince of Peace (Is. 9: 6) became Immanuel—God with us (Is. 7: 14; Matt. 1: 23)— but "God with us" by assuming human nature not as God originally created it but as it became and now is: fallen and therefore sinful, corrupt and vitiated?

The full extent of Christ's humiliation can be seen (though not defined or fathomed) when it is realized that when He became man He assumed fallen human nature and so "exists in the place where we are, in all the remoteness not merely of the creature from the Creator, but of the sinful creature from the Holy Creator."[59]

Christ does not differ from us in His humanity—He assumed the same fallen humanity as we have. The difference between Him and us is according to Barth that in our state and condition He does not do what underlies and produces that state and condition, or what we in that state and condition continually do. Our unholy human existence, assumed and adopted by the Word of God, is a hallowed, and therefore a sinless, human existence; in our unholy human existence the eternal Word draws near to us. In the hallowing of our unholy human existence He draws supremely and helpfully near to us . . . in the likeness of flesh (unholy flesh, marked by sin), there happens the unlike, the new and helpful thing, that sin is condemned by not being committed, by being omitted, by full obedience now being found in the very place where otherwise sin necessarily and irresistibly takes place.[60]

We maintain that Küng could not possibly accept this position. If he did he would have to reject the dogma of the Immaculate Conception—which bars the way to a biblical Christology acceptable to Protestants. Since, in the Roman view, Mary was without original and actual sin, the Son of God did not take upon Himself the sinful flesh of Adam which stood in need of redemption but the sinless flesh of Mary which was already redeemed prior to His incarnation and in view and in anticipation of His redemption.

Here we surely have a divisive factor which belies Küng's optimistic statement that the theological and practical difficulties which face Protestant and Roman Catholics do not lie in the understanding of Christology.

It has already been admitted that the Reformers made statements which cannot be taken as meaning unambiguously that Christ assumed our fallen humanity. Barth thus cannot agree with Calvin when the Reformer "strangely weakens his . . . comment on Jn. 1: 14 by this addition: *Caeterum "caro" minime hic pro corrupta natura accipitur (ut saepe apud Paulum) sed pro homine mortali* [—"The word 'flesh' is not taken here for corrupt nature (as is often used by Paul), but for mortal man.]"[61] Barth asks rightly, "How far, then, was it a *vilis et abjecta conditio* to which the Son of God condescended?"[62]

Must we not ask Küng and the Church of Rome precisely the same question? In becoming man the Son of God took the Virgin Mary's flesh but was it sinful flesh? The Church of Rome teaches, as we have already mentioned, that it was not, for owing to her Immaculate Conception Mary was free of original and actual sin; that she was in fact the sinless mother of the Son of God. In what sense then did the Son of God condescend to a vile and abject condition? In what sense did He become flesh, real flesh, i.e. flesh of our flesh? Is the question of Christ's humanity—fallen or not fallen—not a divisive factor in the understanding of Christology on the part of Protestant and Roman theology?

Küng is, of course, aware of the fact that there is not yet a common understanding of doctrinal matters. But in his view, as we have already seen, the causes of the misunderstanding that still prevails between the different Communions are not the doctrinal matters themselves but the different concepts of the Church held by Protestants and Roman Catholics. He holds—and here we agree with him as we do with what Barth said in 1927—that "this difference in the understanding of the Church . . . has repercussions in differences in the understanding of the sacraments, the justification of the sinner and Christology."[63]

3
Church, Scripture and Tradition

It is not our intention to deal here in detail with the Roman concept of the Church itself. We readily admit, however, that the *Constitutio dogmatica de Ecclesia* (1964) has introduced new aspects into Roman ecclesiology—e.g. it emphasizes that the Church is a *mystery* (not primarily a juridical society) and is the People of God. This might help to bring the different Communions closer together. It is also worth noting that in the decree *de Oecumenismo* it is acknowledged that the members of the separated Christian communities "have been brought, through faith in Christ and Baptism properly received, into a certain though not perfect communion with the [Roman] Catholic Church"—*in Christum credunt et baptismum rite receperunt, in quadam cum Ecclesia catholica communione, etsi non perfecta, constituuntur.*[64] They are in fact incorporated into Christ and therefore brethren.[65] Whether the "separated brethren" on their part are willing to accept this kind of "communion" with the Roman Church, which no doubt implies that they are also in some way under the jurisdiction of that Church, is a different matter.

We contend, however, that neither the Constitution *de Ecclesia* nor the decree *de Oecumenismo* basically affects the Roman understanding of the relation of the Church to Scripture. The difference in the understanding of this relationship is specifically mentioned in the decree *de Oecumenismo* as one of the essential points on which there is dissension between Rome and the Reformation Church.[66] A further point of disagreement also referred to in the same decree is the different understanding of the function of the magisterium in the exposition and proclamation of the written Word of God.[67]

Has the position changed so very much since the sixteenth century? Are the basic points of disagreement between Rome and the Church of the Reformation not the same then and now?

At the time of the Reformation and the Council of Trent one of the main divisive factors preventing the healing of the breach between Rome and evangelical Christendom was the question of the authority and supremacy of Scripture. It is true that in the centuries following the Reformation Protestants could often accuse the Roman Church with a degree of justification of paying only lip-service to the authority of the Bible; of neglecting its study as God's ever actual Word and—to say the least of it—of discouraging the ordinary Christian from reading it and encountering in it the living Christ. Bible Societies, whose chief work was the translation and propagation of the Scriptures amongst the nations were condemned by the *Syllabus Errorum* which described them, together with Socialism, Communism, secret societies and clerico-liberal societies, as "pests".[68]

Protestants would find it difficult to justify similar accusations against the Church of Rome today. The outstanding feature of modern Roman Catholicism is precisely the revival of a genuine biblical theology. As a result of this new interest in the written Word of God the Bible is made available in modern vernaculars in many parts of the world. The Roman layman is not merely allowed but officially encouraged to read the Scriptures, which in many countries are mass-produced and distributed to all and sundry at the lowest possible cost. Not only in theory but also in practice the Roman Church today acknowledges the Bible as the Word of God.

In *Strukturen der Kirche* (Structures of the Church) Küng makes this astounding statement:

> The Church, the great community of those that believe, is the Ecumenical Council of all believers gathered in and under Christ by God Himself. There is but one Lord, even Christ—all the rest are brethren. Even the Pope is not the Lord of the Church but her servant, the servant of all. He cannot be Pope unless he along with all the others is first of all, and ever anew, a simple, humble and believing Christian. Should he not be this, should he act and teach against the Gospel of Jesus Christ, the Church is by no means—as Protestants complain against us—at his mercy for better or worse; rather she may resist him.[69]

It has always been accepted Roman Catholic doctrine that a heretical or schismatic Pope can and must be deposed by the Church. Küng, however, defines unequivocally what constitutes heresy and schism: living, acting and teaching against the Gospel of Jesus Christ; what Küng means by the Gospel of Jesus Christ in this context is Scripture, the Bible, the written Word of God. In *Strukturen der Kirche* he maintains that "[ecclesiastical] office [i.e. of Pope and Councils] does not . . . exalt itself above Scripture as the Apostles' witness to Christ. . . ."[70]

The authority of Scripture thus seems to be fully recognized by the Church of Rome. Its supremacy appears to be such that even a Pope can and must be removed from office if his life, his actions and teaching do not conform to Scripture and its imperative demands.

In the fifteenth century the great champion of the Papacy, the Spanish cardinal Juan de Torquemada, whose works provided later canonists with the legal and theological basis for their debates on the papal primacy, discusses the possibility of proceedings against a heretical or schismatic Pope. Torquemada lists the offences which in his view would make a Pope unfit for office. Some of these are as follows: loss of faith; separation from Christ through disobedience to His law; ordering that which is opposed to divine or natural law; separation from the body of the Church and the college of bishops through non-observance of what is taught by the Universal Church according to the Apostolic Tradition or of what is enjoined by General Councils or the authority of the Apostolic See. Torquemada believes that the Church is in and with the Pope only if he is subject to Christ and lets himself be strengthened by the traditions of the Universal Church which is the Bride of Christ.[71]

When Torquemada speaks of the Law of Christ, the divine Law, the Apostolic Tradition, etc., the implied reference is to Scripture. Yet it is significant that in this context he makes no explicit and unambiguous reference to the written Word of God. In Küng's statement on the other hand there is no ambiguity at all: a Pope who lives, acts and teaches against the Gospel of Jesus Christ can and must be deposed by the Church, and the Gospel of Jesus Christ in this context is Scripture, the Bible, as the Apostolic witness to Christ, above which ecclesiastical office cannot exalt itself.

Since Protestants are assured by a Roman Catholic theologian who is qualified to interpret the teaching of his Communion that the Pope is not the absolute Lord of the Church nor above Scripture (which is the authoritative witness of the Apostles to Jesus Christ) ought they not to re-examine their attitude towards the Roman Church and even the Papacy?

Would Luther have burnt the papal Bull *Exsurge Domine* on December 10, 1520; would Calvin ever have abandoned the comparative security of his career as a scholar in Law and the Arts and exchanged it for that of a reformer of the Church; would there have been a break with Rome at all in the sixteenth century if Pope and hierarchy had then spoken as unequivocally on the authority and supremacy of Scripture as Roman Catholic theologians like Küng are doing today?

It is always dangerous, if not futile, to reinterpret history in the light of events that never happened. In this particular case, however, it is quite safe to say that the Reformation would have taken place even if the Roman Church had given the same assurances regarding Scripture in the sixteenth century as some of its theologians give now. It is very important to remember that even in the sixteenth century what was at stake was not the authority of Scripture but the exclusiveness of this authority over against all other authorities.

For theologians like Küng this question seems now to be settled. ". . . according to what *norm* shall action for the renewal of the Church be measured?"[72] he asks in *The Council and Reunion* and then replies:

> There is only one norm whose authority is adequate. . . . The norm to which we can keep looking, in all our actions, is Jesus Christ, the Lord of the Church, who speaks to the Church of every century in His Gospel, making His demands on her.[73]

Official and authoritative confirmation of this view is found in the *Constitutio de Sacra Liturgia* (1963). In this Constitution the reason why Scripture is and ought to be the supreme norm in the Church is given:

> He [Christ] is present in His Word, since it is He Himself who speaks when the Holy Scriptures are read in Church— (*praesens adest in verbo suo, siquidem ipse loquitur dum sacrae Scripturae in Ecclesia leguntur*).[74]

In his *Rechtfertigung*, Küng explains more fully what is meant when Scripture is accepted as the authoritative norm:

> Holy Scripture has an unchangeable primacy (*Vorrang*) of which it cannot be deprived by any other theological argument.

Scripture is, therefore,

> the inexhaustible source which the theologian can never comfortably enclose within a system. It is always bringing new surprises: problems and solutions which were never before

suspected. . . . If therefore it is not any sort of teaching, but precisely the teaching of Scripture which is to be explained theologically, then all theological-philosophical categories must necessarily be measured and órientated by the categories of the Word of God itself.[75]

In *Strukturen der Kirche*, Küng makes a practical application of what he believes to be the genuine Roman Catholic teaching on the place and the authority of Holy Scripture: it is the supreme norm to which even the magisterium of the Church in the person of the Pope must submit for ecclesiastical office; not even the papal office can elevate itself above Scripture.[76]

If taken by itself, considered, so to speak, in isolation, Scripture, its place and authority in the Church, is thus an area where Protestants and Roman Catholics have discovered much that they hold in common. But once this field is not taken by itself and not considered in isolation, and is related to the authority of the Church itself as understood by Protestants on the one hand and Roman Catholics on the other, much of the common ground already gained has to be given up again. The reason for this is the different understanding of Protestants and Roman Catholics in respect of the authority of the written Word of God *for* and *vis-à-vis* the Church and its authority.

In what sense then is Scripture the norm to which the Church must keep looking in all it does and teaches? What is the teaching of the Church of the Reformation; what does Rome hold?

In what sense is the written Word of God of supreme authority in, for and *vis-à-vis* the Church? According to the Reformation understanding, Scripture is self-authenticating and self-interpretative because the Holy Spirit Himself authenticates and interprets its witness. It is for this reason that it is His Word whose unique authority is sovereign and exclusive over against all other authorities. It is sovereign and exclusive even over against the authority of the Church.

Luther thus says in his *Assertio omnium articolorum* (1520):

Hence it is a manifest error that by saying such things as "it is not allowed to understand Scripture through one's own spirit", we are commanded that we should set Holy Scripture aside and turn to human commentaries on it and believe them. Such an idea, I say, was beyond doubt brought in by Satan himself so as to cause us to stray very far from our, i.e. from Holy Scripture, and give us a desperate knowledge of Scripture. Wherefore this saying is much rather to be understood as meaning Scripture is to be understood through the Spirit alone by whom it was written and nowhere more than in His Scripture which He has written Himself will you find this Spirit present and living. So we ought to strive not to set Scripture aside and turn to the human writings of the Fathers— No! Rather we ought in the first place to set aside the writings of all men and the more present the peril is of understanding Scripture through our own spirit the more assiduous our pains over it alone should be so that the use of this constant endeavour may do away with this danger and finally make us sure of the Spirit of the Scripture who is not to be found at all except in Scripture. For here He has set up His tent and His abode in the heavens (i.e. The Apostles) (Ps. 18: 11) . . .

Or tell me if you are able: who is the judge who settles a question if the statements of the Fathers are in conflict? For here we must decide in accordance with the judgement of Scripture and this cannot be done where we do not give the first place in all that is attributed to the Fathers to Scripture seeing that Scripture itself is through itself most certain, most easily accessible, most easily understood—that which is its own interpreter that proves, judges and casts light on, all that is said . . .

Nothing but the divine words ought therefore to be the first principle of the Christian but all human words are conclusions which being derived from it must be referred back to it and be verified by it . . . I [Luther] do not wish to be praised as more learned than all others but I want that Scripture alone be queen and that it should not be interpreted by my spirit or any other man's. But I want it to be understood through itself and its own Spirit.[77]

In Calvin we find the same insistence on the Holy Spirit's being the authenticator and interpreter of Scripture through whom its unique authority is established. In the *Institutes* he therefore says:

We ought to remember . . . credibility of doctrine is not

established until we are persuaded beyond doubt that God is its author. Thus, the highest proof of Scripture derives in general from the fact that God in person speaks in it.

. . . the testimony of the Spirit is more excellent than all reason. For as God alone is a fit witness of Himself in His Word, so also the Word will not find acceptance in men's hearts before it is sealed by the inward testimony of the Spirit. The same Spirit, therefore, who has spoken through the mouths of the prophets must penetrate into our hearts to persuade us that they faithfully proclaimed what had been divinely commanded . . . [78]

Let this point therefore stand: that those whom the Holy Spirit has inwardly taught truly rest upon Scripture, and that Scripture indeed is self-authenticated; hence, it is not right to subject it to proof and reasoning. And the certainty it deserves with us, it attains by the testimony of the Spirit. [79]

Discussing the threefold form of the Word of God, Barth states:

The revealed Word of God we know only from Scripture adopted by Church proclamation, or from Church proclamation based on Scripture. The written Word of God we know only through the revelation which makes proclamation possible, or through the proclamation made possible by revelation. The proclaimed Word of God we know only by knowing the revelation attested through Scripture, or by knowing the Scripture which attests revelation. [80]

What Barth has to say more particularly of the written form of the Word of God stands in the direct line of the Reformation:

The Apostolic succession of the Church must mean that she is guided by the canon, i.e. by the word of prophets and apostles as by the necessary rule of all expression valid in the Church— that she enters upon the succession of the prophets and apostles in their office of proclamation, and that in such a way that their proclamation comes first, freely and independently, while the proclamation of the Church is related to it, is ventured upon obediently in view of it, is measured by it, only therefore takes its place because and so far as it conforms to it—that she constantly acknowledges its free power over herself. Everything depends for the idea of a living succession upon the *antecessor* being thought of as still alive and possessed of free power as compared with the *successor*. But if, as is the case here, the *antecessor* is one who has long been dead, this can only happen when his proclamation is fixed in writing and when it is recognized that he still has life and free power today over the Church in this very *written* Word of his.[81]

Barth, too, contends that Scripture is self-interpretative and self-authenticating.

... this real or Biblical canon is in a process of continual incorporation into the life, thought and language of the Church, so far as the Bible is continually understood afresh and therefore explained and interpreted. But *exegesis* is always a combination of taking and giving, of expounding and inserting. The very exegesis without which the norm cannot attain to validity as a norm is thus also a sign of the standing danger of a confiscation of the Bible by the Church, of an absorption, a making up of its own life by the Church's life, of a transmutation of its free power into Church authority—in short, of an annulment of its character as the norm, which magisterially confronts the Church. All exegesis of the Bible means the presence of this danger. All exegesis may become predominantly an imposition instead of an exposition, and to that extent deteriorate into a dialogue of the Church with herself. And we shall not banish this danger, but only really begin to conjure it up and render it acute, by making right exposition depend on the verdict of an ultimately decisive Church teaching office, or on the verdict of an historical and critical science, comporting itself with an equal infallibility. If we assume that the one or the other of these authorities is worthy of the Church's highest confidence, in both cases the Church makes a mistake about the Bible, so far as she thinks that in one way or other she can control right exposition and thereby set up a norm over the norm, and ought to and can seize upon the proper norm for herself. Bible exegesis should rather be left open on all sides, not, as this demand was put by Liberalism, for the sake of free *thinking*, but for the sake of a free *Bible*. Self-defence against possible violence to the text must be left here as everywhere to the text itself, which in practice has so far always succeeded, as a merely spiritual-oral tradition simply cannot, in asserting its own life against encroachments by individuals or whole areas and schools in the Church, and in victoriously achieving it in ever-fresh applications, and so in creating recognition of itself as the norm ...

the Bible is the canon just because it *is* so. But it is so because it *imposes* itself as such.[82]

Is it not true that the Church of Rome does precisely what Reformed theology from Luther and Calvin down to Barth refuses to do? Does it not set up a norm over *the* norm by setting its own interpretation of Scripture above Scripture? The First Vatican Council, reiterating the corresponding Tridentine decree (Session 4)[83] teaches

> that is to be held as the true sense of Holy Scripture which our holy Mother Church hath held and holds, to whom it belongs to judge the true sense and interpretation of Holy Scripture and therefore that it is permitted to no one to interpret Holy Scripture contrary to this sense, nor, likewise, contrary to the unanimous consent of the Fathers—(*pro vero sensu sacrae Scripturae habendus sit, quem tenuit ac tenet sancta mater Ecclesia, cuius est iudicare de vero sensu et interpretatione Scripturarum sanctarum; atque ideo nemini licere contra hunc sensum aut etiam contra unanimem consensum Patrum ipsam Scripturam sacram interpretari*).[84]

Is the norm to which the Church of Rome submits Holy Scripture or is the norm the sense and the interpretation which the Roman Church itself has held and does hold?

The First Vatican Council states clearly and unambiguously that it belongs to the Church alone "to judge of the true sense and interpretation of Holy Scripture". This means that the supreme authority to which even the Pope must submit is in actual fact not Scripture itself but the Roman interpretation of Scripture, the sense of Scripture determined by the magisterium of the Church from which there is no appeal to Scripture itself.

As in the Church of the Reformation, so in the Church of Rome, Scripture is the rule of faith which no Christian, not even the Roman Pontiff, can circumvent. But in the Roman view a distinction is to be made between Scripture as *regula fidei remota*—the distant rule of faith—and the interpretation of Scripture by the Roman Church, i.e. by the magisterium of that Church, as *regula fidei proxima*—the proximate rule of faith.

A typical example of the Roman teaching in this respect

245

is the Encyclical *Humani generis* (1950). When the "New Theology" founded by the Jesuits, Henri de Lubac and Jean Daniélou, called in question the time-honoured estimate of Thomism and even the immutability of dogmatic definitions and pleaded for a theology relevant to modern thought and thought-forms, Pius XII—who had himself coined the term "New Theology"—clearly defined in *Humani generis* what the rule of faith was to be:

> . . . although in matters of faith and morals the sacred magisterium must be for every theologian the proximate and universal norm of the truth inasmuch as Christ the Lord has entrusted to it [the magisterium] the task of guarding, protecting and interpreting the whole deposit of faith, Holy Scripture as well as the divine tradition. Yet sometimes people are not aware of the existence of the duty by which the faithful are bound to avoid even those errors which approximate more or less to heresy and therefore "to observe even those constitutions and decrees by which the Holy See rejects and forbids such opinions".[85]
>
> It is also true that theologians must constantly be having recourse to the sources of divine revelation. It is for them to show how that which is taught by the living magisterium is contained explicitly or implicitly in Scripture and in the divine tradition. . . . Together with these sacred sources God has given a living magisterium to His Church; thus He would illuminate and elucidate for us what is contained only obscurely and as it were implicitly in the deposit of faith. The task of authentically interpreting the deposit was not entrusted by our divine Redeemer to individual Christians or even to individual theologians but solely to the magisterium of the Church. And if the Church discharges her office, as she very often has in past ages, whether the way in which it is done is ordinary or extraordinary, it is evident that a method which uses what is obscure to explain what is clear is entirely false. Rather is it necessary that the opposite procedure must be followed by all! Therefore our predecessor of undying memory, Pius IX, in teaching that the noblest office of theology was to show how a doctrine defined by the Church is contained in the sources [of faith] added not without a good reason the words: "in that very sense in which it has been defined [by the Church]". . .[86]
>
> [In the view of some] the teaching of the Holy Fathers and

of the sacred magisterium is as it were to be measured by the standard of Holy Scripture (*ad trutinam Sacrae Scripturae*) as it is interpreted by exegetes according to a purely human method when the same Holy Scripture ought rather to be expounded according to the mind of the Church which has been appointed by Christ the Lord to guard and interpret the whole deposit of the Truth revealed by God.[87] . . . Nobody can fail to see how alien all this is to the principles and norms of interpretation which have been solemnly laid down by our predecessors, of happy memory; by Leo XIII in his Encyclical *Providentissimus*, by Benedict XV in *Spiritus Paraclitus*, and by ourselves in *Divino afflante Spiritu.*[88]

Progressive Roman Catholics claim that *Humani generis* is now out of date. The discussions which took place at the third session of Vatican II in connection with the *schema de Revelatione* show that the Roman Church is now indeed willing to allow its scholars more freedom in research and exposition than *Humani generis* did. But has the fundamental position of *Humani generis* with regard to the relationship between Church and Scripture really changed? Our contention is that it has not!

The text in the *schema de Oecumenismo* which was considered at the third session of Vatican II and in favour of which the great majority of the Council Fathers voted is as follows:

Moved by the Holy Spirit they [the members of the separated communities] find in these same Holy Scriptures God speaking to them in Christ—(*Spiritu Sancto movente, in ipsis Sacris Scripturis Deum inveniunt sibi loquentem in Christo*).[89]

This text, however, was withdrawn and redrafted by some higher authority. It was accepted (or had to be accepted) in this form:

Invoking the Holy Spirit, they [the members of the separated communities] seek God in these same Holy Scriptures speaking as it were to them in Christ—(*Spiritum Sanctum invocantes, in ipsis Sacris Scripturis Deum inquirunt quasi sibi loquentem in Christo*).[90]

In other words the Holy See saw to it that the fundamental teaching of the Reformation was once again rejected by a Council. The Reformers and their heirs teach that God speaks to men through Christ in the Holy Scriptures and that men hear and understand Him through the Holy Spirit. The authoritative text of the decree *de Oecumenismo* as it now stands makes either explicitly or implicitly three assertions with regard to the members of the Reformation Church: 1. they are not moved by the Holy Spirit—they only invoke Him; 2. they do not find God—they only seek Him; 3. (and this is most important in this context) they seek God in the wrong place. Assuming that He can be found in the Scriptures they seek Him there while in fact He can only be found in the Scriptures if they are heard together with Tradition and are interpreted authoritatively by the magisterium of the Roman Church.[91]

Few Roman theologians have come so close to the Reformed position as Küng. Yet once he relates the place and the authority of Scripture to the Roman conception of the authority of the Church he must say, and as a loyal Roman Catholic does say, without hesitation:

> In so far as the binding teaching of the Universal Church is involved and in so far as it is the task of the office (of Pope and Councils) to serve the teaching which binds the Universal Church, this office is in and with the Church the infallible rule for the faith of the individual Christian. The office [of Pope and Councils] does not thereby raise itself above Scripture as the Apostles' witness to Christ but practises in its authoritative teaching its own obedience to the teaching of the Apostles.[92]

Barth's statement about the place and the authority of the Bible in the Roman Church is thus still correct and valid:

> . . . the Church [in the Roman view] has, of course, one Lord and Judge of her action, she, of course, has the Word of God over her. But she has it over her because she has it *in herself*, indistinguishable from herself. The Roman Catholic Church, too, possesses, reads, in fact reverences the Bible, without prejudice to her setting tradition by its side. But, of course, not the Bible by itself, not an emancipated Bible, not a Bible which confronts the Church as the authority. Here [in the Roman Church] it is not acknowledged that the Bible as it stands is the Word of God and, as such, the supreme criterion of Church

doctrine. Here, on the contrary, we are dealing with the Bible authentically interpreted by the Church herself, namely by her teaching office through which Christ yet liveth and speaketh, with the Bible as belonging to the Church, properly understood, properly expounded, properly applied by her teaching office. *It* is the Word of God by which all proclamation is to be measured. Thus the *regula proxima fidei*, the nearest immediate plumb-line of [Roman] Catholic belief is not the verdict of the Bible, but the verdict of the Church's teaching office *on* the Bible. (Cf. Diekamp, *Kath. Dogm.*, Vol. 1, 1930, p. 63f.) By her actual view of the Bible the Church retains *both* proclamation *and* the norm for its needful criticism, in her own hands, i.e. the Bible rightly understood and rightly applied, which actually is the norm which is applied in such criticism. Actually there is only a relative distinction between the two, and the synthesis of them can cause no surprises to the Church who in her head is at once the *norma normata* and the *norma normans*, the *ecclesia audiens* and the *ecclesia docens*; for, at least in her head, i.e. in her teaching office, she has oversight of both and has full authority and power of disposal to complete the synthesis and, therefore, also the dogmatic criticism at her own free judgement.[93]

The question thus arises how and in what way the Church of the Reformation and the Church of Rome understand the authority of Scripture in relation to the Church and its tradition differently. We contend that the reason for this difference is the fact that the Reformers and their heirs apprehend the relationship between Church and Scripture "pneumatically" while Rome introduces the "pseudo-pneumatic".

The term "pneumatic" is used here to indicate that the Church must be continually involved in a confrontation with its Lord. This confrontation—to be true and valid—is brought about pneumatically, i.e. the Holy Spirit brings the Church face to face with its Lord, Jesus Christ, the Son of God, incarnate, crucified, risen and ascended on high. Concretely, this confrontation signifies that through the Holy Spirit the Church in its life and mission, its faith and order, comes continually face to face with Scripture to which its own authority is always subordinate.

Barth puts it forthrightly thus:

... the Body of Christ, the Church, has its Head in heaven, and therefore on earth it is not left to the insight and caprice of its members. Although it consists entirely of human beings, the Church is not a human polity ... in which the discharge of the witness to Jesus Christ committed to it is left to the good pleasure of its members. The Church is governed. And as it is created and maintained by the Word of God, it is also governed by the Word of God: by the Word of God in the form of the testimony to the Revelation of God in Jesus Christ set down in Scripture. To say that Jesus Christ rules the Church is equivalent to saying that Holy Scripture rules the Church. The one explains the other, the one can be understood only through the other. The Son of God in His human nature, and therefore as God revealed, allows this revelation of Himself, this prophetic office of His, to be continued in the prophetic and apostolic witness to His Lordship. In the same way His sovereignty, and therefore the sovereignty of God Himself, confronts the Church in and through this witness. The Holy Spirit, too, is the Spirit of this witness, the Spirit who certifies this witness to be true, the Spirit through whom this witness wins the hearts of men. How else, then, can the Church be ruled except by this witness? And any other rule can only turn the Church into that which is not the Church. [94]

The Reformers saw as clearly as Barth does that the Holy Spirit and the Word cannot be separated. In bearing witness to Christ the Spirit sends men to the Word where Christ is present. The same Spirit certifies to them that this Word is truly the means by which Christ creates, constitutes, maintains and rules His Church.

What Karl Gerhard Steck says concerning Luther applies to all the Reformers of the sixteenth century as well as to Barth. For them

the Word, and so the written Word of the Bible, is the real vehicle of the Spirit. This does not mean that the Church is permitted to forget the promise that the Spirit shall guide it into all truth [Jn. 16: 13]. But the Spirit does not guide it by becoming the Church's soul but He guides it by the Word, and its going forth in the Church. [95]

The understanding of the relationship between Church

and Scripture is thus pneumatic in the sense that the Holy Spirit and the Word are never separated from one another. And because that is so it is recognized that the Church is continually confronted with its Lord in and through the Scriptures as the witness of the Prophets and the Apostles in which, through the Spirit, Christ Himself is present.

This truly pneumatic understanding compelled the Reformers (as it does Barth) wholly to reject all the pseudo-pneumatic. In opposing Romanism and Anabaptist enthusiasm, both Luther and Calvin realized that they were not fighting on two fronts but that they were engaged in a struggle against one and the same error: the identification of the Holy Spirit with subjectivity—collective in the case of the Roman Church and individual in that of the Enthusiasts. On the pretext of the promised guidance of the Holy Spirit the collective subjectivity of the Roman Church induces it to objectivize its own understanding of the truth and exalt it to the level of the objective Truth. On the same pretext the individual subjectivity of the Enthusiast (and of his neo-Protestant heir), i.e. his private judgement or his conscience, is objectivized and becomes the objective Truth.

In both cases the error is one and the same. Spirit and Word are divorced. The Spirit is identified with subjectivity. This identification excludes confrontation with the objective Truth, the Word of God. For the Word which itself is the criterion of its interpretation is now interpreted in the light of the subjective self-understanding of either the Church or the individual.

Both Luther and Calvin were convinced that the Roman Church and the Enthusiasts were labouring under the same mistake: they separated the Holy Spirit from the Word and then substituted their own spirit for the Holy Spirit in the interpretation of the Word.

In the *Schmalkald Articles* Luther writes:

In these matters which concern the spoken (*vocale*) and external Word, it is firmly to be maintained that God gives no one His Spirit or His grace except by or with the preceding external Word: so let us beware of the Enthusiasts . . . who boast that they have the Spirit without and prior to the Word, and therefore judge, turn and twist Scripture or the spoken Word according to their pleasure as Münzer did and others are still doing today who want to distinguish sharply between the Spirit and the letter and do not know what they are saying or trying to prove. [96]

Luther then accuses Papacy and Enthusiasm of the same error:

For the Papacy is also mere Enthusiasm when the Pope boasts that all matter of law (*omnia iura*) are enshrined in his heart and what he thinks (*sentit*) and decrees in his Church shall be spirit and truth even though it is beyond and against Scripture and the spoken Word. [97]

Summing up his argument the German Reformer concludes:

All this is the old devil and serpent who drove Adam and Eve . . . to enthusiasm and led them from the external Word of God to spiritism (*spiritualitates*) and self-conceit (*proprias opiniones*). And this he brought about by other external words. Just as our enthusiasts condemn the external Word yet are not silent themselves but fill the world with their chattering and writing as if the Spirit could not come by Scripture or the spoken Word of the Apostles but would have to come by their writings and words (*scripta et verba*). . . . In short, enthusiasm is innate (*insitus*) in Adam and his children from beginning to end. It is implanted and infused into them by the old dragon and is the source, motive and strength of all heresy, as it is of papacy and Mohammed. Therefore we should and must always insist that God will not act upon us men except through His external Word and Sacrament(s). But all that is boasted of the Spirit apart from this Word and Sacrament(s)—that is the devil. [98]

Calvin, too, appreciates that there is only an apparent opposition between Romanism and Enthusiasm. For him too they are two aspects of one and the same error. Calvin says this most pointedly in his *Reply to Sadolet:*

Well, then, does Chrysostom admonish us to reject all who, under the pretence of the Spirit, lead us away from the simple doctrine of the Gospel—the Spirit having been promised not to reveal a new doctrine, but to impress the truth of the Gospel on our minds. And we, in fact, experience in the present day how necessary the admonition was. We are assailed by two sects which seem to differ most widely from each other. For what similitude is there in appearance between the Pope and the Anabaptists? And yet, that you may see that Satan never transforms himself so cunningly, as not in some measure to betray himself, the principal weapon with which they both assail us is the same. For when they boast extravagantly of the Spirit, the tendency certainly is to sink and bury the Word of God, that they may make room for their own falsehood. And you, Sadolet, by stumbling on the very threshold, have paid the penalty of that affront which you offered to the Holy Spirit, when you separated Him from the Word. For, as if those who seek the way of God were standing where two ways meet, and destitute of any certain sign, you are forced to introduce them as hesitating whether it be more expedient to follow the authority of the Church, or to listen to those whom you call the inventors of new dogmas. Had you known, or been unwilling to disguise the fact, that the Spirit goes before the Church, to enlighten her in understanding the Word, while the Word itself is like the Lydian Stone, by which she tests all doctrines, would you have taken refuge in that most perplexing and thorny question? Learn, then, by your own experience that it is no less unreasonable to boast of the Spirit without the Word, than it would be absurd to bring forward the Word itself without the Spirit. Now, if you can bear to receive a truer definition of the Church than your own, say, in future, that it is the society of all the saints, a society which, spread over the whole world, and existing in all ages, yet bound together by the one doctrine, and the one Spirit of Christ, cultivates and observes unity of faith and brotherly concord. With this Church we deny that we have any disagreement. Nay, rather, as we revere her as our Mother, so we desire to remain in her bosom. [99]

The opposition of the Reformation to the pseudo-pneumatism both of Rome and of Enthusiasm is well summed up by Gottfried W. Locher when he says with reference to Calvin's attack on Pope and Anabaptists:

In both cases [Pope and Anabaptists] the Holy Spirit no longer remained Lord but was subjected to the power of men: in the first, to the power of the hierarchy and its "objective" *magisterium* and in the second, to the power of the "subjective" individual *conscience*. In reality the Holy Spirit transcends the distinctions we draw between the objective and the subjective, He opposes the churchly (*kirchliche*) as well as the non-churchly (*unkirchliche*) principle.[100]

In the case of Rome, the Church or its magisterium displaces and supplants the Holy Spirit. The Church is thus not confronted by the Holy Spirit with its Lord Jesus Christ but, in identifying its own spirit or soul with the Holy Spirit, it administers, interprets and distributes the *depositum fidei* that it claims to possess.

Without in any way doubting the faith and devotion of his Roman Catholic partner, without even unchurching him, the Protestant is yet forced to accuse Rome of confusing the objective truth with its own subjective understanding and interpretation of that truth. Jesus Christ is, to be sure, King, Priest and Prophet for the Roman Catholic as well as for the Protestant but, while in the understanding of the Reformation the Church shares in Christ's own kingly, priestly and prophetic office, which He Himself continues in and by the Church, the Roman view, at least by implication, signifies that the threefold office of the *Christus incarnatus* is still exercised in the threefold office of the *Christus prolongatus*, the *alter Christus*—the Church.

This divergence of opinion between the Protestant and Roman Catholic partners has inevitably an important bearing on their views on the authority of the Church.

Küng, so willing to understand the genuine objective of the Reformation—its understandable concern for the reform of the Church—yet condemns Luther (and the other Reformers) unhesitatingly as a revolutionary on the ground that he arrogated to himself an authority which belongs to the Church alone:

The actual reason for [Roman Catholics] rejecting Luther was this: For all that it included genuine reforms, and despite his conservatism, often stressed today, Luther's Reformation was essentially a revolution. He brought the very essence of the [Roman] Catholic Church into question when (this was the real innovation) he set his personal, subjective, and yet (by his intention) universally binding interpretation of the Scriptures *in principle* above the Church and her tradition. This meant that he rejected the whole teaching office of the Church, not only in the Pope but, after the Leipzig Disputation of 1519, in the Ecumenical Councils as well.[101]

Yves M. J. Congar, who is as much involved as Küng in the Protestant–Roman Catholic dialogue, goes even farther. The question for Congar is whether the rule of faith is the tradition and witness of the Church referring to the fundamental and normative text of Holy Scripture as to its archives or the direct and personal interpretation of a text which could be read outside the Church's tradition. If the latter is the case Congar believes that

> everyone could, as Luther once did, set himself up as the preacher of a new doctrine . . . without commission and *proprio motu* . . . Luther emerged, but so did Carlstadt and Münzer, the "prophets of Zwickau", Storch, Stübner, Zwilling . . .[102]

Küng and Congar argue convincingly against Enthusiasts but also against their own Church.

For Roman Catholics the authority of the Reformation Church is merely the authority of Luther or of Calvin or of any other preacher whose subjective interpretation of Scripture is put in principle above the Church and its tradition. The direct and personal interpretation of Scripture thus becomes the rule of faith. Protestants cannot and will not deny that there are subjective elements in Luther's or Calvin's theology and that *in practice* though not *in principle* these have occasionally been set above the Church and its teaching. Protestants must and do admit that Lutheran and Calvinistic Confessionalism has at times departed from the authority of the Word of God with dire results for the Church. Protestants confess with shame that there have been times— there still are—when the subjectivity of the individual preacher or minister has become the rule of faith for a congregation with truly disastrous consequences for the Church and its authority. But Protestants repudiate the Roman Catholic view that the Church of the Reformation as a Church has ever acknowledged the subjective interpretation of the individual as a binding standard or criterion of truth. It was precisely the pneumatic understanding of the relationship between Church and Scripture which made the Reformers (and Barth) aware of the unbreakable bond between the Holy Spirit and Scripture and prevented them from introducing a subjective rule of faith. In realizing that Spirit and Word cannot be separated Luther and Calvin (as well as Barth) rediscovered at the same time the true authority of the Church.

Since the Spirit sends the Church continually to the Word as the witness of the Prophets and Apostles and illumines it so that the Church hears the voice of Christ Himself, the Church has authority under the Word to proclaim the Gospel of Jesus Christ, being able in so doing to distinguish between the Word of God and the word of man.

There is a significant passage to this effect in the *Babylonian Captivity of the Church* (1520):

> This one thing indeed the Church can do: It can distinguish the Word of God from the words of men; as Augustine confesses that he believed the Gospel because he was moved by the authority of the Church which proclaimed that this is the Gospel.[103]

Luther, however, immediately adds:

> Not that the Church is therefore above the Gospel; if that were true, she would also be above God, in whom we believe because the Church proclaims that He is God. But, as Augustine says elsewhere, the truth itself lays hold on the soul and thus renders it able to judge most certainly of all things; however, the soul is not able to judge the truth, but is compelled to say with unerring certainty that this is the truth. For example, our mind declares with unerring certainty that three and seven are ten; and yet it cannot give a reason why this is true, although it cannot deny that it is true. It is clearly taken captive by the truth; and, rather than judging the truth, it is itself judged by it. There is such a mind also in the Church, when under the enlightenment of the Spirit she judges and approves doctrines; she is unable to prove it, and yet is most certain of having it. For as among philosophers no one judges the general concepts,

but all are judged by them, so it is among us with the mind of the Spirit, who judges all things and is judged by no one, as the Apostle says [1 Cor. 2: 16].[104]

Steck remarks that Luther, following Augustine, compares the ways in which the knowledge and the judgement of the Church proceed (*Erkenntnisvorgang und Urteilsvorgang*) with that of the soul in respect of the truth. The soul is apprehended, overwhelmed by the truth. Since this is so, the soul can arrive at a judgement concerning matters outside the original truth:

> Yet the soul cannot apply its competence of judgement as it were in retrospect to the truth of which it, the soul, is itself apprehended: "*Sed (scil. anima) veritatem iudicare non possit.*" This is also the decisive factor for the relationship between Church and Gospel. The relation of judgement is irreversible. The Church can and should distinguish the Gospel from the doctrine of men but it should not want first as it were to make the Gospel as such effective by its—the Church's —judgement of truth.[105]

Calvin, too, invests the Church with the power and authority to distinguish between the Word of God and the word of man. He is, however, very careful to qualify the statement—made by his Roman Catholic opponents and endorsed by himself—that "the Church cannot err in matters necessary to salvation".[106] This assertion is true but only "in so far as the Church, having forsaken all its own wisdom, allows itself to be taught by the Holy Spirit through God's Word".[107] The possession of power and authority by the Church involves an act of renunciation—the Church renounces its own spirit and lets its place be taken by the Holy Spirit. He leads the Church to the Word which He himself illuminates. Since the Church comes face to face with its Lord Christ in His Word its authority is authority under Christ, i.e. concretely under the Word.

If the Church's authority were separated from the Word it would be "void of that Spirit by whose teaching alone truth is distinguished from falsehood".[108] Calvin's doctrine of the

Church's power and authority may be summed up in his own words:

> The power of the Church . . . is not infinite, but subject to the Lord's Word, and, as it were, enclosed within it. [*subiecta verbo Domini et in eo quasi inclusa*].[109]

As long as it is understood that the power and authority of the Church are *potestas subiecta verbo Domini et in eo quasi inclusa* the Reformers can refer to it in terms which must sound almost "Roman Catholic" to many a "Protestant" ear.

In *Wider Hans Worst* (1541) Luther holds that "the mouth of God is the mouth of the Church and again God indeed cannot lie neither therefore the Church". And why is this so? Because "the Church cannot err for the Word of God which it teaches cannot err".[110]

Calvin adopts the same view. Referring more particularly to the ministers of the Church he is able to say:

> . . . among the many excellent gifts with which God has adorned the human race, it is a singular privilege that He deigns to consecrate to Himself the mouths and tongues of men in order that His voice may resound in them.

The Church through its ministers speaks and proclaims the truth, for its prophets and pastors are "the very mouth of God".[111]

Not only many Roman Catholics but also many Protestants would maintain that, while Roman doctrine asserts the infallibility of the Church, the Protestant teaching rejects it. In actual fact both Rome and Reformation believe in the inerrancy and indefectibility of the Church in all matters necessary to salvation.

In discussing Calvin's views on the authority of the Church Küng recognizes that what the Reformers rejected was not the infallibility of the Church in matters pertaining to salvation. Rather they claimed that in its teaching the Roman Church had gone against or outside and beyond the Word, and was so binding the consciences of men with doctrines established as necessary to salvation on its own authority and without the warrant of Scripture.[112]

Küng realizes that the controversy between the Church of Rome and the Church of the Reformation centres not upon the question of the inerrancy of the Church, its authority and ability to teach all things necessary to salvation but on the question of the infallibility of the hierarchy, i.e. of Pope and Councils. The Reformers assert that Pope and Councils can, and in fact do, err, while the Roman Church holds that Pope and Councils cannot err.

The Reformers had the highest respect for the Councils of the Church which under the promised guidance of the Holy Spirit explicated and expounded or defended the Faith. Their respect, however, never became a blind and uncritical obedience. They knew that though guided by the Holy Spirit the Church is never relieved of the duty to "try the spirits to see whether they are of God" (1 Jn. 4: 1):

> Accordingly, no names of Councils, pastors, bishops . . . can prevent our being taught by the evidence of words and things to test all spirits of all men by the standard of God's Word in order to determine whether or not they are from God.[113]

Barth believes that the failure of the Roman Church is the failure to test the spirits by the standard of God's Word. In his opinion the Church of Rome does not distinguish sufficiently between itself and revelation, but identifies its own word and faith with it.[114]

In answer to Barth's criticism and that of the Reformation, Küng asserts that the definition of the dogma of Papal Infallibility firmly establishes the distinction between Church and revelation, between the Word of God and the word of the Church.

The First Vatican Council makes it clear according to him that ". . . the Holy Spirit was not promised to the successors of Peter, that by His revelation they might make known new doctrine."[115] The definitions of a Pope are therefore in Küng's view merely an authoritative witness to revelation already given. The Holy Spirit is promised to the successors of Peter so that "by His assistance they might inviolably keep and faithfully expound the revelation or deposit of faith delivered through the Apostles."[116]

Küng maintains that Roman Catholic theology is most careful in distinguishing between revelation and the infallible pronouncements of the Pope:

> In contradistinction to the Revelation of God the charism of infallibility given by the Spirit to the successors of Peter signifies (*a*) no new authoritative speaking on the part of God but merely the explanation and defence of already given revelation; (*b*) the main cause [of infallibility] remains always the human subject (the Pope); (*c*) the assistance of the Holy Spirit with regard to infallibility has not the character of a particular inner revelation but only that of an external preservation from error; (*d*) infallibility is therefore not the Word of God but merely a human word about (*um*) the Word of God.[117]

Küng further stresses the distinction between the Word of God and the word of the Church by saying:

> The teaching authority of the Church is never direct-original (*unmittelbar-ursprünglich*) but always merely indirect and derived (*mittelbar-abgeleitet*) from Christ and His Word. The basis, and at the same time the limit, of the teaching authority of the Church is the Word of God which reveals itself in the human word. Even the exercise of the teaching authority of the Church can only be understood as the realization of obedience over against the superior Word of God. God and His Word are above (*oben*), the Church and her word are below (*unten*), no inversion (*Umkehrung*) is possible here. All commissioning (*Beauftragung*), empowering and authorizing comes from above. Nor is an absorption of the Word of God by the Church possible. The authority of God can never be simply annexed (*angeeignet*) by the Church. The obedience of the Church can never become obedience over against herself, her own authority. Only the authority of God is "auto-nomous", the authority of the Church is and will remain "hetero-nomous". No greater harm could be done by the Church to her genuine (!) teaching authority than if she wanted to deify it, make it transcendent. If her authority had no longer God and His Word above it, its source and ground would then be lacking, it would dissolve itself. The Church can strengthen her teaching authority in no better way than if always anew and concretely she sub-

ordinates this authority humbly, modestly and thankfully to the authority of the Word of God, if she hears, proclaims and executes not her own word but the Word of God.[118]

Here it is essential that the Protestant partner in the dialogue should listen most attentively and proceed with the utmost care. Rome and Reformation seem to speak—at least now—with one and the same voice. Both affirm that the Church is inerrant in all matters pertaining to salvation and Küng claims with regard to the Roman Church that this inerrancy is based on an authority which is *subiecta verbo Domini et in eo quasi inclusa*. What more can the Church of Rome do to satisfy the demands of the Reformation? The absolute authority of the Word of God to which the word of the Church is always subordinate seems to be acknowledged. Was the rift in the sixteenth century the result then of a misunderstanding on the part of the Reformers?

The Church has the power and the authority—indeed the duty—to distinguish between the Word of God and the word of man. This position is common to both the Church of Rome and the Church of the Reformation. For the Reformers, however, the judgement of the Church in this connection is merely an act of acknowledgement. The Church acknowledges the Word of God as of God and so distinguishes it from the word of man. The precise area within which the Word of God may be found by the Church is Scripture as the definitive witness of the prophets and the apostles. Anything which is not contained in Scripture cannot be accepted by the Church as the Word of God. What is opposed to Scripture must be rejected by the Church; what is neither opposed to nor contained in Scripture may have the authority of custom and tradition but is always liable to be overruled by the absolute authority of the Word of God. In the view of the Reformers, therefore, the Church possesses neither the power nor the authority to superimpose anything binding the conscience of man upon that which is already given in Scripture. In short, the Church has no suzerainty over the Word of God.

The arrogation of suzerainty over the Word of God was

precisely the charge made by the Reformers against Rome. They claimed that the Roman Church was not only misinterpreting Scripture but adding to it by teaching doctrines and articles of faith not contained in the biblical witness. In other words, the Reformers accused the Church of Rome of having replaced the relative authority which rightly belong to the Church by an absolute authority which rightly belongs to the Word of God alone.

Because the Church has real, though relative, authority Luther is able to say in his sermon on Jn. 7: 17:[119]

> The Christian Church has judged and condemned Arius, Pelagius, and all other heretics. Yes, it has hurled a sea of heretics into the abyss of hell by means of the divine Word, not because it is master over the Word of God, but because it submitted to this Word, because it hears none but Christ and does the will of Him who sent Christ, because it is a pupil of the man Christ and of His Word and teaching. This makes the Church a master over all. On the basis of the Word the Church judges that this doctrine is correct and that doctrine false, and that this man is a heretic and teaches falsehood. "Though I [the Church] can judge which doctrine proceeds from God and which from man, I do not have the authority to rule over God's Word or to reject God's Word. By virtue of being God's pupil I can sit in judgement on human ordinances and teaching, but not on God and His Word".[120]

The realization that the Church can only judge by means of the divine Word to which it remains subject is also found in Calvin. He, too, insists on the real though relative authority of the Church and writes with reference to Councils:

> What then? You ask, will the Councils have no determining authority? Yes, indeed; for I am not arguing here either that all Councils are to be condemned or the acts of all to be rescinded, and (as the saying goes) to be cancelled at one stroke. But, you will say, you degrade everything, so that every man has the right to accept or reject what the Councils decide. Not at all! But whenever a decree of any Council is brought forward, I should like men first of all diligently to ponder at what time it was held, on what issue, and with what intention, what sort of men were present; then to examine by the standard

of Scripture what it dealt with—and to do this in such a way that the definition of the Council may have its weight and be like a provisional judgement, yet not hinder the examination which I have mentioned. . . . Thus Councils would come to have the majesty that is their due; yet in the meantime Scripture would stand out in the higher place, with everything subject to its standard. In this way, we willingly embrace and reverence as holy the early Councils, such as those of Nicaea, Constantinople, Ephesus I, Chalcedon, and the like, which were concerned with refuting errors—in so far as they relate to the teachings of faith. For they contain nothing but the pure and genuine exposition of Scripture, which the holy fathers applied with spiritual prudence to crush the enemies of religion who had then arisen. In some of the later Councils also we see shining forth the true zeal for piety, and clear tokens of insight, doctrine, and prudence.[121]

Because the Church has merely relative and never absolute authority Luther as well as Calvin limits the authority of the Church in two ways: first, the Church is only authorized to interpret, elucidate and apply the Word of God; and second, the Church can only seek the Word of God within the confines of Scripture. Under no circumstances therefore can the Church promulgate new articles of faith.

The scope of the Church's competence in matters of faith and conduct is clearly circumscribed by Luther in his *Artikel wider die ganze Satansschule und alle Pforten der Hölle* (*Articles against the entire School of Satan and all the Gates of Hell*) of 1531:

Article i: The Christian Church has no authority to establish a solitary article of faith, has never yet done it, nor will ever do it.

Article ii: The Christian Church has no authority to establish a solitary command concerning good works, has never yet done it, nor will ever do it.

Article iii: All articles of faith have been sufficiently established in Holy Scripture. Therefore no additional ones need to be established.

Article iv: All commandments concerning good works have been sufficiently established in Holy Scripture. Therefore no additional ones need to be established.

Article v: The Christian Church has no authority to confirm, as a judge or superior, articles of faith or commandments concerning good works, the Gospel, and Holy Scripture, has never yet done it, nor will ever do it.

Article vi: The Christian Church is itself confirmed by the Gospel and Holy Scripture as its judge and superior.

Article vii: The Christian Church confirms the Gospel and Holy Scripture as a subordinate; it bears witness and testimony to them as a servant does to the colours and the coat of arms of his master.[122]

In Calvin the same strict limitation of the Church's power and authority is found.

Let this be a firm principle: No other word is to be held as the Word of God, and given place as such in the Church, than what is contained first in the Law and the Prophets, then in the writings of the Apostles; and the only authorized way of teaching in the Church is by the prescription and standard of His Word.[123]

The proclamation of the Church is the acknowledgement and application of what is contained in Scripture.

Yet this [says Calvin], is the difference between the Apostles and their successors: the former were sure and genuine scribes of the Holy Spirit, and their writings are therefore to be considered oracles of God; but the sole office of others is to teach what is provided and sealed in the Holy Scriptures. We therefore teach that faithful ministers are now not permitted to coin any new doctrine, but that they are simply to cleave to that doctrine to which God has subjected all men without exception.[124]

In matters of faith and doctrine Calvin excluded subjectivity both on the part of the individual and of the whole Church.

... here is a universal rule that we ought to heed: God deprives men of the capacity to put forth new doctrine in order that He alone may be our schoolmaster in spiritual doctrine as He alone is true [Rom. 3: 4] who can neither lie nor deceive. This rule pertains as much to the whole Church as to individual believers.[125]

It would of course be a complete misunderstanding of the

Reformation teaching were it assumed that the Reformers claimed no authority for the Church's interpretation of Scripture. They claimed authority not only for the written but also for the spoken Word, not only for the prophetic and apostolic witness as such, but also for its interpretation and elucidation in the proclamation of the Church and in its Creeds and Confessions. The central place given by the Reformation to the preaching of the Word can only be explained and justified if it is meant to be not the reciting of Bible verses and passages but their authoritative interpretation and application to the human situation here and now.

The distinction made by the Reformers was between the absolute authority of the Word and the relative authority of the Church in its interpretation, between the authority of the Word itself and the authority of the Church under the Word. The Reformers thus taught that the norm of everything the Church says or does is and always remains the witness of the Prophets and the Apostles as it is contained in Scripture. The Church of the Reformation, realizing that its own authority is never merged with, nor set above, the authority of the written Word of God in which Christ Himself speaks to it through the Holy Spirit, has always believed that Scripture is the final court of appeal which rejects all doctrines opposed or added to the biblical witness.

The principle that even the authoritative pronouncements of the Church remain subject to the authority of Scripture and may at any time be cited to appear at the bar of the written Word of God is manifest in, e.g. *the Scots Confession* of 1560. In the preface to the *Confessio Scoticana* John Knox and his fellow authors acknowledge the supreme authority of Scripture as the final court of appeal by saying:

> . . . if any man will note in this our Confession any article or sentence repugnant to God's Holy Word that it would please him of his gentleness and for Christian charity's sake to admonish us of the same in writing; and we upon our honour and fidelity, by God's grace do promise unto him satisfaction from the mouth of God, that is, from His Holy Scriptures, or else reformation of that which he shall prove to be amiss.[126]

The Church of Rome makes no such promise and stipulation nor, indeed, does it need to, for in the Roman view the promised guidance of the Holy Spirit guarantees not only the infallibility of the Church but also that of ecclesiastical office, i.e. of Pope and Councils, that teaches the Church.
Küng holds the view that

> the infallibility of the Church and the infallibility of ecclesiastical office [i.e. of Pope and Councils] are essentially connected. Since Christ has promised to keep the Church as a whole in His Spirit from apostasy through His eschatologically victorious grace, He will also keep [ecclesiastical] office as a whole . . . from apostasy: from the apostasy of faith and from an essential error which would destroy the message of Christ. There is no dilemma between the Church of the faith of the Apostles and the Church of the office of the Apostles. [127]

The pronouncements of the magisterium, of Pope and Councils, like all other human statements, are certainly regarded by Roman theology as finite. Owing to their finite nature they may indeed be incomplete and therefore may require fuller and more adequate expression and formulation. The infallibility of ecclesiastical office, however, prevents any doctrinal statement made by Pope or Councils from being false. It may in principle be "surpassed" by a more adequate statement but it continues to be true.

The Protestant interlocutor in the dialogue must ask his Roman Catholic partner what practical difference the distinction drawn by Küng and others between the direct and original and therefore absolute authority of God and the indirect and derived and therefore relative authority of the Church can possibly make to the believer. Since the doctrinal and dogmatic pronouncements of the Church, or rather of its magisterium, though finite, are never false, and cannot be, the word of the Church, however ingeniously distinguished by Roman theologians from the Word of God, arrogates to itself the authority of the latter, in fact poses as the Word of God—infallible and irreformable.

In *Überlieferung—Tradition und Schrift in der evangelischen und katholischen Theologie der Gegenwart* (*Tradition—Tradition*

and Scripture in Protestant and Catholic Theology of Today) Peter
Lengsfeld ascribes the contradiction Protestant theology
finds between Scripture and divine-apostolic Tradition (in
the Roman Catholic sense) in the ecclesiastical formation of
(Roman Catholic) dogma to the prejudice that the Church
cannot be permeated by the Holy Spirit or guided by Him
in its interpretation of Scripture expressed in its dogmas.[128]
Protestant theology has no such prejudice but rejects the
Roman Catholic assumption that the (Roman) Church
cannot but be guided by the Holy Spirit in all its doctrinal
pronouncements. Protestant theology claims that in fact the
Roman Church was not guided by the Holy Spirit in the
formulation of some of its dogmas, i.e. it was not led to
Scripture nor did it keep within the confines of Scripture, but
refusing to renounce its own wisdom promulgated new
dogmas not contained in the witness of the Prophets and the
Apostles.

Roman theologians are now at great pains to prove that all
the dogmas of their Church are rooted in Scripture itself. In
his *Scripture, Tradition and the Church: An Ecumenical Problem*,
Josef Rupert Geiselmann maintains that the difference of
opinion between Roman Catholics and Protestants does not
concern the Scriptural root of dogma but "the authoritative
interpretation of Holy Scripture by the teaching office of the
Church, the explanation of Scripture 'in accordance with
that meaning which the Church has always held and now
holds', the 'development' of the data of Holy Scripture in the
historical process of their interpretation through centuries."[129]

Geiselmann emphatically rejects the two sources-theory,
i.e. the view so prevalent amongst post-Tridentine theologians that revelation is contained partly in Scripture and
partly in Tradition. "One cannot emphasize enough", he
says, "that nothing, absolutely nothing, was decided at the
Council of Trent concerning the relation of Scripture and
Tradition."[130] When the Council of Trent adopted the
formula that saving truth and moral discipline *contineri in
libris scriptis et sine scripto traditionibus* (are contained in the
written books (i.e. Scripture) *and* the unwritten traditions),[131]

instead of the earlier version that they are contained *partim-partim*, partly in the written books and partly in the unwritten traditions, according to Geiselmann the Tridentine Fathers deliberately avoided a decision about the relation of Scripture and Tradition.[132]

Roman Catholic theology is faced with a serious difficulty, especially in the Protestant–Roman Catholic dialogue. If it interprets the *"et"* of Trent in the sense of two sources of revelation it can explain dogmas not contained in Scripture, i.e. the Immaculate Conception and the Bodily Assumption of Mary, by pointing to the unwritten tradition as their source. H. Schauf, for instance, holds that "oral tradition . . . as to its contents goes beyond Holy Scripture. Holy Scripture therefore cannot be an absolute standard." He goes on to say that "whoever is not convinced that the Bodily Assumption of Mary into Heaven is to be found in the stated way in Holy Scripture must seek and find this truth in the oral tradition."[133]

This, of course, re-echoes what one of the greatest advocates of the *partim-partim* theory, Cardinal Bellarmine, taught:

> When the universal Church embraces as a dogma of the faith something which is not found in Holy Scripture, we must say that it is held from a tradition of the Apostles. When the universal Church observes some practice which no one could appoint save God, but which is nevertheless nowhere found in Scripture, we must say that it is a tradition from Christ and His Apostles.[134]

Since the *partim-partim* theory maintains that there are two sources of revelation, Scripture and Tradition, both of which must be received and venerated *pari pietatis affectu ac reverentia* (with an equal affection of piety and reverence),[135] the Church of the Reformation, holding Scripture to be the sole source of, or rather witness to, revelation, has no hesitation in rejecting any dogma or doctrine not contained in the biblical record.

The position, however, becomes more complicated when the Roman Catholic partner in the dialogue does not hold the two sources-theory of revelation but claims that all Roman dogma and doctrine are sprung from "roots" contained in the one and only source of Revelation, i.e. Holy Scripture.

Geiselmann believes that Holy Scripture with regard to its contents and in respect of faith is sufficient. Tradition for him is the interpreter of Scripture. Holy Scripture as the revealed Word, i.e. according to its nature (*Sein*), is, as far as its contents are concerned, *ultimum fundamentum*, and therefore absolutely (*schlechthin*) *norma normans*. Scripture, however, "is not *sui ipsius interpres* [its own interpreter] but needs the living tradition of the Church as its interpreter". While Scripture is sufficient in respect of faith it would be incorrect to say "that Holy Scripture is sufficient in every respect with regard to its contents. There is no absolute sufficiency of Scripture."[136]

Geiselmann thus maintains that concerning faith Holy Scripture is as to its contents sufficient. The function of tradition is to interpret Scripture: it is *traditio interpretiva*. Furthermore Holy Scripture depends, for the explanation of its contents which concern faith and *mores*, on the *sensus* to which the Church holds and will hold. Geiselmann's final conclusion is this:

> In respect of faith it is to be held: *totum in sacra scriptura et iterum totum in traditione*, wholly in Scripture and wholly in tradition.
>
> It is different with regard to the *mores et consuetudines* of the Church. Here Scripture is insufficient and for the completion of its contents needs tradition which is in this case *traditio constitutiva*.
>
> With regard to the *mores* and *consuetudines* it is to be held: *partim in sacra scriptura, partim in sine scripto traditionibus*, partly in Holy Scripture, partly in tradition.[137]

This is not the place to examine the question of how far the Church is entitled to introduce, and to claim authority for, *mores* and *consuetudines* which have their origin in tradition and not in Scripture. Nor is it necessary to debate again the Roman error of claiming, in principle and practice, absolute instead of relative authority for the Church's interpretation of Scripture.

The real point at issue is the addition of new articles of faith to the witness of the Prophets and Apostles contained in Scripture. As long as Roman theology taught that Revelation had two sources, Scripture and Tradition, there was from a Protestant point of view some logical explanation for the emergence of new dogmas in the Roman Church. In the nineteenth century, however, beginning with Johann Adam Möhler and the Tübingen School, a gradual change took place. The two sources-theory began to be questioned, and the idea that Scripture is the sole source of revelation and that tradition is its interpretation is gaining ground. The Protestant interlocutor in the dialogue must therefore ask how—if Scripture is the sole source of revelation—the already mentioned dogmas of the Immaculate Conception and of the Bodily Assumption can be justified by the Roman Church?

The Roman Catholic answer to Protestant queries would undoubtedly be that a development of dogma has taken place from a biblical root to the authoritative definition by the magisterium of the Church. But can Rome maintain that all its dogmas and doctrines are explicit statements of what is implicitly rooted or contained in Scripture?

From a Roman point of view the theory of dogmatic development is so important that it is necessary to find out how it is used by Roman Catholic theology. It was Johann Adam Möhler of the Tübingen School in Germany and Cardinal J. H. Newman in England who, applying the categories and insights of idealistic philosophy to Roman theology, defined the doctrines of their Church in terms of development and progress. The latest Roman dogma to which we referred before—the Bodily Assumption of Mary—has, however, compelled Roman theologians to "develop" even more the theory of dogmatic development to uncover the biblical roots of that dogma. One of the most important exponents of the idea of the development of dogma is Karl Rahner. His essay on *The Development of Dogma*[138] written with special reference to the dogma of the Bodily Assumption is so important that it must be discussed at some length.

While all Roman Catholic theologians regard new doctrinal formulations as already being contained in an earlier form of the Church's consciousness in faith, Rahner points out that they have failed to reach agreement on the question of "how this 'being contained' . . . is to be understood *objectively* . . .".[139]

Rahner argues that the connection between earlier and later knowledge has been viewed in terms of the explication of what is implicit (or virtually so) in earlier knowledge. But he maintains that it cannot be assumed that the starting-point of a dogmatic explication is *always* a proposition in the usual sense of the term. Even in the natural order there exists "a kind of knowledge, which, while it is itself not articulated in 'propositions', is the starting-point of an intellectual process which develops into propositions."[140]

For example, a young man has the "experience" of a great love. "His love *itself* is his 'experience'" about which "he 'knows' much more than he can 'state'."[141] Yet he might come to the point of being able to state what he knows about his love. In such a case we have not merely logical development and inference of new propositions from earlier ones, but the formulation for the first time of propositions about an already possessed knowledge. Thus "root and shoot are not the same thing but each lives by *the other*".[142]

> The question now arises whether in the development of dogma there is to be found an inter-relationship of types of explication, (analogically) similar to that . . . in the natural order.[143]

Rahner believes that it is possible to reply in the affirmative.

> . . . it may be supposed that the *Apostles* themselves had a global experience of this kind, lying behind propositions and forming an inexhaustible source for the articulation and explication of the faith in propositions. Christ, as the living link between God and the world, whom they have seen with their eyes and touched with their hands, is the objective content of an experience which is more elemental and concentrated, simpler and yet richer than the individual propositions coined in an attempt to express this experience—an attempt which can in principle never be finally successful. . . .[144]

It is not only propositions about their experience that the Apostles bequeath, but their Spirit, the Holy Spirit of God, the very reality, then, of what they have experienced in Christ. Their own experience is preserved and present together with their Word. Spirit and Word together form the permanent active potentiality of an experience which is in principle the same as that of the Apostles . . .[145]

It is this *successio apostolica* which "hands on to the post-Apostolic Church . . . not simply a body of propositions but living experience: the Holy Spirit, the Lord, who is ever present in the Church; the keen flair and instinct of faith . . .".[146]

In contradistinction to mathematical propositions, a normal human proposition states unambiguously only "the minimum but not the maximum of what may in fact be its intelligible content".[147] The hearer of such a proposition may hear not only the minimum but "concomitantly all that further content of the speaker's unreflexive awareness not yet propositionally objectified; and he hears it *as* something known to the speaker".[148]

This sort of communication must also exist in the sphere of revelation because it, too, "works with human concepts and propositions".[149] "When, for example, someone says, 'Christ "died" for us', everybody understands what is meant by dying or death in this statement."[150] But what is meant by "death" in this statement is not or at least need not be merely a "physiological exit".[151] If the hearer should arrive "at a reflexive propositional analysis of what the word 'death' has always meant to him, it is then perfectly *possible* . . . that what has been analysed in this way and minted into propositional coin, may still be conceived of precisely *as* communicated by the speaker."[152]

In other words, apart from the minimum which can be stated unambiguously, analysis reveals that other matters were "compresent" in mind and "com-municated" though not in propositional form:

This leaves room for an explication of a more complex kind. . . .
It need not always be the case that from a proposition A . . . a

proposition B is deduced as formally, or above all, as virtually, contained in A. It might happen that . . . B . . . should follow from what is *com-municated* in A or what is "formally" contained in this com-munication.[153]

In this case the explication must run as follows:

The immediately intelligible and express statements of revelation in its manifold variety (propositional series A) are heard and questioned with a view to discovering what is compresent to mind and com-municated by them, that is, their background and the principle which comprehends the whole of this variety and gives it unity. This basic idea compresent to mind and con-signified (*mit-gesagte*) is extracted by making use of the individual propositions to give a view of the *res* on which they are based; in this way the basic idea is formulated expressly in propositions (proposition B). It is only from this intermediate proposition B that the desired terminal proposition is deduced, i.e. recognized as con-signified.[154]

If this is correct, "the procedure described does not (or need not in every case) move outside the sphere of what is properly speaking revealed."[155]

Rahner concludes that

where we have an explication of faith in which it is possible to demonstrate historically that theological reflection has co-operated (whether this be in a properly scientific way or merely prescientifically, for there is no essential difference between the two inasmuch as both work with the same instruments), the magisterium, assisted by the Spirit, has a double function. Firstly, it can in certain circumstances guarantee the correctness of this theological activity even where (in principle or up to now *de facto*) the activity, just as such, has led to no strict consequence but only to a *convenientia*. (We have at least left this possibility open.) Moreover it [the magisterium] guarantees not only that the consequence is correct, but also that it is still God's Word.[156]

It must be clearly stated that Protestant theology does not reject the idea of dogmatic and doctrinal development if properly understood. Scripture is the witness of the Prophets and the Apostles to the mighty deeds of God in Jesus Christ. This witness, however, though it is the place where men encounter Jesus Christ through the Holy Spirit, is not a system or body of doctrinal statements or propositions. Times of stress and strain have often compelled the Church to elucidate the original biblical witness in connection with a particular aspect of revelation by formulating doctrines and dogmas in defence of the faith against heresy and unbelief. In such a case the biblical witness—its explicit and implicit meaning—is first interpreted and then systematized and stated as doctrine or dogma. In a certain sense a development thus takes place from biblical roots to formulated doctrine or dogma, from the original witness of the Prophets and the Apostles in the language of their own day and generation to the witness of the Church at any one time in the language of its own day and generation.

Rahner says nothing new when he maintains that

> many of the Church's doctrines are characterized by the fact that they have not always been present in the Church and in her consciousness in faith in an expressly apprehensible form.[157]

The best example is perhaps the doctrine of the Trinity. In the early Church it was attacked on the grounds that it was not biblical, i.e. that the form in which it was taught by the Church is not to be found in the Bible. Yet Calvin upbraids those who object to the use of non-biblical terms like "person", etc., with regard to the doctrine of the Trinity. He tells them that it is wicked "to disapprove of words that explain nothing else than what is attested and sealed by Scripture".[158] In his view, to "call a foreign word one that cannot be shown to stand written syllable by syllable in Scripture", is to impose "an unjust law which condemns all interpretation not patched together out of the fabric of Scripture."[159]

Does Calvin not accept a development of doctrine and dogma in the sense of a clarification of the Church's understanding and presentation of the truth when he asks:

> . . . what prevents us from explaining in clearer words those matters in Scripture which perplex and hinder our understanding, yet which conscientiously and faithfully serve the truth of Scripture itself, and are made use of sparingly and modestly and on due occasion?[160]

Since the truth always transcends human statements about and formulations of it, Rahner is also right when he writes:

> . . . because our statements about the infinite divine realities are finite and hence in this sense inadequate—that is, while actually corresponding to reality, yet not simply congruent with it—so every formula in which the faith is expressed can in principle be surpassed while still retaining its truth. That is to say, in principle at least it can be replaced by another which states the same thing, and, what is more, states it not only without excluding more extensive, more delicately nuanced prospects, but positively opening them up: prospects on to facts, realities, truths, which had not been seen explicitly in the earlier formulation and which make it possible to see the same reality from a new point of view, in a fresh perspective.[161]

Pope John XXIII made his most important theological statement when he declared in his opening address to the first session of Vatican II (1962): "One thing is the substance of the ancient doctrine of the *depositum fidei*, and another is the way in which it is presented."[162]

The Church, ever willing to hear its Lord, formulates the truth anew in obedience to the command of that Lord to proclaim it. Without changing the substance of the truth, the Church makes use of the language and terminology of its own day and expresses the truth in new formulations which are better and more adequate than the old ones. Did Calvin not recognize this type of dogmatic development more than 400 years ago when he writes:

> Indeed, I could wish they [i.e. non-biblical Trinitarian terms like "person", "essence", etc.], were buried, if only among all men this faith were agreed on: that Father and Son and Spirit are one God, yet the Son is not the Father, nor the Spirit the Son, but that they are differentiated by a peculiar quality.[163]

As the understanding of the Church deepens, any term or word previously used to express the truth may in Calvin's view be "buried" if a new one is capable of presenting the same truth better and more fully.

Few theologians have stressed the central place of the

275

doctrine of the Trinity as strongly as Barth. Yet he recognizes that it would be a mistake to "expect to find the doctrine of the Trinity actually expressed in the Old or New Testament".[164] There are explicit indications of it "wrapped up in a perfect network of implicit indications" so that "the problems which developed later in the doctrine of the Trinity are not foreign to the Bible but at least preformed in it."[165] Yet the fact remains that

> as such this doctrine is not to be found in the texts of the Old and New Testament witness to God's revelation. It did not arise out of the historical situations to which these texts belong. It is the exegesis of these texts in the language which means also in the light, of the questions arising out of a later situation. It belongs to the Church. It is a theologoumenon. It is a dogma.[166]

Perhaps Barth expresses his view here a little incautiously, which could lead to misunderstandings. The material content of the doctrine of the Trinity is certainly contained in Scripture. On the ground of biblical exegesis and of the knowledge of God mediated in this way the Church was compelled to state the doctrine of the Trinity as it does in its Creeds and Confessions. What is not found in Scripture and had therefore to be "developed" are the precise dogmatic statements on the Trinity which formalize (as far as this is possible) what is materially contained in the witness of the Prophets and the Apostles. These dogmatic statements were (and are being) made by the Church as the result not of a development of the truth but of a development in the understanding of the truth. In making and developing formalized dogmatic statements the Church is thus not engaged in a creative, but in a perceptive and receptive activity, which through the Holy Spirit is capable of development.

The theology of the Reformation—and more particularly "Reformed" theology—has always worked with the idea of dogmatic development in the sense of a clarification of the biblical message in the language and the light of a concrete situation prevailing at any one time in the history of the Church. A development of doctrine and dogma in this sense is the necessary and inevitable result of the fact that God did not only speak to men in the past but is speaking to them here and now through the Holy Spirit in the witness of the Church.

"Reformed" theology realized this even more than "Lutheran" theology. Otto Weber points out that "the Reformed Churches have always assigned to Confessions [i.e. doctrinal and credal statements] only provisional authority, one which is subordinate to the living norm of Holy Scripture. . . ." He then asks whether "it was salutary for the Lutherans to have stopped writing Confessions in 1580"[167] and concludes that "such an historical or geographical 'freezing' of the Church's Confessions is in any case impossible for the 'Reformed' Churches."[168]

The disagreement between Protestant and Roman Catholic theology is therefore not over the idea of a dogmatic development but over what is developed—the understanding of the truth or the truth itself—and about the role assigned to the Church in this development. The Reformation made it clear that all doctrinal and credal statements are subordinate to the living norm of Scripture. If these statements are further developed, i.e. if there are clarifications and reformulations in the language and light of the concrete situation at any one time, they too are subject to the final authority of the Word of God.

Rahner admits that there may be an "anxious" theologian asking: "How are we to get anywhere, if no adequate laws of this [dogmatic] development can be formulated? Are we not leaving the field open to the rankest proliferations of pseudo-theological speculation and callow visionary enthusiasm?"[169] Rahner tells the enquiring theologian that there are three reasons why he should not be anxious:

1. Certain laws of development exist "even if they can be applied only in the Church and in the last resort only *by* the Church herself; for applications made by individual Christians and theologians are never more than appeals to the Church herself, who consequently has to be recognized as the court of last appeal."[170]

2. "The fuller and clearer truth becomes, the more strict it becomes, and more thoroughly excludes possibilities of future error."[171]

3. "And this is the decisive point, the danger of the human factor simply remains a danger. . . . [But] it is the promise of the Spirit and that alone which prevents the final realization of an ever-present danger."[172]

Once again the vicious circle is complete. The interpretation of Scripture (by the Roman Church) is prevented from being false by the promised guidance of the Holy Spirit. The verdict that the Word of God and its interpretation by the Church are in agreement is given by the Church whose verdict cannot be wrong because it is guaranteed to be right by the promised guidance of the Holy Spirit.

When the Protestant theologian asks his Roman Catholic partner in the dialogue where the dogma of the Bodily Assumption of Mary into Heaven, for example, is referred to either explicitly or implicitly in the Bible, Rahner would agree that it has not always been in existence as an explicit statement. Yet in his view this dogma has developed from a Scriptural root. According to Rahner's theory it would appear that the Apostolic *kerygma* contained the doctrine of Mary's Assumption in an inarticulate and non-propositional form. It was "compresent" to the mind of the Apostles and thus "con-signified" and "com-municated" in their witness so as to be finally deducible and definable in its present apprehensible form. Whether a particular doctrine was in fact "compresent", "con-signified" and "com-municated" in the Apostolic witness is for the magisterium of the Church to decide.

The Church possesses an organ of perception by which she can tell whether something which, from our point of view, emerges as a result of theological activity, is in fact objectively something more than the result of human speculation; whether it is still God's Word, though now expressed propositionally, in a new form, in a new articulation and explication. At any rate it need not necessarily be the case that what to us seems to be the fruit of theologically complex exegesis and speculation should in actual fact lack the character of revelation, even if in a given case this character is only guaranteed by the verdict of the magisterium.[173]

Barth maintains that

the *proof of the truth of dogma*, which as such "is not in the Bible", is not led by the fact that it is now a dogma once for all, but only by the fact that we may and must regard it as a *just interpretation of the Bible*.

There remains therefore

the need for dogmatics to *prove* dogma, in the sense of indicating its basis, its root in revelation, i.e. in the biblical witness to revelation. If dogma had no such root, if it could be shown that at its formation it was chiefly or entirely inserted in instead of excerpted from revelation, if in short it could not be regarded as the analysis of revelation, it could not be regarded as dogma.[174]

Can Rahner really maintain that the dogma of Mary's Assumption has a biblical root which is uncovered by the analysis of revelation or the Scriptural witness to it? The biblical witness shows quite clearly that every reference to Mary in the New Testament points away from her to Christ to whom alone attention is drawn. "That Christ and the Apostles do not expressly stress and celebrate Mary's glory" —says M. J. Scheeben—"is abundantly explained by the fact that to begin with the whole attention of believers had to be turned upon Christ Himself."[175]

Have believers changed so much that their whole attention does not still need to be turned upon Christ Himself? Or is the real explanation of the lack of stress on, and celebration of, Mary's glory on the part of Christ and His Apostles that there is nothing to be stressed and celebrated? Rahner says quite rightly that "died" in the statement "Christ 'died' for us" communicates more than merely a "physiological exit". But what is communicated and con-signified in the word "died" here is contained in other express and explicit statements of the Apostolic *kerygma*. With regard to Mary the express statements of the New Testament—e.g. Matt. 12: 47–50; Luke 11: 27–28; Jn. 2: 4–5—repudiate any idea of a privileged Mary being placed outside the fellowship of redeemed sinners through her Immaculate Conception or, of a Mary, who, already perfectly redeemed through her Bodily Assumption, is exempt from the necessity of waiting for the coming of the Lord and the redemption of the body. In other words, the whole tenor of the biblical witness contradicts any celebration of Mary and her glory so that the roots of the Immaculate Conception and of the Bodily Assumption wherever they may be, are not to be found in the Apostolic witness.

The decisive factor in Rahner's explanation of dogmatic development, and for the whole theory as it is generally taught by Roman theology is, of course, the concept of the actualization and prolongation of the Apostolic experience in the present-day Church. The *successio apostolica* as understood by the Church of Rome leads that Church not to excerpt what is contained in the Apostolic witness but to insert new elements into it. Thus the development of the doctrine of Mary's Assumption, as of other Roman doctrines, is the result not of the analysis of the written Word of God but of the synthesis of the New Testament witness with the subjective self-understanding of the Roman Church.

The Reformers rediscovered the unbreakable bond between the Holy Spirit and the Word of God; their understanding of the relationship between Church and Scripture was truly pneumatic in the sense that the Church led by the Spirit to the Word of God, i.e. concretely to Scripture, is confronted by its Lord there.

In nothing can the Church go against, past or beyond its Lord, i.e. concretely against, past or beyond Scripture. The Church must exercise a legitimate magisterium in the course of which the will of the Church's Lord must be interpreted, elucidated and applied here and now. But the authority of the Church and its magisterium remain relative, always subject to the absolute authority of Jesus Christ, i.e. concretely of Scripture as the witness to revelation which is the court of final appeal.

The Roman Church, identifying its own spirit with the

Holy Spirit, is confronted, not with Scripture, but its own interpretation of Scripture subject to its own self-understanding. With the help of its own spirit and self-understanding, i.e. the pseudo-pneumatic, the Roman Church blends its own understanding of Scripture and its insertions into it and so, guaranteeing the result to be the Word of God, adds new articles of faith. In a very real sense when some of its dogmas and doctrines are considered, the Roman Church is not *creatura verbi* but it makes the word *creatura ecclesiae*.

A consideration of the *schema de Divina Revelatione* which was discussed at the end of the third session (1964) of Vatican II will show that our judgement is not too harsh in respect of the Church of Rome and its attitude towards the authority of the written Word of God.

The history of this particular *schema* is important. *De Divina Revelatione* replaces a draft drawn up before the opening of Vatican II. The original title of the *schema* was *de Fontibus Revelationis*. In this draft it was implied that revelation is contained not only in Scripture but in Scripture and Tradition as in two sources (*tamquam in duplici fonte*). When the original *schema* was presented to the Council the majority of the Fathers rejected it and it was then withdrawn by John XXIII who appointed a new mixed commission to deal with what was obviously a controversial subject even within the Roman Church. A further draft produced in 1963 was not satisfactory. Revised for the third time the *schema de Divina Revelatione* was submitted to the third session Vatican II for discussion.

The change of title—from "The Sources of Revelation" to "The Divine Revelation"—is at first sight hopeful and promising. But as far as one can see—only summaries and comments[176] on the *schema*, whose text is still *sub secreto*, are available—the new draft is obviously a compromise which evades the issue by simply not answering controversial questions. For example, no answer is given to the question of the material sufficiency or insufficiency of Scripture. In other words, no answer is given to the controversial question of whether all revealed truths are contained in Scripture or whether some of them are only to be found in the oral tradition. This means that the existence of two sources of revelation is neither affirmed nor denied.

But is not the place and the authority of Scripture *vis-à-vis* the Church sufficiently safeguarded by what is said in chapter 6 of the *schema*: *Scripture in the Life of the Church:*

> The Church has therefore always honoured them [the Scriptures] and offered them to the faithful like the Body of the Lord itself.[177]

The proclamation of the Church (*praedicatio ecclesiastica*) and the Christian religion must always look back to Scripture as the supreme norm and authority by which they are ruled and judged:

> The faithful receive from Scripture the power of faith and in Scripture the Church possesses the source of its spiritual life.[178]

But is the unique place and authority of the written Word of God still assured when chapter 6 is read in the light of chapter 2 of the same *schema*? Chapter 2: *The Transmission of the Divine Revelation* deals *inter alia* with the relationship between Scripture and Tradition. Scripture and Tradition are not two unconnected sources but rather two modes of transmission in which the one mystery of salvation continues to live in the one Church. Christ, in whom the entire revelation is consummated, commissioned the Apostles "to preach the Gospel to all men as the source of the whole truth of salvation and of the moral order".[179] This was done "by the Apostles who through oral preaching, examples and institutions transmitted what they had received through association with Christ, out of His mouth and by His works or what they had learned through the inspiration of the Holy Spirit."[180] The Christian message was fixed in writing either by the Apostles themselves or by "apostolic men" (*viris apostolis*) through the inspiration of the Holy Spirit.

Tradition originates in the *praedicatio apostolica* "which is contained in the inspired writings in 'a special way'."[181] The

Apostles instructed the faithful to preserve and follow everything that is required for a holy life and for the faith of the People of God:

> The Church preserves it in her teaching, life and worship and she transmits to all generations what she herself is, what she has, and what she believes.[182]

Tradition thus does not consist merely in the transmission of revealed truths through the living Word but in the total being, teaching and action of the Church. Scripture does not stand beside Tradition but belongs to it and contains it or, more precisely, contains the transmitted *praedicatio apostolica* in a special way. The connecting link between Scripture and Tradition is the Church, for both Tradition and Scripture (as the special mode of Tradition) live in the Church. By the assistance of the Holy Spirit the living Tradition grows in the Church.

For the first time the doctrine of development is clearly stated in what is proposed to become a conciliar text. Tradition is not only alive but it is capable of development and growth. Tradition is the total being, teaching and action of the Church. Scripture, of course, is held to be a special part of Tradition, embodying it in a particular way. But this leaves unanswered the question whether revealed truths are contained in Scripture alone or partly in Scripture and partly in oral tradition.

In the event does it not follow that both Tradition and Scripture are so completely merged with, or even absorbed by, the Church that they become one with it and so grow with it? This development does not lead to an increase in the content of Tradition but to a progressive apprehension of the mystery of salvation through contemplation and spiritual experience.[183] God's colloquy with man is not a communication of truths completed in the past but is carried on continually in the uninterrupted dialogue of the Son of God with His Bride the Church through the never-ending influence of the Holy Spirit.

In this manner Tradition lives also in all the members of

the Church but its authentic interpretation is entrusted to the magisterium, not in the sense that ecclesiastical authority has any power over the Word of God, but in the sense that it has a mandate to preserve and to proclaim the Word of God with faithfulness and vigilance.

Development, as the *schema* understands it, seems to apply not to the content of the *depositum fidei* but only to its understanding. Is this really the case? Who, for example, decided that the dogmas of the Immaculate Conception and of the Bodily Assumption were not an increase of the content of Tradition but only a development and deepening of its understanding? Did not ecclesiastical authority decide that those dogmas were not expressions of popular piety but already part of the *depositum fidei* and that since the understanding of the Church had developed they had to be officially defined? Yet Scripture makes no reference either to the Immaculate Conception or to the Bodily Assumption.

The *schema de Divina Revelatione* states that ecclesiastical authority has no power over the Word of God. But does it need any? The magisterial interpretation of the Word of God, prevented from erring by the assistance of the Holy Spirit, makes the question who has authority over whom futile because in the Roman system this problem does not really arise. Much more important is the question whether the quasi-identification of Tradition (and so of Scripture which belongs to it and contains it in a special way) with the total being, teaching and action of the Church does not mean that ultimately it is not Tradition (in any sense of the term) or Scripture that is the source of revelation but the Church itself. In any case, how can Scripture stand *vis-à-vis* the Church as its superior and judge it, when its total being, teaching and action are equated with Tradition to which Scripture belongs?

In our opinion, the *schema de Divina Revelatione* confirms views expressed, for instance, by Carl Feckes. In 1950 he said, in connection with the then expected definition of the dogma of the Bodily Assumption:

The primary norm of my [Roman] Catholic faith is by no means Holy Scripture but the living consciousness of the present-day Church of Christ. If the Church of Christ is indeed—as we all believe enthusiastically—the *alter Christus*, the other, the ever living Christ, then she has within herself the clear consciousness of her faith. . . . The Church therefore does not need in principle Holy Scripture. . . . With or without Holy Scripture the Church carries the revelation of God within herself and she alone knows what is or is not contained in it. "The Spirit Himself beareth witness with her spirit".[184]

If the summaries of and comments on *de Divina Revelatione* are correct, and reflect the true intention of the *schema*, we can only say that the gulf separating the Church of Rome and the Church of the Reformation remains as wide as ever. The relationship between Church and Scripture as envisaged by the *schema de Divina Revelatione*—to say the very least—comes dangerously near to making the Word of God *creatura ecclesiae*.

It is to be hoped that a future session of Vatican II will amend the present text of the *schema de Divina Revelatione* so that, in its final and authoritative form, no doubt is left that the Church of Rome understands itself as *creatura verbi* also.

* * * * * * * * *

In ecumenical circles there is a tendency to give great prominence to what the various Churches hold in common and to minimize their differences. The continued schism of the Christian Church is excused by the somewhat trite and irritating formula of so many ecumenicists: what unites us is more than what divides us.

There are times when those who take part in the Protestant–Roman Catholic dialogue are also liable to yield to the temptation of introducing the arithmetical categories of quantity and number into their theological discussion on the unity of the Church. If it were a question of counting and adding up the number of points on which the Church of the Reformation and the Church of Rome agree or disagree, the result might well be encouraging. Arithmetically it could be that the points of agreement outnumber the points of disagreement.

But this kind of ecumenical arithmetic does not do away with one all-important and undeniable fact: the schism of the Christian Church continues. The Protestant–Roman Catholic dialogue has certainly helped to remove misunderstandings and to break down imaginary barriers, but it has not yet been able to overcome the real obstacles which still keep the two Churches apart: their different understanding of grace, of justification, of faith, of authority, etc.

Whether these obstacles are counted as so many points of disagreement compared with a greater number of points on which the two Churches agree is irrelevant. What matters is that the issues on which the two Churches disagree are so important, vital and fundamental that they prevent the unity of the Church of Jesus Christ from becoming a visible reality.

The question underlying our whole inquiry was: the Church of Rome—opponent or partner, adversary or ally? There cannot be any doubt that with regard to the dialogue, i.e. the determination to examine together differences and disagreements from a truly theological instead of a merely historical, psychological or emotional point of view, the Church of Rome and the Church of the Reformation are today partners and allies. But there cannot be any doubt either that with regard to important areas of theology the two Churches remain opponents and adversaries. The real achievement of the dialogue is the fact that even in their opposition to each other, in their calling each other in question, they feel responsible for each other. Love prevents them from letting each other go.

What gives us hope and the courage to go on in spite of our disagreements is the fact that in the last resort even the reunion of separated Christians is the work of Christ Himself. It could not be otherwise, for it is His Body which is torn and only He can ultimately heal its wounds. In the meantime, what is required of Protestants and Roman Catholics is not to try to hide from Him the wounds they themselves have inflicted on His own Body. Christians should certainly rejoice that in spite of schism and separation they are yet one in Christ. At the same time, however, they ought not to conceal their divisions which prevent them from becoming visibly one, but should, as it were, frankly expose them to Christ that He may heal them. And heal them He will; but He will do it in His own good time. This we must and do believe: "Lord, I believe; help thou mine unbelief" (Mark 9: 24).

NOTES ON PART III

1. Cf. H. U. von Balthasar, *Karl Barth*, p. 20; Karl Barth, *Credo, A Presentation of the Chief Problems of Dogmatics with reference to the Apostles' Creed*, sixteen lectures delivered at the University of Utrecht in February and March, 1935, trans. by J. Strathearn McNab, London, 1936, p. 147.

2. Cf. H. U. von Balthasar *Karl Barth*, p. 20.

3. Karl Barth, *The Concept of the Church*, p. 156.

4. Cf. *ibid.*, pp. 155–6.

5. Karl Barth, *Roman Catholicism: A Question to the Protestant Church* (1928), in *Theology and Church, Shorter Writings, 1920–8*, trans. by Louise Pettibone Smith, London, 1962, p. 315.

6. *Ibid.*, p. 322.

7. *Ibid.*, pp. 322–3.

8. *Ibid.*, p. 323.

9. H. U. von Balthasar, *Karl Barth*, p. 20.

10. *Ibid.*, p. 20.

11. *Ibid.*, p. 20.

12. Vincent Wilkin, S.J., *From Limbo to Heaven. An Essay on the Economy of the Redemption*, London and New York, 1961, p. 13.

13. Joseph Klein, *Skandalon um das Wesen des Katholizismus*, Tübingen, 1958, pp. vi–vii.

14. Cf. *ibid.*, p. 33.

15. *Ibid.*, p. 86.

16. *Ibid.*, p. 19.

17. *Ibid.*, p. 19.

18. *Ibid.*, p. 19.

19. *Ibid.*, pp. 78–79.

20. *Ibid.*, p. v.

21. Cf. A.A.S., 56, 20.8.1964, Nr. 10, p. 630.

22. Cf. *ibid.*, p. 639.

23. Cf. *ibid.*, p. 639.

24. *Ibid.*, p. 639.

25. Cf. *ibid.*, p. 655.

26. *Sacrosanctum Oecumenicum Concilium Vaticanum Secundum, Decretum De Oecumenismo*, Typis Polyglottis Vaticanis, 1965, II, 9, p. 13 (hereafter referred to as *De Oecumenismo*).

27. Mass was concelebrated by the Pope and twenty-four bishops.

28. A.A.S., 56, 24.10.1964, Nr. 13, pp. 805–806. Translation (slightly altered) taken from *Herder Correspondence*, Dublin, London, New York, etc., Vol. I, Nr. 2, November 1964, p. 315.

29. A.E., 40, pp. 231–2.

30. Part I; S.B., p. 47; Schaff III, pp. 26–27.

31. *Ibid.*, S.B., p. 48; Schaff III, p. 27.

32. A.E., 26, pp. 24–26.

33. O.S., I, p. 475; *Tracts I*, p. 44.

34. O.S., I, p. 476; *Tracts I*, p. 45.

35. O.S., I, p. 476; *Tracts I*, p. 45.

36. *Institutes*, IV, 2. 12.

37. *Institutes*, IV, 2. 12.

38. *Institutes*, IV, 2. 12.

39. *The Works of John Knox* (collected and edited by D. Laing), Vol. VI, Edinburgh, 1864, p. 497 and p. 507.

40. A.E., 40, p. 232.

41. C.R., 52, 199; John Calvin, *Commentary on the Second Epistle to the Thessalonians* (editors, David W. Torrance and Thomas F. Torrance), trans. by Ross Mackenzie, Edinburgh and London, 1961, p. 402.

42. A.E., 12, pp. 271–2.

43. *Part II, Article 4*; S.B., p. 307

44. *Institutes*, IV, 7. 24.

45. *Institutes*, IV, 7. 24.

46. Hans Küng, *The Council and Reunion*, trans. by Cecily Hastings, London and New York, 1961, p. 97 (hereafter referred to as H. Küng, *Council*).

47. *Ibid.*, pp. 97–98.

48. *Ibid.*, p. 101.

49. *Institutes*, IV, 7. 26.

50. *Institutes*, IV, 7. 26.

51. *Institutes*, IV, 7. 25.

52. Cf. Karl Gerhard Steck, *Kirche des Wortes oder Kirche des Lehramtes?*, *Theologische Studien*, ed. by Karl Barth and Max Geiger, Nr. 66, Zürich, 1962, p. 10 (hereafter referred to as K. G. Steck, *Kirche*).

53. Edmund Schlink, *Der Kommende Christus und die kirchlichen Traditionen. Beiträge zum Gespräch zwischen den getrennten Kirchen*, Göttingen, 1961, p. 95.

54. *De Oecumenismo*, III, 22, p. 20.

55. *Ibid.*, I, 4, p. 9.

56. Karl Barth, *The Concept of the Church*, p. 161.

57. Hans Küng, *The Living Church, Reflections on the Second Vatican Council*, trans. by Cecily Hastings and N. D. Smith, London and New York, 1963, p. 333 (hereafter referred to as H. Küng, *The Living Church*).

58. C.D., I/2, p. 151.

59. C.D., I/2, p. 155.

60. C.D., I/2, pp. 155–6.

61. C.D., I/2, p. 153.

62. C.D., I/2, p. 153.

63. H. Küng, *The Living Church*, p. 333.

64. *De Oecumenismo*, I, 3, p. 6.

65. Cf. *ibid.*, I, 3, p. 7.

66. Cf. *ibid.*, III, 21, p. 20.

67. Cf. *ibid.*, III. 21, p. 20.

68. Para. 4; Denz. 2918 (1718a) Schaff II, p. 218.

69. Hans Küng, *Strukturen der Kirche*, Freiburg, Basel, Wien, 1962, pp. 283–4 (hereafter referred to as H. Küng, *Strukturen*).

70. *Ibid.*, p. 318.

71. Juan de Torquemada, *Summa de Ecclesia*, lib. II, cap. 102, 241 and lib. IV; pars. I, cap. 11, 369v–370; cf. H. Küng, *Strukturen*, pp. 276–9.

72. H. Küng, *Council*, p. 78.

73. *Ibid.*, pp. 78–79.

74. A.A.S., 56, 15.2.1964, Nr. 2, p. 101.

75. R., pp. 117–18.

76. Cf. H. Küng, *Strukturen*, pp. 283–4.

77. W.A., 7, pp. 96–98.

78. *Institutes*, I, 7. 4.

79. *Institutes*, I, 7. 5.

80. C.D., I/1, p. 136.

81. C.D., I/1, p. 117.

82. C.D., I/1, pp. 119–21.

83. Denz. 1507 (786); Schaff II, p. 83.

84. Session 3, Chapter 2; Denz. 3007 (1788); Schaff II, p. 242.

85. Denz. 3884 (2313).

86. Denz. 3886 (2314).

87. Denz. 3887 (2315).

88. Denz. 3889 (2316).

89. Cf. Gottfried Maron, *Brief aus Rom*, Schweiz. Evang. Pressedienst, Informations-Sonderdienst zum Konzil III, Nr. 11, Zürich, November 26, 1964, p. 3.

90. *De Oecumenismo*, III, 21. p. 20.

91. Cf. Gottfried Maron, *op. cit.*, p. 3.

92. H. Küng, *Strukturen*, p. 318.

93. C.D., I/1, p. 295.

94. C.D., I/2, p. 693.

95. K. G. Steck, *Kirche*, p. 18.

96. Part III. 8; S.B., p. 321.

97. *Ibid.*, S.B., pp. 321–2.

98. *Ibid.*, S.B., p. 322.

99. O.S., I, pp. 465–6; *Tracts I*, pp. 33–34.

100. Gottfried W. Locher, *Calvin Auwalt der Ökumene, Theologische Studien*, Nr. 60, Zollikon, 1960, p. 25.

101. H. Küng, *Council*, p. 106.

102. Yves M. J. Congar, *Vraie et Fausse Réforme dans l'Église*, Paris 1950, pp. 518–19.

103. A.E., 36, p. 107.

104. *Ibid.*, pp. 107–8.

105. K. G. Steck, *Kirche*, p. 21.

106. *Institutes*, IV, 8. 13.

107. *Institutes*, IV, 8. 13.

108. *Institutes*, IV, 8. 11.

109. *Institutes*, IV, 8. 4.

110. W.A., 51, pp. 516 and 518.

111. *Institutes*, IV, 1. 5 and *42nd Homily* on 1 Sam. 12, C.R., 29. 705.

112. Cf. H. Küng, *Strukturen*, pp. 309–17.

113. *Institutes*, IV, 9. 12.

114. Cf. C.D., I/2, pp. 606–37.

115. Session 4, Chapter 4, Denz. 3070 (1836); Schaff II, p. 269.

116. *Ibid.*

117. H. Küng, *Strukturen*, p. 326.

118. *Ibid.*, p. 327.

119. Luther preached his sermons on St. John 6–8 in Wittenberg from November 5, 1530, to March 9, 1532.

120. A.E., 23, p. 231.

121. *Institutes*, IV, 9. 8.

122. W.A., 30, 2, p. 424; translation (in part) taken from Ewald M. Plass, *op. cit.*, Vol. I, p. 286.

123. *Institutes*, IV, 8. 8.

124. *Institutes*, IV, 8. 9.

125. *Institutes*, IV, 8. 9.

126. *Scots Confession*, 1560, and *Negative Confession*, 1581, with Introduction by G. D. Henderson, Edinburgh, Glasgow and Aberdeen, 1937, p. 41; Schaff III, p. 438.

127. H. Küng, *Strukturen*, p. 318.

128. Cf. Peter Lengsfeld, *Überlieferung, Tradition und Schrift in der evangelischen und katholischen Theologie der Gegenwart*, Paderborn, 1960, p. 252.

129. Josef Rupert Geiselmann, *Scripture, Tradition, and the Church: An Ecumenical Problem* in *Christianity Divided*, *op. cit.*, p. 61 (hereafter referred to as J. R. Geiselmann, *Scripture, Tradition and the Church*).

130. *Ibid.*, pp. 47–48.

131. Session 4, Denz. 1501 (783); Schaff II, p. 80.

132. Cf. J. R. Geiselmann, *Scripture, Tradition and the Church*, p. 48.

133. H. Schauf, *Kirchenzeitung für das Bistum Aachen*, Nr. 34, 26.8.1961, p. 11; quoted from Josef Rupert Geiselmann, *Die Heilige Schrift und die Traditionen. Zu den Neueren Kontroversen über das Verhältnis der Heiligen Schrift zu den Nichtgeschriebenen Traditionen*, Freiburg, Basel, Wien, 1962, p. 272 (hereafter referred to as J. R. Geiselmann, *Die Heilige Schrift und die Traditionen*).

134. Cardinal Bellarmine, *De Verbo Dei*, IV, Chapter 9, quoted from J. R. Geiselmann, *Scripture, Tradition and the Church*, p. 47.

135. Trent, Session 4; Denz. 1501 (783), Schaff II, p. 80.

136. J. R. Geiselmann, *Die Heilige Schrift und die Traditionen*, p. 272; cf. also J. R. Geiselmann, *Das Konzil von Trient über das Verständnis der Heiligen Schrift und der nichtgeschriebenen Traditionen. Sein Missverständnis in der nach-tridentinischen Theologie und die Überwindung dieses Missverständnisses* in Michael Schmaus (editor), *Die Mündliche Überlieferung*, München, 1957, pp. 123–206.

137. J. R. Geiselmann, *Die Heilige Schrift und die Traditionen*, p. 282.

138. Karl Rahner, *The Development of Dogma* (hereafter referred to as Karl Rahner, *Development*) in *Theological Investigations*, Vol. I (*op. cit.*), pp. 39–77.

139. *Ibid.*, p. 55.

140. *Ibid.*, p. 63.

141. *Ibid.*, p. 63.

142. *Ibid.*, p. 65.

143. *Ibid.*, p. 65.

144. *Ibid.*, p. 65.

145. *Ibid.*, p. 68.

146. *Ibid.*, p. 68.

147. *Ibid.*, p. 69.

148. *Ibid.*, p. 70.

149. *Ibid.*, p. 72.

150. *Ibid.*, p. 72.

151. *Ibid.*, p. 72.

152. *Ibid.*, p. 72.

153. *Ibid.*, p. 73.

154. *Ibid.*, p. 73.

155. *Ibid.*, p. 73.

156. *Ibid.*, p. 75.

157. *Ibid.*, p. 39.

158. *Institutes*, I, 13. 3.

159. *Institutes*, I, 13. 3.

160. *Institutes*, I, 13. 3.

161. Karl Rahner, *Development*, p. 44.

162. Quoted from H. Küng, *The Living Church*, pp. 99–100.

163. *Institutes*, I, 13. 5.

164. C.D., I/1, p. 360.

165. C.D., I/1, p. 360.

166. C.D., I/1, p. 431.

167. The reference is to the *Book of Concord*, published in 1580 at Dresden. It contains the *Apostles' Creed*, the *Nicene* and the *Athanasian Creed*, the *Augsburg Confession*, the *Apology of the Augsburg Confession*, the *Schmalkald Articles*, Luther's *Short* and *Large Catechisms* and the *Formula of Concord*.

168. Otto Weber, *A New Edition of Reformed Confessions* in *The Reformed and Presbyterian World*, Geneva, Vol. 27, Nr. 6, June 1963, p. 256.

169. Karl Rahner, *Development*, p. 42.

170. *Ibid.*, p. 42.

171. *Ibid.*, p. 42.

172. *Ibid.*, p. 43.

173. *Ibid.*, p. 75.

174. C.D., I/1, p. 356.

175. M. J. Scheeben, *Handbuch der Katholischen Dogmatik*, Vol. 3, 1882 and 1925, p. 458, quoted from C.D., I/2, p. 140.

176. Cf. *Die Offenbarung und ihre Weitergabe* in *Herder-Korrespondenz*, December 1964, Nr. 3, XIX, Freiburg, pp. 130–7; *Concilio Ecumenico Vaticano* II, Dritte Session, Pressedokumentationen, Nr. 10, Citta del Vaticano, 25.9.1964, etc.

177. *Herder-Korrespondenz*, December 1964, Nr. 3, p. 133.

178. *Ibid.*, p. 133.

179. *Ibid.*, p. 131.

180. *Ibid.*, p. 131.

181. *Ibid.*, p. 131.

182. *Ibid.*, p. 131.

183. Cf. *ibid.*, p. 132.

184. Carl Feckes, *Zur kommenden Definierung der Himmelfahrt Mariens*, Leutersdorf am Rhein, 1950, pp. 1–2.

Index